The NFT Revolution

in 50 Use Cases

ISBN: 978-1-4475-4038-0

Image credits: Canva, Freepik.

The

NFT

Revolution
in 50 Use Cases

Maxime
MONTFORT

Table of Contents

DISCLAIMER

Dear reader,

Before delving into the reading of this book, I would like to draw your attention to the following points:

1. No investment advice

This book does not provide any investment advice. Its sole purpose is educational. When a project is mentioned in the book, it is for informational purposes only. You are solely responsible for your investment choices.

2. The world of NFTs is evolving rapidly

Blockchain technology, particularly NFTs, is advancing rapidly. What was valid six months ago may no longer be applicable today, and what is valid today may not be so in six months. Therefore, some information presented in this book may no longer be up to date.

3. This book does not aim to explain how NFTs work

If you are seeking to understand the technical aspects of NFTs, do not purchase this book. That is not its purpose, and you will not find the information you are looking for. This book is primarily intended for the general public who are curious about the potential use cases of NFTs.

4. This book should be approached with a forward-looking perspective

This book is primarily experimental, an attempt to project into the future. Therefore, I invite you to consider the information presented in this book as a forward-looking vision at a specific moment. Use it as a foundation to deepen your knowledge, fuel your reflection, and explore new perspectives.

FOREWORD

Thank you for making the decision to read this book. You could have chosen to do a billion other things with your time, but you have chosen to devote your attention to this book. If you have done so, it means you are interested in NFTs and how they will impact our lives.

Indeed, NFTs represent much more than just a technological evolution. They are the beginnings of a profound transformation in our interactions with the digital world. Understanding the potential of NFTs means grasping the opportunities they offer, as well as the challenges they present to us.

NFTs, still relatively unknown a few years ago, are gradually permeating the digital universe, disrupting established norms and offering new perspectives. Through these carefully selected 50 use cases, I aimed to create a synthesis that had not been done before.

However, this book goes beyond a mere list of use cases. My goal is to provide you with a comprehensive perspective by exploring the socio-economic, cultural, and technological implications of this revolution. NFTs will completely transform our relationship with digital ownership.

I would like to take this opportunity to express my gratitude to all the people who contributed to the creation of this book, including artists, collectors, experts, and those who simply shared their passion for NFTs with me. Thank you also to those who proofread this book.

I hope that this book serves as a source of inspiration for you.

Happy reading!

INTRODUCTION

We are on December 5, 2000. The Daily Mail publishes an article claiming that the internet, born a few years earlier, is just a passing fad and that millions of Britons are already abandoning ship. However, those predictions were far from reality...

20 years later, we can't live without it. The internet is omnipresent, connecting billions of people around the world. It has profoundly transformed our society and has become an essential tool in many aspects of our daily lives.

Far from abandoning ship, the British enthusiastically immersed themselves in this new digital era. The internet has become the preferred means of communication, information search, and interaction with the world around us.

It is true that in 2000, even sending an email was a daunting task. We face similar challenges today with Blockchain and NFTs. Even today, advanced technical knowledge is required to directly interact with the blockchain.

And yet, it is highly likely that in 10 years, everyone will be using the blockchain and NFTs without even realizing it. They will become indispensable for the reasons I invoke in this book.

But to understand this, we need to grasp the transition between what is known as "Web 1," "Web 2," and "Web 3. »

INTERNET IS EVOLVING: FROM WEB 1 TO WEB 3

The internet has evolved since the creation of the World Wide Web on March 12, 1989, at CERN in Geneva (back when connections were made through the telephone network and computers took up all the space on the desk). Initially, it was only possible to read content on the internet (Web 1), then it became possible to share content (Web 2). Today, the blockchain has enabled the emergence of Web 3, which will allow us to truly own digital content. To fully grasp the significance of this innovation, it is necessary to understand the different stages of the web's evolution.

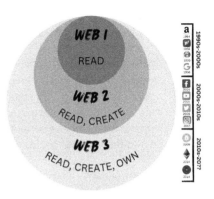

WEB 1: READING CONTENT

Web 1 was largely focused on information reading. The original web had the essential purpose of helping everyone find information more easily. Users could navigate between web pages by clicking on links, but interactions were limited. Professionals were on one side and internet users on the other, with no interaction between the two parties. There were no links and exchanges between these two sides. Content was published on the internet and could be read, but that was the extent of it. Search engines played a vital role in exploring Web 1. Popular search engines like AltaVista and Yahoo! allowed users to find relevant websites by entering keywords. However, the quality of the results was not always optimal, and users often had to navigate through multiple pages before finding the desired information.

WEB 2: CREATING AND SHARING CONTENT

The main problem with Web 1 was its lack of interactivity and user participation. Users were mainly passive consumers of content. However, the advent of Web 2 brought significant changes. Unlike Web 1, which only offered static content, Web 2 now provides dynamic content (HTML). Data is no longer distributed from static files but from a database. Users now have the ability to interact with the content and actively contribute to the creation and dissemination of new information. This evolution gave rise to social networking platforms, blogs, forums, and other interactive sites that have profoundly transformed the web landscape.

WEB 3: OWNING CONTENT

Web 2 brought many improvements in terms of interactivity and user participation, but it also presented certain problems. One of the main issues with Web 2 is the centralization of data and power in the hands of tech giants like GAFAM (Google, Apple, Facebook, Amazon, Microsoft). These companies have accumulated vast amounts of user data and exerted significant influence over users' choices and online experiences. Privacy and data security have become major concerns in the Web 2 era. Users have had to consent to sharing substantial amounts of personal information to access certain online services, thereby relinquishing control of their data to the GAFAM companies.

These concerns have led to the emergence of Web 3. The concept of Web 3 was introduced by Gavin Wood in 2014[1]. At that time, Bitcoin's blockchain had already been in existence for 5 years, and Wood had recently co-founded Ethereum with Vitalik Buterin. In essence, Wood's definition of Web 3 is to give individuals the tools to do everything they need without relying on trusted intermediaries. This includes simple actions like buying a baguette of bread without depending on banks to facilitate the transaction. This form of peer-to-peer electronic cash should remind you of something: Bitcoin.

THE BIRTH OF BITCOIN, THE FIRST GENERATION OF BLOCKCHAIN (2009)

UNDERSTANDING THE DIFFERENCE BETWEEN BLOCKCHAIN AND BITCOIN

To understand Satoshi Nakamoto's innovation, the creator of Bitcoin, it's important to differentiate it from the concept of blockchain.

In fact, blockchain has existed for 40 years already. In simple terms, blockchain, as a computer concept, allows cryptographic proofs to be linked together in an immutable chain. If you touch one proof, you touch the entire chain. This concept existed 30 years before the invention of Bitcoin.

Satoshi Nakamoto's innovation doesn't pertain to the blockchain itself. What he introduced in 2008/2009 was the addition of a consensus mechanism to the blockchain, enabling the creation of a distributed network that functions peer-to-peer and allows value transfer without intermediaries.

Let's consider a concrete example with a network of 50 computers. How can they all agree on an account state, for example, that Mr. X has $100 in his account? Before Bitcoin, we didn't know how to achieve this. The only solution was to introduce trusted intermediaries, such as banks.

To solve this problem, Nakamoto invented a form of consensus known as Proof of Work. Without delving into technical details[2], simply understand that it's a security mechanism that generates economic incentives (in the form of bitcoins) for computers that secure the network.

The participants in the network would have no economic incentive to attempt to corrupt the network since they would be immediately identified thanks to the blockchain. For example, if someone tries to claim that Mr. X has $150 instead of $100, all other consensus participants would immediately detect it since it would alter the entire chain.

FROM "COPY/PASTE" TO "CUT/PASTE"

With the emergence of the Internet, when conducting online transactions, we are obliged to rely on trusted intermediaries. In the physical world, we don't need intermediaries. If you hand someone a $20 note, you no longer possess it, and the other person does. We exchange directly, hand to hand, without intermediaries. In the digital world, we couldn't do that before Bitcoin. When making a transfer or transaction, there was always at least one intermediary involved: the bank.

However, with Bitcoin, it became possible to transfer digital value directly from one party to another without depending on intermediaries. It was the equivalent of cash but in the digital world.

Why couldn't we do this before? In the Web 2 era, the nature of the internet allows for easy duplication of everything on it. For example, an image can be copied 10,000 times without issue. Similarly, when you send an email, you're actually sending a copy of that email, and the original remains in your mailbox. You haven't destroyed the email on your computer to send it (unlike in the physical world, where sending a postcard means you no longer possess it).

When you send something on the internet, it's naturally copied for transmission. This is convenient for quickly disseminating content, particularly on social media. However, this copying mechanism doesn't work for currency. Imagine if you could send someone 10 dollars and still retain those 10 dollars! The money would quickly become worthless.

To address this problem, intermediaries like banks had to be introduced. Their role isn't to physically transfer anything since, as we've seen, that's impossible. They can't do anything beyond what the internet allows. Their role is simply to maintain accounting records (who owns what and when), which they update throughout the day.

In contrast, Bitcoin, for the first time, enabled "Cut/Paste" on the internet. It became possible to send a Bitcoin to someone and prove to everyone that you had indeed sent a Bitcoin to another person and no longer had it in your possession.

This was made possible through the consensus mechanism explained earlier.

THE BIRTH OF ETHEREUM, THE SECOND GENERATION OF BLOCKCHAIN (2014)

PROFILE OF VITALIK BUTERIN, THE CREATOR OF ETHEREUM

Vitalik Buterin is one of the most influential figures in the blockchain world and can be considered a computer genius. At the age of 4, his parents gave him his first computer, and he developed a fascination for Microsoft Excel spreadsheets.
In 2011, his father introduced him to Bitcoin. At that time, Bitcoin was still a niche domain, and only cryptographers or highly tech-savvy individuals had heard of it. Bitcoin became an obvious interest for Vitalik at that moment.

Also in 2011, he co-founded Bitcoin Magazine with Mihai Alisie, who invited him to join. This allowed Vitalik to combine his interests and get paid for writing articles for the magazine. He dedicated between 10 and 20 hours per week to it alongside his studies. The magazine published its first print version the following year.

In 2014, he made the decision to leave university and fully commit his time to Bitcoin, founding Ethereum.

The myth suggests that Vitalik got the idea to create Ethereum following the unilateral decision of game developer Blizzard to weaken the abilities of his favorite class in World of Warcraft. It was supposedly at that moment he realized the "horror" of centralized services[3].

SMART CONTRACTS: ADDING PROGRAMMABILITY TO BLOCKCHAIN

We've seen why Bitcoin was created and the significant innovations it introduced. However, Bitcoin's sole use case was digital cash transfer; it couldn't do much else. But how could one send something other than money? How could one, for example, send an image through "Cut/Paste"?

To address this issue, Vitalik Buterin created Ethereum in 2014, aiming to add more programmability to the Bitcoin blockchain. He developed a new programming language called Solidity. Thanks to this language, it became possible to create smart contracts. A smart contract is simply a piece of code deployed on the blockchain (specifically Ethereum) that automatically executes actions. Ethereum thus gave birth to NFTs, decentralized applications (dApps) and decentralized finance (DeFi).

AND WHAT ABOUT NFTS?

WHAT IS AN NFT?

Reflecting the times, the term NFT entered the Larousse dictionary in 2022, alongside words like "wokeness" or "distanciel" (remote). The dictionary defines it as follows: "non-fungible digital file that is non-reproducible and unalterable, representing a unique asset, either virtual or physical (artwork, tweet, music piece, etc.), listed on a blockchain and associated with a digital certificate of authenticity and ownership."

An NFT is something that is non-reproducible or non-fungible (NFT = Non-Fungible Token). This is a crucial aspect to understand. Fungible things are interchangeable, like cash: a $1 banknote is equivalent to another $1 banknote. On the contrary, non-fungible tokens are unique. For example, the Mona Lisa painting is unique; there is only one original. Similarly, if you have a ticket for a concert with no assigned seats, it is fungible, but if each ticket has an assigned seat, it becomes non-fungible.

Fungible	Non Fungible
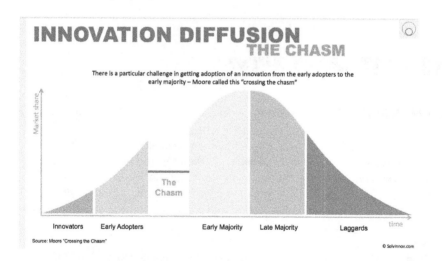	

ADOPTION IS UNDERWAY: A LOOK AT SOME FIGURES

INNOVATION DIFFUSION
THE CHASM

There is a particular challenge in getting adoption of an innovation from the early adopters to the early majority – Moore called this "crossing the chasm"

Market share

The Chasm

Innovators   Early Adopters   Early Majority   Late Majority   Laggards   time

Source: Moore "Crossing the Chasm"

© Solvinnov.com

According to Everett Rogers' theory of innovation diffusion proposed in 1962, every innovation goes through various phases. Regarding blockchain technology, we are still in the "early adopters" stage. Approximatively 425 millions of people had crypto in December 2022[4]. That represented approximately 5% of the world's population. However, this figure hides a significant disparity: for example, in the United States, this figure stands at 15%, and in Russia, it is 17%.

While we can celebrate the growing adoption of cryptocurrencies, we are still far from reaching the "chasm" (a concept introduced by Geoffrey Moore in 1991), which represents the transition from early adopters to the early majority, from a niche market to the mass market. Early adopters are easy to convince as they are receptive to innovation. However, to convince the early majority, concrete value propositions need to be offered, something that blockchain and NFTs have not yet fully achieved because the technology is not yet ready.

We were in the same situation with the internet in the early 2000s. The transition to Web 2.0 was gradual, with early users and use cases, but the technology was not yet fully prepared. Today, there are approximately 430 million people who own cryptocurrencies. In the early 2000s, the number of internet users was also around 400 million. When NFT technology is ready, mass adoption will likely occur, and perhaps much faster than anticipated, considering that everyone now has a smartphone, unlike in the early 2000s.

Adoption is indeed underway, and this book aims to help you understand why through 50 use cases.

I. REAL ESTATE

NFTS IN REAL ESTATE

COST REDUCTION OF TRANSACTIONS

As mentioned earlier, purchasing real estate involves numerous intermediaries and time-consuming, costly processes. With NFTs, transaction costs such as administrative procedures and multiple visits to a notary for paperwork will be significantly reduced. Property deeds will be directly recorded on the blockchain, and property transfers will happen quickly. The blockchain's timestamping system will certify that the transfer has taken place between the parties. Dynamic NFTs (whose characteristics change based on factors like renovations) will allow real-time tracking of the property's evolution, eliminating the need to search for documents in physical files.

A DISTRIBUTED AND IMMUTABLE REGISTRY

Real estate ownership could also benefit from Blockchain due to its ability to provide a distributed and immutable registry. Blockchain operates as a distributed ledger, meaning there is no single central entity with access to all documents and the power to arbitrarily delete them. Once information is recorded on the Blockchain, it is impossible to reverse. Therefore, if you have completed a sale, you can be certain that a trace of that transaction will always remain on the Blockchain. This inherent transparency and permanence provided by Blockchain technology offer a higher level of trust and security in real estate transactions. With a decentralized registry, the risk of fraud, tampering, or data loss is significantly reduced, instilling confidence among buyers, sellers, and other stakeholders involved in property transactions.

RENTAL MARKET: VERIFYING APPLICANTS WITH TWO CLICKS

Today, real estate purchases seem to be giving way to rentals as younger generations are less inclined to commit to buying a property. This situation can benefit property owners. However, renting out a property can sometimes be complicated, especially when it comes to verifying prospective tenants' applications. Any property owner can attest that there is always a concern with each new tenant arrival that they might provide false documents and prove to be financially unreliable. NFTs can help solve part of this problem. With two clicks, you can verify that the applicant's documents have indeed been provided by the relevant authorities and recorded on a blockchain. You can also verify their financial solvency, eliminating the possibility of deception for tenants.

BOOSTING REAL ESTATE TRANSACTIONS

Real estate investment is often seen as an attractive way to generate additional income and build a solid asset base. However, for those unfamiliar with the field or with limited financial resources, venturing into real estate investment can be a real challenge. Nevertheless, the tokenization of real estate presents new opportunities. Real estate tokenization platforms enable investors to purchase tokens representing fractional ownership in a property. These tokens can be acquired with smaller amounts, allowing a larger number of people to invest. For example, a student who saves $50 per month could invest that amount in real estate with potential returns of 5 to 10%.

PROPY: A HISTORIC MILESTONE

Propy was one of the first companies to sell real estate using blockchain[5]. It involved the sale of an apartment in Ukraine purchased by Michael Arrington for $60,000 paid in ETH. In the same year, the apartment was resold for 36 ETH (around $90,000 at the time of purchase). The price difference was due to the sale being organized through an auction of an NFT representing ownership of the apartment, an innovation at the time (although technically, the NFT represented ownership of a U.S. LLC that owned the property in Ukraine). Currently, it is not yet possible to directly tokenize real estate in France, the United States, or Ukraine; it must be done through a company that holds the property.

THE CHRISTOPHER COLUMBUSES OF THE 21ST CENTURY: REAL ESTATE AND THE METAVERSE

THE CONCEPT OF THE METAVERSE IS NOT A RECENT INVENTION

Can we say that we are already living in the metaverse? Considering that we spend a significant portion of our days in front of screens, the idea seems plausible. The concept of the metaverse is not as recent as it may seem. The term first appeared in Neal Stephenson's 1992 science fiction novel _Snow Crash_. Eleven years later, the game Second Life was created, enabling the creation of virtual avatars and interaction with other virtual avatars in a virtual world. The film industry has also explored the metaverse concept, as seen in the release of "Ready Player One" in 2018, based on the eponymous book published in 2011.

EARNING RENT FROM VIRTUAL PROPERTY? IT'S POSSIBLE!

Why would someone buy virtual land at exorbitant prices when they can do so in the real world? The answer lies in the economic potential. Virtual lands offer opportunities to develop projects and monetize them. It is not surprising that major brands such as Nike and LVMH are investing millions in virtual lands and buildings. Imagine a new world opening up, a world where possibilities are limitless, except for space. To have space in the metaverse, you need to have space on the blockchain.

THE HYPE OF VIRTUAL LANDS IN THE METAVERSE

Two essential elements have contributed to the emergence of the metaverse in public debate in France: the COVID-19 pandemic and Facebook. In March 2020, the government implemented lockdown measures. With free time on their hands, people started exploring the world of blockchain and cryptocurrencies. The term metaverse began gaining attention. However, it was on October 28, 2021, when Facebook announced its transformation into Meta, that the idea of the metaverse truly gained popularity. The prices of crypto-assets related to the metaverse skyrocketed, with some like $SAND increasing by a factor of 10 in just one month[6]. In the midst of this euphoria, many people bought virtual lands, sometimes for tens of thousands of dollars.

THE BURSTING OF THE BUBBLE?

The hype of November 2021 quickly subsided, and it appears that the bubble has burst. When analyzing the numerous projects trying to capitalize on the metaverse hype, a significant portion will fail (as is the price of any innovation—many failures for few successes). The market is not yet ready, and as Vitalik Buterin said in a July 2022 tweet, "The 'metaverse' is going to happen, but I don't think any of the existing corporate attempts to intentionally create the metaverse are going anywhere." You are entitled to disagree with his statement; after all, everyone has their own perspective.

<u>EXAMPLE</u>

 RealT is a platform for tokenized real estate sales. It is possible to invest starting from $50 with an annual return of around 10%. The properties are primarily located in the United States.

2. MUSIC

MUSIC INDUSTRY: THE SAME OLD SONG? NO!

MUSIC CONSTANTLY REINVENTS ITSELF: FROM VINYL TO STREAMING

The music industry has undoubtedly been one of the sectors most transformed by technology in the past fifty years (see the excellent animated infographic by VisualCapitalist on this topic[7]). As early as 1948, the introduction of vinyl records allowed people to store music at home for the first time. In 1979, the advent of the Walkman made it possible to have music not just at home but directly on the go. This innovation paved the way for widespread accessibility to music. In 1982, the emergence of CDs marked the decline of vinyl: with laser reading, the sound quality was significantly improved and required less storage space. However, CDs themselves were soon replaced by the iPod starting in 2001. This time, it became possible to carry thousands of songs in the palm of one's hand! In the 2010s, the rise of music streaming further disrupted the industry. Who still carries an iPod around to listen to music? Everything is done on smartphones now!

NEW CHALLENGES FOR THE MUSIC INDUSTRY TO OVERCOME

All these innovations have led to a significant democratization of music, opening it up to a much broader audience than before. Many artists have emerged over the past decade, including the most famous ones, as well as numerous independent creators. The competition is fierce, and very few manage to make a living from their passion. Streaming platforms have driven down revenue, forcing artists to modify the structure of their songs since plays are only counted as monetized after 30 seconds. As a result, nearly all artists have adopted the same strategy to please algorithms: placing the chorus at the beginning to captivate attention beyond the initial 30 seconds. Unfortunately, this has gradually stifled artists' creativity.

MUSICAL NFTS WILL BE THE NEXT WAVE...

AN EL DORADO FOR COLLECTORS

NFTs, non-fungible tokens, digital collectibles... Call them what you will. One thing is certain: musical NFTs will be the new El Dorado for collectors. In the past, collectors would amass vinyl records or merchandise from their favorite artists. In the future, it will be songs in the form of collector NFTs. Imagine, for example, if

Michael Jackson had released a limited edition of his famous *Thriller* music video, restricted to only 10,000 copies (no more). They would have sold like hotcakes and today would likely be valued well beyond their initial sale price.

PRESERVING ARTISTS' RIGHTS OVER THEIR CREATIONS

The numerous copyright issues in music clearly demonstrate the interest of artists in providing irrefutable and transparent proof of their rights over the lyrics or sounds they have created. For this purpose, NFTs are the ideal medium. They would allow for secure and permanent recording of the contributors involved in the creation of a song, whether it be for the lyrics or the music. The information would be timestamped using the Blockchain and made publicly accessible, at least for the relevant stakeholders. NFTs would enable the creation of a safer and more transparent global database, even though previous attempts to create such a database have failed (for example, the European Commission's Global Repertoire Database initiative, which had a budget of 12 million dollars). The transition to the Blockchain will likely initially occur on a private Blockchain, with authenticated collective management organizations giving information about the rights holders of the works.

AUTOMATING AND CUSTOMIZING COPYRIGHT MANAGEMENT

In a world where you can listen to music from anywhere on the planet with just a few clicks, the payment system for rights holders seems to be lagging behind. Payments sometimes take months to reach the bank accounts of rights holders. This slow and outdated system could be improved through blockchain technology, enabling the automation and personalization of copyright management. In the smart contract of a music NFT, the artist could not only be automatically paid for each play but also have finer control over how much they charge each party. For example, they could decide to charge a different percentage for nightclubs and radio stations. They could also choose to allocate 5% of the music's revenue to those who own the NFT.

EASIER ALBUM FUNDING

Funding an album can quickly become complicated, especially when subsidies are needed. The processes involved are lengthy, costly, and tedious. With NFTs, artists will have the opportunity to directly fundraise from their community. Imagine you want to finance your album with $100,000. You can simply launch a collection of 100 NFTs priced at $1,000 each. In the smart contract of each NFT, it would be stated that each NFT holder receives a 0.5% royalty. By giving away 50% of your rights, you can quickly finance your album with $100,000. The key is to have a dedicated community that believes in you and is willing to invest in you. Of course, if the target amount of $100,000 is not reached, the funds are automatically returned to the various contributors.

NEW ADVANTAGES FOR FANS

Beyond their financial aspect, NFTs can also grant exclusive rights to fans who own them. For example, they may have access to exclusive songs, receive a special dedication from the artist, listen to a song in advance, appear as extras in a music video, receive discounts on the next album, or even have the opportunity to meet the artist backstage after an incredible concert. For instance, in July 2022, L'Olympia (a renowned concert hall in Paris) sold 250 membership cards in the form of NFTs[8], granting certain benefits.

PROVING THAT YOU WERE THERE FROM THE BEGINNING OF AN EMERGING ARTIST

Imagine discovering an artist on Spotify when they only had 15,000 streams. A few months later, you see their streams have reached 150,000. You regret not being able to prove that you were there from the start, that you believed in their talent, and contributed to their early success. What if you could be rewarded for that? That's precisely what NFTs enable. They offer a unique opportunity to establish a direct and authentic connection with emerging artists. They allow recognition and appreciation for early supporters, offering them special rewards and the ability to feel involved in the artist's growing success.

A BETTER REMUNERATION FOR ARTISTS

One of the major problems faced by the majority of independent artists is the lack of remuneration. It is very difficult to make a decent living from streaming. For instance, Spotify pays artists between $0.003 - $0.005 per stream on average[9]. It means that an artist would need millions of streams just to earn a substantial amount of money. The Blockchain, by enabling artists to bypass intermediaries, could allow them to obtain better income. Similarly, artists could also receive royalties. Thus, with each resale of an NFT (for example, an NFT that grants the right to discounts on all of the artist's albums), the artist can be remunerated with a percentage of the sale. This offers a significant additional source of income.

CONCERT TICKETS IN THE FORM OF NFTS

Concerts are the primary source of revenue for musicians. However, concerts also involve tickets, and where there are tickets... there are scams. Scams involving fake tickets are becoming increasingly common in the music industry. It has become relatively easy to sell counterfeit tickets shortly before a major concert when the demand for obtaining those coveted tickets is at its peak. Fake tickets circulate, and it is difficult to distinguish the real ones from the fakes. Tickets in the form of NFTs, being secure and fully traceable, could be a solution to this problem. They would provide a level of security for both individuals and event organizers. Additionally, to prevent speculation on the black market, it would even be possible to include in the ticket's smart contract a provision that prohibits selling the ticket at a price higher than its original value. Many artists have already implemented NFT-based tickets for their concerts, such as The Weeknd in collaboration with TicketMaster[10].

STIMULATING FAN ENGAGEMENT

In today's music industry, artists provide content while fans have a passive role as consumers, with their interactions limited to likes and shares on social media or streaming platforms. NFTs rebalance the relationship between artists and their communities. The relationship is no longer one-sided. Unlike consuming music on centralized platforms, purchasing an artist's music NFT allows fans to directly contribute to their compensation. It's even possible to imagine a system where each play of a song requires a micro-transaction on the blockchain, and through a smart contract, the revenue from that track is automatically sent to the rights holders who own the NFT for the song.

ALL SECTORS OF THE MUSIC INDUSTRY WILL BE IMPACTED

Streaming platforms will be the first to suffer from the emergence of decentralized music platforms, as they will offer more attractive remuneration terms for artists (transparency, automatic payments, fairer distribution) while also providing space for new forms of exclusive rights for fans. Labels and record companies, although they will continue to play a significant role in artist promotion, will face challenges from these new decentralized models. Copyright management societies will no longer be able to collect rights from decentralized platforms, as they will be directly handled by a DAO* and smart contracts. All these stakeholders will be forced to adapt and gradually turn toward NFTs.

12 MILLION PEOPLE IN A METAVERSE CONCERT? YES, IT'S POSSIBLE!

Take a moment and try to recall: What do you think was the largest concert in history? 500,000 attendees? 1 million? 2 million? You're still far off! It was actually a concert by Jean-Michel Jarre in 1997 in Moscow, which gathered (brace yourself) 3.5 million spectators[11]! But in comparison, that's still far behind the 12.3 million players who gathered at Travis Scott's virtual concert in Fortnite[12]. For his show titled "Astronomical," Epic Games (the game's publisher and developer) created a special stage with giant inflatable balloons and Travis Scott heads. The video of the show received over 200 million views on YouTube[13]. Similarly, the Decentraland Metaverse Music Festival 2022 brought together over 200 artists, including celebrities like Ozzy Osbourne, Motörhead, and Megadeth[14]. Of course, a concert in a metaverse is not the same as a real concert, but it offers a more captivating experience than a simple live stream.

ASSOCIATING MUSIC WITH... SOMETHING OTHER THAN MUSIC

Perrine Guyomard, Head of Business Development & Innovation at Warner Music France, highlights the numerous opportunities NFTs offer to artists: *"For highly creative individuals, it allows them to connect different universes and further reveal their personality by expanding their field of expression. Some artists in our company came to us saying they kept a handwritten journal or made drawings but didn't know what to do with them. I told them that with NFTs, for example, they could link a track with the notes used to write the lyrics, including the scribbles and changes made. It may not fit into traditional formats, but it suits NFTs very well. It's a tool that enables the creation of very interesting complete works."*[15]

GENERATIVE MUSIC THROUGH NFTs

Today, when you listen to music, it can be considered "static": whether you listen to it in winter or summer, for the first or thousandth time, it remains the same. However, dynamic NFTs could change that. As the name suggests, these are NFTs that change based on specific criteria. This would work well with music: songs could evolve based on criteria chosen by the artist. The possibilities would be vast. Imagine the ambiance of the music changing based on the weather, time of day, or location where you're listening to it... or envision collectible NFTs that can be combined to create unique music compositions... The only limit will be our imagination!

MAJOR PLATFORMS AND ARTISTS EMBRACING NFTs

Since 2021, many artists have ventured into NFTs. Some have formed partnerships, such as Snoop Dogg and Eminem with BAYC* (their music video has garnered over 70 million views[16]), or Pharell Williams with Doodles. Others have launched NFT collections, including Rihanna, Muse, Kings of Leon, Shawn Mendes, Booba, Mike Shinoda of Linkin Park, and many more. Muse, for instance, became the first UK number one album to incorporate NFT technology[17]. The music video for their song "Will of the People" is heavily inspired by the cypherpunk* universe.

EXAMPLES

 Audius is a fully decentralized music streaming platform founded in 2018 by Roneil Rumburg and Forrest Browning. It provides artists with greater control over their music creations.

Pianity allows to collect music from artists through limited editions in the form of NFTs. Currently, there are four levels of rarity: Unique, Legendary, Epic, and Rare.

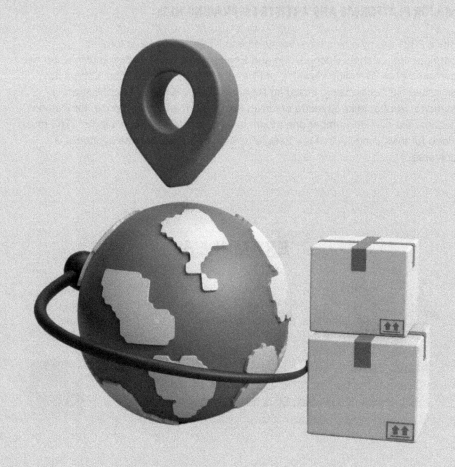

3. SUPPLY CHAIN

THE SUPPLY CHAIN: A SIGNIFICANT MARKET FACING NUMEROUS CHALLENGES

THE SUPPLY CHAIN: A MASSIVE $15 TRILLION MARKET...

The supply chain market is substantial because it is essential everywhere, whether it's purchasing pharmaceutical products, fresh vegetables, or the latest iPhone that has just been released, we inevitably rely on the upstream supply chain. We have indeed witnessed during the pandemic how the supply chain can pose problems. The size of the supply chain management market was estimated to be around $20 billion in 2022[18], and this figure is expected to double by 2030.

...BUT TRACEABILITY ISSUES PERSIST

Even though the supply chain plays a significant role in our economy, it is not without problems, especially when it comes to traceability. Traceability is a crucial issue because the actors in this sector cannot afford to "accidentally" lose packages. But losses can also be more subtle than package loss: for example, did you know that large distributors can lose up to 20% of their pallets each year? When you consider that the price of a standard pallet is at least $40, the costs can add up quickly. Moreover, not all standards and accounting models are the same, which generates significant transaction costs.

A LACK OF FLEXIBILITY

Flexibility is currently a major problem in the supply chain. Data management is one of the most concerning aspects because many systems used date back more than 20 years. As a result, some software is not compatible with each other, leading to integration and information sharing difficulties. Additionally, package tracking often relies on human interventions, exposing the process to risks of errors. Some parts of the supply chain are even managed on paper. These technological limitations and outdated practices have a direct impact on the efficiency and transparency of the supply chain.

IT'S NOT ME SAYING IT, IT'S THE BLOCKCHAIN

A REAL CONTRACT OF TRUST THROUGH SMART CONTRACTS

What if Darty's "contract of trust" was genuinely a contract of trust? For a long time, this retailer has committed to offering its customers low prices and quality after-sales service. However, the reality of this promise of transparency and honesty towards customers does not always meet their expectations. Technological advancements will strengthen this trust through smart contracts. These intelligent contracts are programmed to execute automatically once certain predefined conditions are met. They enable faster, secure, and transparent management of transactions between the company and its customers. They are open source, and anyone can read them. Being immutable, they cannot be modified once recorded on the blockchain.

REDUCING TRANSACTION COSTS

Previously, the supply chain was linear with few actors. However, since the 1990s, with globalization and the emergence of the Internet, supply chain networks have become considerably complex. These networks are now multi-tiered and involve a large number of suppliers, manufacturers, logistics partners, storage partners, etc. When some networks have hundreds of participants and thousands of daily transactions, errors are more frequent (missed shipments, payment issues, etc.), especially since many verifications are still performed manually or on paper. The use of NFTs at each level of the supply chain would be a way to reduce these "transaction costs" (in terms of time and money) as they enable faster data verification without relying on trusted intermediaries.

MINIMIZING PRODUCT RECALL COSTS

Product recalls are a nuisance that companies strive to avoid as they can cause considerable financial losses and damage to the brand's reputation. Blockchain is a solution to this problem as it allows tracking the entire journey of a product, from raw materials to the finished product. Let's take the example of canned tuna. Suppose a supermarket detects a quality issue with its cans of tuna. It immediately contacts its suppliers, who contact the manufacturer. If the manufacturer sources from multiple suppliers and processes tuna in multiple factories, it can be challenging for them to precisely locate the defective cans. Blockchain technology resolves this problem by ensuring better traceability. With this technology, the manufacturer can trace each can of tuna back to the specific shipping vessel it came from. Each step of the logistics chain is recorded using NFTs, ensuring complete transparency and immutability. With blockchain, information can be quickly communicated, avoiding the recall of entire batches when only a few products are affected.

PREVENTING FRAUD: THE CASE OF HORSEMEAT FRAUD

One can even go further and assert with certainty that in the future, consumers themselves will demand certified traceability on a blockchain, just as we expect a confirmation email after an online purchase. The case of the agri-food industry is a compelling example of fraud problems in the supply chain, as fraud amounts to $40 billion per year[19]. The horsemeat fraud in 2013 in Europe is significant in this regard, with 4.5 million ready meals and tens of millions of consumers impacted[20]. In 2013, the DGCCRF identified 750 tons distributed in thirteen countries. The entire production chain was involved (abattoirs, traders, processors, etc.), and it was challenging to trace the entire journey of the prepared meals.

TRACKING THE LOGISTICS THREAD

The lack of transparency in the supply chain is detrimental to both consumers (who don't have the means to verify the origin of goods) and companies (who sometimes lack visibility on their supply chain, especially when many actors are involved). Associating products with NFTs to track them on a permanent, transparent, and more secure register is a good idea. In the near future, it will seem obvious to track our packages directly on the blockchain, just as it seems obvious to expect a confirmation email after making an online purchase. It will seem logical to sign the proper receipt of a package with one's wallet through a blockchain transaction.

HAVING A BETTER BRAND IMAGE

For companies emphasizing environmental commitment in their marketing strategy, NFTs offer the opportunity to transparently and publicly prove that their products are indeed sourced sustainably or made from local raw materials. Customers will no longer need to blindly trust; they can verify the information provided by the company themselves because everything will be recorded directly on the blockchain. Consumers can be assured that a label "says the truth" and adjust their purchasing behavior accordingly.

HOMOGENIZING DATA

One of the major problems in the supply chain is that all the involved actors are siloed and may not necessarily have the same version of payment or delivery documents (often in paper format). By using NFTs, all these documents would be recorded and accessible from a single location, requiring only the possession of the private key (provided along with the NFT) to access the documents. Thus, these documents would have the advantage of being both accessible and confidential through data encryption. Each delivery of a package would be recorded on the blockchain, and the documents would be automatically updated. With NFTs, companies could grant access to specific individuals while benefiting from the transparency offered by the blockchain.

EXAMPLES

 Morpheus Network enables its clients to automate and optimize their operations, streamlining the entire supply chain process

Ownest focuses on the transfer of responsibility through NFTs rather than just ownership. They specialize in traceability and cost optimization to minimize expenses in the supply chain.

4. SOCIAL MEDIA

SOCIAL MEDIA AND CENTRALIZATION

"ACCEPT THE TERMS OF USE"

"I have read and agree to the terms and conditions of use": perhaps this is the most widespread lie on the Internet. In 2013, a study conducted by researchers from Carnegie Mellon University (located in Pittsburgh) revealed that it would take 76 days a year, 8 hours a day, to read all the terms and conditions of the services they use[21]. Needless to say, nobody does it! In 2013, the terms and conditions of the top 75 most popular websites on the Internet averaged around 2,500 words. Today, that number has only increased. The terms and conditions are not designed for you to read them; quite the opposite. It's no wonder that everyone clicks on "Accept" without even paying attention. The problem is that by doing so, we give consent to tech giants to use and exploit our personal data.

LARGEST SOCIAL MEDIA PLATFORMS EMBRACING NFTs

On October 28, 2021, Facebook announced a complete rebranding as Meta[22]. In 2022, the Meta group announced that NFTs were being integrated into Instagram[23]... only to reverse that decision just 10 months later[24]. As for Twitter, in March 2021, Jack Dorsey, the founder, sold the NFT of the first tweet from the platform for $2.9 million to Sina Estavi, the CEO of Bridge Oracle. Interestingly, that tweet is now valued at less than $280[25]. In October 2022, after 7 months of negotiations, Elon Musk (a fan of Dogecoin, by the way) acquired Twitter for $44 billion, bringing the social media platform into the Web3 era. In January 2022, Twitter enabled users to associate their profile pictures with NFTs directly on their accounts[26]. In October 2022, Reddit (with 52 million daily users) made a notable entry into the Web3 space by onboarding over 3 million users[27].

...BUT IT RAISES THE ISSUE OF CENTRALIZATION

One step forward for adoption, two steps backward for decentralization? Reddit's onboarding seems to prove this, as most people who created a Vault digital wallet to obtain an avatar were not aware that they were holding an NFT. According to data from Dune Analytics[28], only around 15,000 addresses are truly active and engage in other interactions on the blockchain. Very few people are aware of the centralization issues associated with blockchain and NFTs. These issues arise, for example, in relation to the question of custodial or non-custodial wallets. If the wallets are custodial, it means that the platform holds your private key, not you. The entire purpose of the blockchain as a decentralized system is then lost.

BENEFITS OF NFTS FOR DECENTRALIZED SOCIAL MEDIA

AVOIDING CENSORSHIP: THE EXAMPLE OF TRUMP

In January 2021, Twitter suspended Donald Trump's account and deleted some of his tweets, citing "incitement of violence" as the reason. This decision sparked debates about the issue of censorship on social media platforms. Some argued that the suspension of Trump's account was a necessary step to limit the spread of messages that could incite violence and harm public safety. Others saw it as a form of censorship that restricts freedom of speech. Regardless of one's opinion, it is highly likely that social media influencers will gradually move towards decentralized models (such as Lens Protocol) to be less dependent on unilateral decisions by these platforms. Spending all that time creating content only to see it disappear in seconds based on the platform's sole decision? Content creators are well aware of this issue and will switch to a decentralized alternative as soon as it becomes possible. By associating their content and followers with NFTs recorded on the blockchain, they can ensure that no centralized entity can censor them.

AVOIDING FAKE PROFILES AND SCAMS

You have probably noticed the increasing number of fake profiles on social media platforms, particularly on Twitter. Some scammers pretend to be well-known figures in the ecosystem to push their followers to invest in scams. Others create pages that mimic official brands or artists, launching identical collections. Users who don't conduct minimum verification end up purchasing NFTs that hold no value. Social media platforms are aware of the problem, and some (like Twitter or OpenSea) offer a form of blue badge to identify "legit" accounts. While this is a good initiative, NFTs could further enhance account legitimacy by offering more transparency without relying on these platforms as intermediaries of trust.

BETTER COMPENSATION FOR CONTENT CREATORS

The compensation of content creators on social media platforms is a significant issue, especially on video platforms like TikTok and YouTube. On average, creators earn around $1 per 1,000 views on YouTube and $0.02 to $0.04 per 1,000 views on TikTok[29]. These platforms take a substantial margin from the creators' efforts. Content creators are forced to collaborate with brands or sell their own products or courses to make ends meet. Moreover, these platforms can decide to demonetize their content at any time. To address this problem, solutions like Patreon have emerged to allow fans to financially support creators in exchange for exclusive content. NFTs could further enhance this system by enabling artists to grant exclusive rights to those who support their work. Additionally, NFTs could facilitate project financing through crowdfunding.

ALL YOUR CONTENT AND FOLLOWERS IN YOUR WALLET

Today, if you regularly publish content on social media, you don't actually own it. Since your content is hosted on centralized servers, the social media platform can easily censor or delete your account at any time. For example, many content creators on LinkedIn have complained about their accounts being suspended without apparent reason, despite having been active for years and having created significant value for others. In Web3, you will have all your content and followers directly in your wallet, regardless of the social media platform you use. If a platform decides to exclude you, it won't be a problem because you will still have access to what you have posted (including likes and comments) and all your followers.

THE HYPE OF PROFILE PICTURES (PFPs)

It's impossible to talk about the use of NFTs on social media without mentioning PFPs (Profile Pictures). As the name suggests, PFPs are simply profile pictures derived from famous NFT collections. There isn't any practical use for this type of NFT, apart from showing off with a JPEG image worth hundreds of thousands of dollars (exaggerating a bit!). It mainly serves to prove that you have the means to afford it and that you support the project. Many celebrities have displayed their PFPs on social media: Eminem with Bored Ape Yacht Club #9055, Serena Williams with Cryptopunk #2950, Reese Witherspoon with World of Women #6403, Jimmy Fallon with Bored Ape Yacht Club #599, and the list goes on.

EXAMPLES

Lens Protocol is an infrastructure that enables the construction of decentralized social networks such as Lenster and Lenstube. It was created by Aave, a well-known lending platform in the DeFi ecosystem.

Nostr is an open-source protocol that utilizes blockchain to build the world's first fully decentralized and censorship-resistant social network. Jack Dorsey, the founder of Twitter, is a big fan!

5. DOMAIN NAMES

THE FUNCTIONING OF DOMAIN NAMES IN WEB2

THE FUNCTIONING OF IP ADDRESSES AND DOMAIN NAMES

In 1983, a group of researchers consisting of Jon Postel, Paul Mockapetris, and Craig Patrige invented the Domain Name System (DNS), which is at the core of Internet functioning today. The DNS (Domain Name Service) has significantly facilitated internet navigation by linking the IP address of a website to its domain name. For example, to access Facebook's services, you only need to type their domain name, facebook.com, instead of typing the IP address 69.63.176.13, which is much easier to remember. Similarly, the IP address 216.58.217.206 is linked to google.com.

THE BUSINESS OF WEB2 DOMAIN NAMES (SEDO, GODADDY, ...)

Today, having an online presence is essential for any business, whether it involves placing orders, managing customer returns, or responding to quote requests. Having a website provides access to numerous services and significantly enhances visibility. However, to have a website, you also need a domain name; otherwise, it would be impossible to find you. Domain names are like postal addresses: they are how customers know where to go to access your products or services. They have become so essential that a genuine market for buying, selling, and leasing them has developed. Several players have positioned themselves in this market, such as GoDaddy, Sedo, Dan, and more. They all acquire domain names to resell or lease them. As a result, GoDaddy is the world's largest domain registrar, currently managing over 75 million domains for 17 million customers worldwide[30].

DOMAIN NAMES: FOCUS ON ICANN

It is impossible to talk about domain names without mentioning ICANN. ICANN (Internet Corporation for Assigned Names and Numbers) is a non-profit organization created in 1998. It is, in a way, at the top of the domain name hierarchy: it decides on the opening of any new extension and manages the list of Top-Level Domains (TLDs) such as .com, .net, .org, .fr, .uk, etc., which it entrusts the technical management to organizations called registrars. Its main mission is to regulate IP addressing and domain names used on the web. It is closely linked to the U.S. government, which gives it international legitimacy in decision-making. It does not have control over the content published on the web, nor does it have the rights to manage internet access. Nevertheless, it plays a crucial role on the Internet, which can sometimes pose centralization issues.

THE DECEMBER 2021 CONTROVERSY INVOLVING ICANN AND NFTs

It all started in December 2021 when ICANN refused to transfer 23 domain names owned by the UNR registry (domiciled in the Cayman Islands). The controversy began when UNR put up its batch of domain names for auction as NFTs on the Ethereum blockchain, raising $40 million from these sales[31]. ICANN did not appreciate this sale at all because it meant that it no longer had authority over these domain names, as they now belonged to the Ethereum blockchain rather than ICANN. Since Ethereum is decentralized, no central authority has control over it, which obviously did not sit well with ICANN. Currently, none of these 23 domain names have been transferred to the winners of the auctions. This controversy reveals two major issues related to Web 2 domain names: centralization and censorship.

THE INTEREST OF NFTS IN DOMAIN NAMES

A FEW REMINDERS: HOW A WALLET WORKS IN WEB3

To use web3 domain names, you need a wallet. This wallet contains two types of cryptographic keys:
- A **private key**: It allows you to control your wallet and digital assets (crypto, NFTs). You can access it with your password or speed phrase*. It is like the key to your house (or mailbox), and it must be kept secret to prevent theft. If you lose it, it is permanently lost.
- A **public key** : It represents the public address of your wallet and allows you to receive digital assets. On Ethereum, it consists of a string of 42 characters (numbers or letters). This type of public key can be associated with a web3 domain name.

A MORE READABLE ADDRESS FOR YOUR WALLET

Just as web addresses have replaced IP addresses, public keys of our wallets will soon be replaced by web3 domain names. The most common web3 domain name extension is currently .eth (for Ethereum). It is definitely easier to remember a wallet address like "name.eth" compared to a much more complex address like "0xb9b39e5DA023E3560e85C33d5cD6843c3B3a87C6"! If the mass adoption of NFTs depends on various factors, one of them is certainly the ability to replace the hard-to-read 42-character address with a simple and understandable name.

EASIER RECEIPT OF CRYPTOCURRENCIES

To send cryptocurrency or an NFT to someone, you no longer need to ask, "Does your address start with 0xb9b and end with a87C6?" You can simply say, "Send the transaction to: name.eth," which represents the receiving address. It will soon be as easy as sending an email with your email address. This will be an incredibly convenient feature for everyday use, whether for transferring funds between your own addresses or simply facilitating the receipt of funds from family or employers.

NO CENTRALIZATION OR CENSORSHIP (OR ALMOST)

While Web2 domain names are managed by a handful of entities, Web3 domain names are decentralized. In practical terms, if ICANN decides to revoke your right to use the domain name "name.com" tomorrow, it can do so because it has control over it. This is not the case with Web3 domain names. For example, the domain name "name.eth" is impossible to censor because it is stored in a decentralized manner on the Ethereum blockchain, and no entity can censor it. Similarly, launching a DDoS attack (Denial of Service) on a Web3 website is much more difficult because even if one server is down, others can continue to function.

OWNING YOUR WEB3 IDENTITY

Imagine being one of the top players in a popular blockchain game, but your digital identity on the leaderboard appears as "0xb9b (...) a87C6". It's hard to claim that little moment of glory! You would definitely want to associate your pseudonym with that leaderboard. Beyond the realm of blockchain games, the core of web3 domain names lies in digital identity. We know how much our identity is becoming increasingly digital. For some, it is the heart of their business (think of Instagram influencers, for example!). However, currently, you don't truly own your digital identity; it is controlled by tech giants. Web3 domain names are specifically created to allow everyone to take control of their digital identity.

EASIER CREATION AND HOSTING OF WEBSITES

In just a few clicks, it will soon be possible to create your own decentralized website with a domain name that you truly own. Such websites already exist[32], but they are still relatively inaccessible. Accessing them requires using browsers like Brave, which also give users the option to enable optional ads that pay users in BAT (Basic Attention Tokens). Users can then send contributions to content creators through cryptocurrency tips. As of February 2023, Brave had 21 million daily active users[33], which is still relatively small compared to Google but indicates a significant level of interest.

THE SURGE OF ENS DOMAIN NAMES IN 2021-2022

The Ethereum blockchain utilizes domain names with the .eth extension, which are generated by the Ethereum Name Service (ENS). Their numbers skyrocketed in 2021-2022. This was partly due to the massive airdrop* of 25 million ENS tokens to those who had purchased a .eth domain name before October 2021. Some people made fortunes, which further increased the visibility of web3 domain names. According to statistics from Dune Analytics, 137,689 wallet addresses were eligible for the airdrop[34]. On platforms like OpenSea, nearing The Merge* (September 15, 2022), the trading volume of ENS domains even surpassed well-known collections (such as BAYC*, CloneX, or Moonbirds), reaching a volume of 3,762 ETH (equivalent to $6.6 million) in a week. The peak trading volume reached 8,488 ETH on May 2, 2022[35].

LARGE BRANDS WILL NEED TO GET INVOLVED (CYBERSQUATTING)

Despite the explosion of web3 domain names since 2021, their quantity remains relatively low compared to web2 domain names. However, that does not mean they won't be widely used in the years to come. If that is the case, a problem will arise due to the nature of the blockchain: its irreversibility. It is easy to imagine how this new category of domain names would become a perfect playing field for cybersquatters. Pursuing legal action would be complicated for the reasons mentioned above. Therefore, large brands have a strong interest in engaging in defensive registrations to protect themselves from potential cybersquatters who would have no qualms about selling them the domain name for a hefty price.

Unless they enjoy playing poker and relying on the failure of Web3 and associated domain names, which seems like a risky bet...

EXAMPLES

 ENS (Ethereum Name Service) is a website that allows users to register names with the .eth extension. It is managed by True Names, an organization based in Singapore. ENS operates exclusively on the Ethereum blockchain, and the registered names need to be renewed periodically.

Unstoppable Domains was created in 2018 and offers a wider range of domain extensions such as .nft, .crypto, .blockchain, and more. Unlike ENS, once you purchase a domain name from Unstoppable Domains, it belongs to you forever, and there is no need for renewal.

6. BOOKS

SELF-PUBLISHED NFT BOOKS: THE ADVANTAGES OF SELF-PUBLISHING...

A PERSPECTIVE THAT HAS CHANGED IN RECENT YEARS

There's no denying that just a few years ago, when we saw a book labeled as "self-published," we tended to think that it had been rejected by all publishers and that the author wanted to publish it anyway out of desperation. It was seen as a choice of last resort. As readers, we would assume that self-published books were somehow "inferior" because traditional publishers hadn't wanted them. However, self-published books have gained significant popularity in recent times, and many best-selling books are, in fact, self-published. Examples include _Eragon_, _Rich Dad Poor Dad_, _Fifty Shades of Grey_, and many more. Similarly, crowdfunding platforms like Kickstarter or Ulule have allowed numerous independent authors to finance their own books, sometimes raising substantial amounts[36]. It's not surprising to witness this recent shift, as self-published books offer numerous advantages, as we will explore.

A BETTER INCOME FOR AUTHORS

On average, out of a book sold for $20, the author only earns 10% of the book price, which is $2. A significant portion of the sale price is dedicated to the publisher ($4, or 20%). This is how the market works: if you publish your book with a publishing house, you have to relinquish your rights as an author to the publisher in exchange for a compensation equivalent to a percentage of the book's sale price. On the other hand, if you choose self-publishing, you retain full ownership of your rights as an author and you receive the profits from each book sold, based on the price you have set.

AUTONOMY AND FREEDOM (IN THEORY, AT LEAST)

When you self-publish your book, you are the sole master on board. You don't have to answer to anyone, and you can freely choose the title, cover, desired format, content of the book, price, etc. You are not dependent on a traditional publishing house that would tell you what to do: through self-publishing, you retain complete autonomy. Some publishing houses "shackle" their authors by obliging them to publish their next books with them. Publishing contracts are often heavy and complex, filled with pitfalls to avoid. Of course, not relying on a publishing house comes with its disadvantages. Knowing how to write is not the only condition for success in self-publishing: it requires a significant personal investment, sometimes challenging for authors to manage. A self-published author must wear all the hats of a traditional publisher: proofreading, editing, cover design... and above all, book promotion.

IMMEDIACY OF PUBLICATION

When going through a traditional publisher, response times are often long, and rejections are numerous (J.K. Rowling can testify to that!). Furthermore, publishing houses usually only accept manuscripts in physical format, so you must bear the costs of printing and shipping your books. This investment is often lost for three-quarters of the submissions, as manuscripts are rarely returned. Even if you manage to navigate this arduous process and have the opportunity to see a publisher accept your manuscript, you still have to wait several months before seeing it on the shelves of your favorite bookstores. In addition, authors can generally only publish a maximum of one book per year, which penalizes productive authors who would like to publish multiple books each year.

PRINT ON DEMAND, NO STORAGE COSTS

Print on Demand (POD) has become popular in recent years, especially among self-published authors. When you use Print on Demand, you no longer have to deal with book production, delivery costs, storage, or returns, and you also don't have to manage customer support. This greatly simplifies management and reduces costs, allowing you to devote more time to the promotional aspect of the book. You also have the option to print a single copy of your book. POD enables greater responsiveness and adaptability: for example, if you want to make a slight modification to your cover or add a paragraph to your book, you simply need to send the new PDFs (and soon NFTs!) to the service provider, and the new versions will be incorporated instantaneously.

...AND E-BOOKS...

GREATER SCALABILITY

E-books offer even more advantages than POD because they are 100% digital. Readers can buy and download them instantly from anywhere in the world, at any time of the day. This allows authors (and publishers) to reach a wider audience. Similarly, the production costs of an e-book are often much lower than those of a physical book because there are no printing, storage, or physical distribution costs. As a result, authors and publishers can sell e-books at a lower price while still making a similar profit.

MORE INTERACTIVE THAN PRINT BOOKS

When you have an e-book in hand (whether on a tablet or phone), you have the ability to customize your reading experience by adjusting the font size (ideal for dyslexic readers), background color, or screen brightness (great for reading at night). You also have the ability to check the book's sources in real-time by simply clicking on the link at the bottom of the page, which immediately takes you to the website. Similarly, if you're looking for a specific keyword in the book (let's say "Julius Caesar" for a history book), you have a search tab that allows you to do so, saving you several minutes of searching. If you want to improve your foreign language skills, e-books make it easy because a dictionary can be directly integrated. Additionally, you can highlight favorite passages and quickly find them in one file, or add comments without damaging the book.

YOUR ENTIRE LIBRARY ON-THE-GO WITH E-READERS

E-readers have made their way into our daily lives in recent years. Whether for avid readers or occasional readers, they have become a practical tool to carry everywhere. Amazon has reportedly sold between 20 and 90 million Kindle e-readers since its launch in 2007[37]. E-readers weigh only a few grams but can hold a library of thousands of books! Whether on a train, at the beach, or on the other side of the world, it is possible to carry your entire library without having to preselect which books you want to bring. But even if you don't travel often, e-readers offer significant space savings at home.

THE AUDIOBOOK MARKET

How can we talk about e-books without mentioning audiobooks? It is a booming market that represents billions of dollars today. Spotify, for instance, recently entered this field with the acquisition of Findaway in 2021[38], offering a service with over 300,000 audiobook titles. Audiobooks are advantageous for multiple reasons. First and foremost, they allow readers to relax and unwind while listening to a story (e.g., during a walk in the forest). They also provide a more immersive experience with accompanying melodies, sound effects, and character voices. Finally, they save time by allowing people to "read" a book while doing the dishes, exercising, or commuting to work.

... BUT EVEN MORE WITH NFTS!

YOU TRULY OWN YOUR BOOK

You may not know it, but all the e-books you have purchased and can read on dedicated platforms do not belong to you. Without considering PDF books, all the books you have on your Kindle, for example, actually belong to Amazon, not to you. The only thing you have is a license to read the book on their platform. If Kindle were to disappear one day, your book would also disappear. Similarly, if for any reason Kindle servers don't work, you will no longer have access to your books. In contrast, on a blockchain, since the servers are decentralized, you are sure to always have access to your books. And the books truly belong to you! Once they are minted* in your wallet*, no one else but you has access to them, not even the platform on which you minted your book.

THE ABILITY TO RESALE YOUR BOOK IN TWO CLICKS

One of the major advantages of owning your own e-book is that it will now be possible to sell it in two clicks on a dedicated marketplace! Indeed, the problem with buying a book in PDF format is that there is no secondary market: once you have read it, you cannot resell it. With NFT technology, you will be able to do so. You simply need to put your book up for sale on the marketplace, and when someone buys your book, it will be automatically transferred to their wallet (so you will no longer have yours). The money will be automatically refunded to you. You won't have to worry about finding someone willing to buy your book. In exchange for this service, the marketplace will take a small commission.

NO MORE ILLEGAL DOWNLOADS!

One of the problems with e-books today is that once you buy them, they are in PDF format. However, you can easily give this PDF book to your friends with a few clicks. This is a problem for authors and represents a significant loss of revenue for them. It is not uncommon to see authors complaining that the book they spent months writing ends up freely circulating on the Internet and that anyone can get it for free. The solution to this problem lies in NFT books because, unlike PDF books, they cannot be duplicated, they are unique. Of course, this is not a miracle solution: just as Netflix did not put an end to illegal downloads, NFT books will not prevent the circulation of books without the consent of the authors. However, they offer a very interesting alternative for both authors and readers.

CREATING A COMMUNITY WITH EXCLUSIVE RIGHTS

Self-published authors are well aware that in order to be read, they need to build a community of readers. But since they don't benefit from the network of a publishing house, they are the only ones who have to promote their book. And one of the best ways to do this is to foster closeness with readers by communicating with them, especially on social media. By maintaining a direct relationship with their readers, they build loyalty over time. NFT books will go beyond simple communication with readers; they will create real communities by granting exclusive rights to the most engaged readers. For example, a reader who owns all of an author's books in NFT format will have the opportunity to meet the author in person in a small group. Those who bought the collector's edition of a book will, for example, have access to a Discord server* (only accessible with the NFT's private key) to communicate directly with the author.

IDEAL FOR LIMITED EDITIONS

A few years ago, it was impossible to create true limited editions for ebooks. But NFTs will change that: for the first time in history, they will allow the creation of digital scarcity. Each NFT book will be associated with a unique serial number authenticated by the blockchain. If a collector's edition book is released in 2000 copies and you have number 167, you can prove it through the blockchain. Even if someone manages to get their hands on it, take screenshots, and reproduce the book identically, they won't be able to prove that it's an official version of the book.

MORE REVENUE FOR AUTHORS

Based on what we've just seen, it becomes apparent that authors would have a lot to gain by adopting NFT books, as it would allow them to increase their revenue in three different ways. Firstly, limited edition NFT books could enable authors to sell their books at higher prices due to their rarity. These books could be of interest to collectors who would be willing to pay a premium to obtain an NFT book from the author, especially if it's their first book (and especially if they can benefit from exclusive rights as we've seen). Secondly, authors could receive royalties for each resale of their book on the secondary market. These royalties (e.g., 5%) would be directly written into the smart contract of the NFT book. With each resale, the author could receive royalties for as long as the book is being resold/purchased. Lastly, the blockchain, as an automatic trust tool, would eliminate intermediaries, allowing authors to sell their books directly to readers without having to go through intermediaries that take significant margins.

BOOK SIGNING EVENTS

Imagine attending a book signing event with your favorite author. You've bought their latest book and are eager to have it signed. You wait in line for hours, and finally, it's your turn. The author signs your book, writes a personal dedication, and you're thrilled. But what will you do with your book now? Keep it safely in your library? Of course, but why not do something more interesting with it? This is where NFTs come in. Instead of just getting your book signed, the author can also create a unique NFT for your dedication. This NFT can take the form of an image or a video of the author signing your book. You can then sell or trade this NFT with other fans of the author or the series, and even keep it as a precious memento of your encounter with the author.

UNCENSORABLE, UNFORGEABLE, AND ANONYMOUS BOOKS

Just as Satoshi Nakamoto created uncensorable currency while remaining anonymous, NFTs could make books uncensorable due to their decentralized and immutable nature. When a book is registered as an NFT on a blockchain, it becomes an integral part of that blockchain. This means that if a public or private entity wants to censor the book for any reason, they cannot do so because there will always be at least one intact copy on the blockchain. NFTs, therefore, allow authors to publish their work without fearing censorship or the removal of their book by third parties. Furthermore, zero-knowledge proof (ZKP) technology could enable authors to publish a book anonymously while still having the ability to prove that they are the authors[39].

EASIER COLLABORATIVE CONTENT

In the world of publishing, the issue of fair remuneration for co-authors of a book often poses a problem. It's not uncommon for copyright royalties to be unevenly distributed, leaving some authors with a minimal share of the revenue generated from book sales. This is where blockchain technology can provide an innovative solution. It can be directly written into the smart contract of the book that, with each sale, the revenues are automatically distributed to the co-authors of the book. Through the use of the blockchain, each co-author could verify the payments received and be assured of receiving fair compensation for their contribution to the work.

NEW MARKETING STRATEGY: THE EXAMPLE OF GARY VEE

1 million book pre-orders in 24 hours[40]... That's the feat Gary Vee accomplished with a well-crafted marketing strategy... using NFTs! It's worth mentioning that he was no stranger to NFTs, as he had already created VeeFriends in May 2021, an NFT project designed to help people explore and understand NFTs. It offered exclusive access to a pass for VeeCon, a conference that brings together people from around the world every year. Riding on the success of VeeFriends[41], he promised anyone who purchased 12 copies of his new book titled "Twelve and a Half" an NFT connected to the newly created franchise in May 2021 (without revealing what it was to fuel the mystery). This created an incredible FOMO (fear of missing out) movement that skyrocketed book sales. It's worth noting that French publishing houses have also started using NFTs in their marketing strategies, like Fayard Editions[42].

{QUICK PUBLICITY}

(And yes, this book is self-published, I can do whatever I want :p)

I am planning to develop my own startup in the book industry, leveraging all the advantages of Blockchain and NFTs. The brand is trademarked but not yet registered, so I can't talk about it here just yet. If you're interested in this project, you can follow me on Linkedin starting now, and I will definitely share more information there!

7. EMAILS

THE EMAIL REVOLUTION

THE BIRTH OF EMAIL

Since its creation, email has completely revolutionized our way of communicating on the internet. Here are a few milestones:

- **1965**: The first appearance of email, known as the "Mailbox" program, happened at MIT. Users could leave messages on the university's computers for others to read.
- **1969**: The creation of the ARPANET network enabled the first communication between two computers spanning a distance of 500 km.
- **1971**: Ray Tomlinson, an American engineer, introduced the "@" symbol to link the username and destination address.
- **1982**: The Simple Mail Transfer Protocol (SMTP) was developed as a communication protocol used to transfer electronic messages to email servers.
- **1998**: Microsoft launched Outlook 2000 and acquired Hotmail.
- **Late 1990s**: Email gained popularity, and HTML format messages emerged, allowing the use of different fonts, colors, images, and formats.
- **2004**: Google announced the launch of its free email service, Gmail.
- **2018**: The General Data Protection Regulation (GDPR) came into effect, regulating email marketing.

OVER 300 BILLION EMAILS... PER DAY!

Today, email is a part of our daily lives. It is ubiquitous, with people sending and receiving emails every day. There are short emails, long ones, well-crafted ones, poorly crafted ones, spam, phishing attempts, and more. The number of emails sent each day is staggering: 300 billion! To be more precise, in 2020, there were exactly 306.4 billion daily emails[43], including 1.4 billion in France for 42.2 million users. These numbers demonstrate the extent of email usage and its importance in our daily lives. Email has become a cornerstone of modern life, and its usage shows no signs of diminishing.

THE WELL-KNWON ORDER CONFIRMATION EMAIL

Within the vast ocean of emails sent worldwide every day, a significant portion consists of order confirmation emails. While not always seen as crucial a few years ago, they have become indispensable. Not receiving an order confirmation email can cause anxiety, as it may indicate a problem with the order. These transactional emails, which are sent automatically without human intervention, are opened in

70% of cases[44], demonstrating their importance. Some brands take advantage of these emails to suggest the purchase of other products since the average reading time for this type of email is typically longer.

NFT EMAILS: MORE THAN JUST EMAILS...

A WAY TO COMBAT EMAIL CENTRALIZATION

Who doesn't have a Gmail or Outlook address these days? If you're reading this, there's a good chance you have at least one! This situation highlights a significant problem: email centralization around a few major players. It's not surprising given that the email market was valued at over $46.8 billion in 2020 and is expected to surpass $84.2 billion by the end of 2024[45]. In 2018, Gmail already had over 1.5 billion active users. The top three email services used in France—Gmail, Outlook, and Orange Mail—account for more than 57 million unique visitors each month[46]. Blockchain technology could decentralize email management, offering users more control over their data and privacy.

ENSURING EMAILS ARE NOT DELETED AGAINST OUR WILL

Today, when you send an email, it can be deleted by a third party, whether maliciously or unintentionally. This can happen for security reasons or to comply with company policies. Technical issues like server outages or software errors can also lead to email deletion. Additionally, emails may be archived or stored for a limited time, resulting in automatic deletion. In contrast, NFT-based emails are stored on the blockchain, making them immutable and undeletable. No central entity has control over them, and they are forever recorded in the digital ledger.

FRAUDULENT EMAILS AND PHISHING ATTEMPTS

As mentioned earlier, 300 billion emails are sent each day. With such a large volume, it's easy to fall victim to a phishing attempt. Phishing is the preferred method for cybercriminals to gain access to sensitive data and introduce malware—it requires little effort for significant results. Currently, 96% of phishing attacks occur via email[47]. Phishing websites are constantly created and used in these scams. In 2021, approximately 1.5 million new phishing URLs were identified each month[48]. This issue is particularly important as emails often contain critical information for businesses, such as contracts and personal data. By providing more transparency and better traceability, NFTs can partially address this problem.

GOOD NEWS FOR GDPR COMPLIANCE

The General Data Protection Regulation (GDPR) is a European regulation implemented in May 2018. It aims to protect the personal data of European citizens and enhance their control over its usage. Concerning emails, the GDPR imposes several obligations on companies and organizations that collect and process user data. Companies must obtain explicit consent from each user before collecting and processing their personal data. NFTs could be used to ensure that the user has given consent by signing a transaction.

NFTs TO CELEBRATE OR AS REMEMBRANCES OF OLD EMAILS

Most of the emails in our inbox hold little value to us. However, there are certain emails that we may want to immortalize on the blockchain by transforming them into NFTs. It could be an email received from someone significant to us or an important work-related email. Due to their uniqueness, there would be an interest in collecting these NFT emails and preserving them for the long term, similar to digital mementos. Some emails might even become precious documents to us. In the future, there might be a feature directly integrated into email applications to automatically transform emails into NFTs.

AN INTERESTING SOLUTION FOR LEGAL SUMMONSES

Emails currently do not have evidentiary value in legal disputes or other judicial actions. They do not hold the same legal weight as documents issued by a notary or bailiff. The reason behind this limitation is that the certain identification of the sender and the integrity of email content can be disputed. This limitation could be overcome with NFTs, as they rely on traceable technology where both the sender and recipient can be definitively identified. This could prove useful in many ways.

REPLACING EMAIL ADDRESSES WITH WALLET ADDRESSES?

In the future, it is likely that our most important messages will be sent directly from our wallet addresses rather than email addresses. Similar to how an email address has a unique identifier (e.g., example@gmail.com), a wallet address also has a unique identifier (e.g., 0x5b4...5eg2). To ensure that your email has been successfully sent and received by the intended recipient, it would be simplest to use your wallet address. Of course, this replacement would only apply to a small portion of email addresses, as 98% of emails we send won't require blockchain technology.

EXAMPLE

 MailStone is a solution that records a digital fingerprint of emails on the blockchain to ensure their integrity and security.

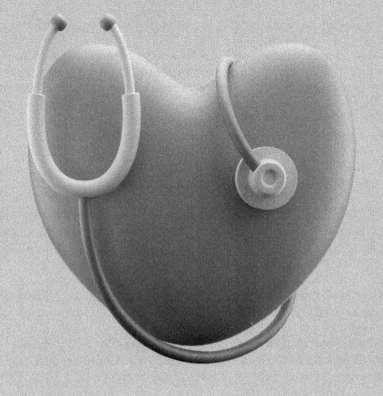

8. HEALTH

DATA AND HEALTH: HEAD-SPINNING NUMBERS

THE HEALTH DATA MARKET: $230 BILLION

The digital health market is expected to reach over $230 billion worldwide in 2023, representing a 160% increase compared to 2019[49]. This growth can be attributed to the increasing adoption of technology in the healthcare sector and the emergence of new players in the market. These new players are becoming more numerous and diverse. In addition to large technology companies, numerous startups specialized in digital health are emerging, developing new solutions to meet market needs. These include telemedicine and teleconsultation platforms that facilitate access to care for patients who are geographically distant from healthcare centers.

WHO HAS ACCESS TO OUR MEDICAL DATA AND HOW IS IT MANAGED?

Have you ever wondered how your health data is stored, who has access to it, and for what purposes? Even if you haven't, it's worth knowing that doctors are not the only ones with access to your sensitive data. This data is regularly and legally accessible and exchanged on marketplaces (often without the patients' awareness). Our current healthcare system heavily relies on the collection, processing, and utilization of data, and medical researchers and companies purchase large sets of anonymized data. This data can be used to discover new disease markers, train diagnostic algorithms, or create risk calculators. In the United States, pharmaceutical companies, often referred to as "Big Pharma," pay substantial amounts for some of this data. As an illustration, health data can be sold at a price up to 20 times higher than that of financial data[50].

RANSOMWARE, WHEN IT GRIPS US...

Your medical data is highly valuable, and there are many actors who covet it for strategic purposes, including hackers! The high-profile hacking of medical records for millions of patients in the UK, the US, and dozens of French hospitals is clear evidence that medical data is particularly vulnerable. The objective of these attacks is to hold websites or personal databases hostage by injecting ransomware. This ransomware encrypts the data and demands that the owners send money in exchange for the decryption key. The victims have no choice but to pay the ransom, fearing the loss of their valuable data. These attacks are made possible by "Single Points of Failure" because health data relies on centralized systems. This is not possible on the blockchain since data storage is decentralized.

HEALTH AND NFTS: ALIVE AND KICKING!

HENRIETTA LACKS: A CASE STUDY

Henrietta Lacks is an interesting case to reflect on the ownership of health data. Henrietta Lacks was a patient whose tumor samples were taken without her consent during the treatment of her cervical cancer in 1951. These cells were successfully cultured in vitro - a first at the time - and have been used in numerous medical studies on gene therapy, cloning, and the development of a polio vaccine. Her family has never been able to gain ownership or control over the commercial exploitation of her cells. According to bioethicist Marelle Gross, "There is no reason why patients should not own their own samples - as well as derivatives." In other words, tumors removed from patients or cells cultivated in the laboratory from human tissues could be "tagged" with an NFT so that patients remain the owners.

OWNERSHIP OF HEALTH DATA AND ACCESS MANAGEMENT

As we have seen, nobody truly owns their medical data. This becomes a significant issue when we consider that most health data is stored in American data centers. Blockchain technology could reverse this trend and make patients the true owners of their health data. For example, in the case of a medical record, once configured, the only way to access it would be through the NFT that grants access. The owner of the medical record could maintain an access registry, control or even sell access to their health data. They could also grant access to their health data exclusively to their primary physician or designated healthcare providers.

VERIFYING THE AUTHENTICITY OF PHARMACEUTICAL PRODUCTS

The prevalence of counterfeit pharmaceutical products is a significant problem worldwide. According to the World Health Organization (WHO), 10% of drugs in circulation in developing countries are counterfeit[51], rising up to 70% in some regions of Africa. This poses serious consequences, resulting in 800,000 deaths annually worldwide. The counterfeit drug market generates an estimated $200 billion per year[52]. Blockchain could provide a solution by associating medications with NFTs, enabling quick verification of their authenticity, which is currently not possible.

INSURANCE: FRAUD PREVENTION AND AUTOMATIC REIMBURSEMENT

Insurers could also benefit from a distributed ledger of health data. It is conceivable that insurers could process reimbursements to their clients using a smart contract that automatically executes payments if the insured's health data meets the required conditions. This use case would automate administrative tasks, reduce costs, and importantly, combat health insurance fraud. In France, healthcare fraud cost $200 million in 2014[53]…! With Blockchain, cheating would be eliminated as medical documents such as prescriptions would be recorded directly on the Blockchain by the treating physician, allowing other parties such as pharmacists to verify the authenticity of the document.

USE CASES FOR TELECONSULTATION

Teleconsultation through applications like Livi has saved a significant amount of time for patients. However, ensuring the authenticity of digital prescriptions is crucial. By associating an NFT with digital prescriptions, their authenticity (the issuer, date, content, etc.) could be guaranteed. Blockchain technology would enable pharmacists to verify the authenticity of prescriptions presented to them. Additionally, the medications purchased using the prescription could be recorded directly on the NFT.

IMPROVING PRODUCT TRACEABILITY

We have seen in the Supply Chain chapter how NFTs can improve the logistics of a product. Let's now take a concrete example in the healthcare context:
1. A pharmaceutical company produces a batch of medications and assigns a unique NFT to it. All relevant information is included in the NFT, such as batch number, production date, manufacturing location, expiration date, and more.
2. The batch of medications is transported to a distributor. The distributor adds their information to the NFT.
3. The batch is then sold to a retailer, who also adds their transaction information to the Blockchain, associating it with the NFT of the medication batch.
4. Finally, the medication is sold to a patient, who can verify its authenticity by scanning a QR code or entering a unique code associated with the NFT. The patient can access all the recorded information about the medication on the Blockchain.

By recording the entire supply chain process of medications on the Blockchain using NFTs, there is an immutable proof that all relevant parties have been informed about the new or modified data. This will restore confidence in the product and its authenticity. All stakeholders in the supply chain will have the ability to verify the origin and integrity of the medications.

INCREASING TRANSPARENCY IN SCIENTIFIC RESEARCH

The issue of authenticity in the pharmaceutical industry extends beyond medications and prescriptions. Research and development programs for new drugs are often criticized for their lack of transparency. The validity of research and clinical trials conducted is regularly questioned, with some estimating that 60 to 80% of research projects are scientifically unfounded[54]. However, once again, blockchain technology can bring more transparency and trust to this area.

IMPROVING COMMUNICATION AMONG HEALTHCARE STAKEHOLDERS

According to Premier Healthcare Alliance, the lack of interoperability among healthcare stakeholders costs an average of 150,000 lives and 18.6 billion dollars per year[55]. This situation is due to a lack of standardization in protocols and information systems used. All involved parties, including hospitals, laboratories, insurance companies, and others, struggle to access the same data. However, blockchain, as a distributed ledger, could address this problem. It would allow storing and sharing healthcare data among different stakeholders. Access to this data could be permissioned for NFT holders while preserving patient data confidentiality. This would enable more efficient handling of emergency cases, providing healthcare professionals with access to all necessary information such as blood type, allergies, recent or ongoing treatments, pregnancy, and more. Another example is the scenario where you want to donate a kidney to a family member, but you're not compatible. Similarly, in another part of the country, a similar situation exists. Currently, due to the isolation of hospital data, it's impossible to detect such situations. However, with blockchain, it's possible to imagine a system where the detection of these cross donations happens privately, notifying only the two hospitals involved to organize the transfer.

BENEFITS OF A HEALTH RECORD 3.0

You may have had a paper health record during your childhood. However, over time, you may have lost it, which can be problematic, especially in emergency situations. The absence of this information during emergencies can lead to less precise patient care. That's why utilizing blockchain and having a "health record 3.0" is valuable. It would allow assembling all patient-related data throughout their life from various sources, including general practitioners, hospitals, telemedicine, insurance providers, pharmacists, and medical laboratories. Healthcare professionals would then have direct access to the patient's health history, complete visibility into their family medical history, vaccinations, allergies, current and past treatments, and disease history.

ENCOURAGING "COOPETITION" IN THE HEALTHCARE INDUSTRY

In the medical field, two opposing logic camps clash: the competitive nature of the pharmaceutical industry and the cooperative nature of the medical field. How can we reconcile economic interests with the common good? The answer lies in using blockchain and NFTs, particularly Zero-Knowledge Proofs (ZKPs), which allow companies to share data without disclosing it. Researchers could share the results of their research without revealing the entire research process. This solution is still in development and is currently in its early stages[56].

REDUCING ADMINISTRATIVE PAPERWORK

The administrative paperwork is a problem that also affects the healthcare industry. Whether it's medical records, patient forms, or any other document, there are numerous hidden costs associated with paperwork. The issues associated with all this paperwork are as follows:

Document duplication Document loss Slow processing time

All of this can lead to medical errors, poor patient care, and sometimes disastrous consequences. The use of NFTs would significantly reduce the amount of paper in circulation and retain only the necessary documents that cannot or should not be digitized. This would eliminate unnecessary frictions and allow for more time and resources to be devoted to patients.

THE CASE OF BLOOD DONATION

NFTs can be used to track and manage blood donations. An NFT could be provided to each blood donor, and their information could be traced through the blockchain. In emergency situations, these NFTs can save lives by quickly providing hospital services with blood type information. Unfortunately, this is not always the case, leading to errors, sometimes fatal. With NFTs that securely certify blood types (along with their origin), this situation could be avoided.

THE CASE OF ESTONIA: A PIONEER IN MEDICAL DIGITALIZATION

In some countries, the shift from paper to digital formats is gradually taking place to make the healthcare system more efficient and faster. Estonia has been a notable example since 2017, with nearly 97% of the population having a "digital identity card." This card centralizes a patient's medical information at the national level on the *National Electronic Health Record*[57]. This initiative is supported by the Estonian eHealth Foundation, which has implemented a secure data storage solution on the blockchain for medical data. This technology allows registering patient fingerprints to ensure their identity and secure access to their medical information. To date, more than one million patient records have been secured using this solution. It represents a significant advancement in the digitization of the healthcare sector and could inspire other countries to adopt similar initiatives.

HEALTH AND NFTS: A BITTER PILL TO SWALLOW...

LIMITATIONS IN DATA STORAGE

After reading these different arguments in favor of health tokenization, you might think it's fantastic. Well, not so fast... There are still many limitations. One of these limitations is of a technical nature. Databases in the healthcare world are massive: just in the United States, they measure in the exabyte scale (1 billion gigabytes)[58]. It is currently impossible to store all this information on a blockchain, no matter how powerful it is. Similarly, the intensity of data exchange flows is too high to be supported by a blockchain at the present time.

AN INCOMPLETE DIGITAL TRANSFORMATION

The healthcare sector is still relatively behind in terms of digitalization. For example, in the United States, a significant portion of healthcare institutions still do not have a proper data storage system. In Europe, the digital transformation of healthcare is not yet fully complete. In Africa and Asia, the lag is considerable. The deployment of blockchain technology in this sector seems to be far off…

LEGAL LIMITATIONS

The healthcare sector is highly regulated, especially when it comes to health data, and regulations vary from country to country, making it challenging to achieve interoperability of health data between countries. Traditional authentication systems (e.g., health insurance cards, healthcare professional cards) are valid only within individual countries. Similarly, there is currently no legally valid unique digital health identity at the European level.

DIGITAL PASSES TO "PROTECT OUR HEALTH"?

Ethical questions also arise. We have seen with the COVID crisis how easy it is to control a significant portion of the population with digital passes. Blockchain is a powerful tool, and we must carefully consider its use to avoid creating a society of widespread surveillance. The advantages of this technology are undeniable, but we must take into account the risks associated with its use, such as the creation of automated control systems that could be used for discriminatory purposes. To prevent these abuses, it is necessary to establish safeguards, strict controls, and involve citizens in the debates regarding the use of blockchain in the healthcare sector.

EXAMPLES

Galeon is a French startup founded in August 2015 by Loïc Brotons. Its objective is to value health data, support research, and facilitate projects through a community launchpad.

MedicalChain was founded by Dr. Abdullah Albeyatti and Mo Tayeb in 2016. The company completed its ICO in 2018, raising $24 million.

9. DIPLOMA AND RESUMES

CANDIDATES, THEY DECEIVE A LOT...

78% OF CANDIDATES "CHEAT" ON THEIR RESUMES

According to a study conducted by the Florian Mentionne Institute, 78% of candidates lie to their employers[59]. Of course, there are different degrees of deception. Most of the time, it involves either lying by omission or embellishing an experience. According to the study, a simple training course magically transforms into a degree (33%). The duration of previous employment is also subject to alterations. Candidates often overstate their proficiency in a foreign language (62%). And unsurprisingly, salespeople take the lead as the biggest liars!

INVENTED DEGREES FROM SCRATCH?

Presenting oneself in the best light on a resume and slightly embellishing experiences is quite normal and usually not a significant issue. However, lying about degrees can be more dangerous. Some individuals pretend to have obtained a degree from a prestigious school when they have merely participated in a program in partnership with their own school. Others, more audacious, fabricate degrees entirely or purchase them illegally. In any case, it represents a real problem for human resources departments, resulting in millions of dollars lost each year (due to recruitment errors, lawsuits, damage to the company's image, etc.).

VERIFYING A RESUME IS A LENGTHY AND TEDIOUS TASK...

Interestingly, the practice of lying doesn't seem to bother recruiters: only one-third verify the accuracy of the information provided on resumes[60]. Yes, a lie takes much longer to dismantle than to create... (unless you use the Blockchain!). Verifying a resume takes a lot of time, and recruiters often don't allocate the necessary time to check everything, except for the most important positions.

NO CERTIFICATION ON THE BLOCKCHAIN? DISQUALIFIED!

HOW DOES CERTIFICATION ON THE BLOCKCHAIN WORK?

Educational institutions publish their students' diplomas on a specialized platform for blockchain certification. Subsequently, each diploma holder can share a link to it using a QR code or URL. Recruiters only need to follow this link to verify the diploma in question. This link is permanent and provides easy access to the diploma and all evidence of its authenticity. As long as the entity issuing the digital certificates is considered trustworthy, the authenticity of the documents stored on the blockchain cannot be challenged.

BLOCKCHAIN RESUMES DIRECTLY IN YOUR WALLET

When we talk about the Blockchain, we inevitably mention wallets. The wallet is at the heart of the Blockchain. It's where you store all your cryptocurrencies and NFTs. And among these NFTs will likely be your diplomas or any documents substantiating your professional experience. Eventually, it is highly likely that everything will be stored in your wallet. It will be like your CV 3.0, directly inscribed on the Blockchain.

DIGITAL CREDENTIALS: SOON IN THE FORM OF NFTs?

Digital credentials are increasingly used nowadays. They are the digital versions of our paper documents (passports, driver's licenses, identity cards, diplomas, etc.). However, they are not simply scanned versions of your paper documents; they are fully digital documents. They are issued by authorized entities such as universities, banks, etc. Unlike a photocopy of a diploma, which holds less value than the original diploma, a digital credential has the same value as the original diploma. But digital credentials are not limited to diplomas. They also include micro-certifications (certifications of specific skills issued by accredited organizations such as schools, universities, or companies).

POAPs, SOON INTEGRATED INTO BLOCKCHAIN RESUMES?

POAPs (Proof of Attendance Protocol) are a unique form of digital credential. They are literally proof (on the blockchain) that you have attended a particular event. POAPs are increasingly common as a complement to diplomas. They are issued in the form of badges, fully traceable on the blockchain. Unlike other NFTs, they cannot be transferred; they are simply created to demonstrate that you were present at a specific moment or that you obtained a particular certification. They are useful tools to highlight your resume. For example, if you have attended the CES in Las Vegas every year for the past 10 years and have the corresponding POAPs to prove it, including them on your resume would be a good idea.

ENSURING YOU DON'T LOSE YOUR DIPLOMAS

As mentioned earlier, all your diplomas will be in your wallet. You will have your entire educational history at your fingertips, right in your pocket. You can be sure not to lose anything, including your diplomas (as long as you don't lose access to your wallet...!). This solution also benefits educational institutions, as they can be certain not to lose the diplomas they issue. Thanks to the decentralization of the blockchain across multiple servers, they are no longer dependent on a single server to store all their diplomas. Therefore, even in the event of a server failure, the diplomas will remain accessible and secure on other network nodes.

FASTER FOR RECRUITERS

One of the advantages of using NFTs for diplomas is speed. Recruiters do not have to verify the diplomas provided by candidates themselves. The Blockchain automatically does it for them. The Blockchain will certify the match between the candidate and the diploma automatically, thanks to a simple link or file provided by the candidate. Employers can instantly verify the accuracy of the information provided. A 100% verified and accessible resume in just three clicks. Simple and efficient. Why bother with anything else?

EXAMPLE

BCDiploma is a French company founded in 2017 by Luc Jarry-Lacombe and Vincent Langard. It specializes in the certification of digitized documents on the blockchain, known as Digital Credentials.

10. TICKETING

THE FIASCO OF THE STADE DE FRANCE: A REVELATORY INCIDENT

RECAP OF THE SITUATION (May 28, 2022)

It is 6:00 pm when English supporters start gathering near the Stade de France to watch the UEFA Champions League final between Real Madrid and Liverpool. Between 10,000 and 15,000 Liverpool fans arrive simultaneously at Gate U of the Stade de France. Many of them unknowingly possess fake tickets. Around 7:45 pm, the influx of supporters becomes overwhelming, and the staff is unable to keep up. The British supporters start getting restless, leading to police intervention and multiple charges into the crowd using tear gas. In the aftermath of the incident, Gérald Darmanin, then Minister of the Interior, states that it is "a massive, industrial, and organized fraud of fake tickets since the pre-screening procedures mentioned by the staff, the Stade de France, and the FFF (French Football Federation) allowed for over 70% of fake tickets... 30,000 to 40,000 English supporters found themselves at the Stade de France, either without tickets or with counterfeit ones." Unfortunately, this situation is not an isolated incident, as evidenced by events like the Lyon New Year's Eve festival, where hundreds of people found themselves with invalid tickets at the concert entrance[61].

TICKET SCALPING: ONE OF THE PROBLEMS BEHIND THE FIASCO

Ticket scalping involves purchasing a large quantity of tickets (anticipating their sell-out) to resell them at inflated prices as the event approaches. Let's consider an example: suppose there are 30,000 tickets available for the upcoming Justin Bieber concert. A bot purchases 3,000 tickets at once and holds onto them until closer to the concert date to resell them for double the price to Justin's fans who were unable to secure tickets initially. High demand with limited supply inevitably drives up prices. Another common practice is selling already scanned tickets near the event venue. The buyer's entry is then denied since entry is only authorized when the ticket is scanned for the first time. As these tickets appear authentic, buyers have no way of knowing if a ticket has been used or not. However, it's worth noting that in France, only 2% of events are sold out, primarily large-scale events being susceptible to ticket scalping.

TICKETS AND NFTS: COUNT ME IN!

ELIMINATING FRAUD

The most apparent advantage of using NFTs in ticketing is the prevention of fraud. Currently, tickets are QR codes printed on PDFs received via email, making them easily duplicable and falsifiable. One can generate multiple copies to resell them. With NFTs, each ticket is uniquely identified and cannot be duplicated or falsified. This provides increased security for event organizers and ticket buyers since it becomes impossible for fraudsters to replicate an NFT ticket, as its lack of authenticity would be immediately evident. Furthermore, in the case of bulk purchases, it would be easy to trace the purchase back to its source, thus limiting ticket scalping.

SETTING RULES FOR TICKET RESALE

Once a ticket is purchased, it is relatively easy to resell it at a much higher price near the event venue. Even if one is acting in good faith and not reselling the ticket for profit but out of necessity, it can be tempting to sell it to the highest bidder. As long as there are buyers willing to pay more for the ticket, why not take advantage of the situation? While the logic holds, the ethics are questionable. With NFT tickets, the smart contract could specify that reselling the ticket above the purchase price is not permitted (or only allowed with a 20% increase, with a portion going to the artist or venue). A legitimate secondary market could then be established with clear and ethical rules.

NFT TICKETS FOR THE 2024 OLYMPICS?

To prevent incidents like the one at the Stade de France from recurring, France is considering adopting blockchain technology to secure ticketing for the 2024 Olympics[62]. Michel Cadot, the French government's envoy for the Paris 2024 Olympics, has proposed implementing NFT tickets for the upcoming games. One of the recommendations suggests paying particular attention to the dedicated ticketing system for the event. Non-transferable tickets would be issued shortly before the competition, ensuring increased security. Their issuance would be based on NFT technology and a rotating QR code. Each spectator would register upon entry to the site, which would result in ticket deactivation.

NO MORE SINGLE-USE TICKETS!

More and more companies are abandoning single-use tickets in favor of rechargeable passes. For instance, the RATP (the Paris public transportation authority) has gradually phased out the sale of single-use "t+" tickets since October

2021, with complete discontinuation expected in 2023. Several reasons are cited, including demagnetization (nearly 5 million tickets are demagnetized each year due to their proximity to keys or coins), ticket loss (on average, 1 out of 10 tickets in a booklet goes unused due to loss, damage, or forgetting), and security (contactless supports improve speed and sanitary safety). It is highly likely that NFT technology will be adopted for these rechargeable passes, as they offer the aforementioned advantages along with improved traceability and transparency.

MEMORIES FOR A LIFETIME

We all cherish something, especially when it brings back positive memories. Do you remember your first concert? Most likely, yes. Well, with NFTs, you can preserve that memory for a lifetime, as it will be permanently stored on the blockchain and accessible in your wallet. In this way, you can show your grandchildren that you were at Justin Bieber's concert and that this piece of your history is indelibly engraved on the blockchain! NFTs will breathe new life into your tickets.

PERSONALIZED TICKETS

Rather than having a ticket that looks like all the others, it's always more enjoyable to have a personalized ticket. If you browse through platforms like OpenSea and look at examples of tickets, you'll see how various collections strive to stand out. Soon, you'll take pleasure in showing your friends the unique version of your backstage pass to the Justin Bieber concert. Of course, it is also possible to make physical tickets unique by using holographic security features (similar to banknotes or passports). This method makes ticket reproduction extremely challenging, but it is much more expensive to produce. NFT tickets remain a more practical and cost-effective solution.

DIFFERENTS LEVELS OF TICKETS FOR DIFFERENT ADVANTAGES

As NFTs allow for the inclusion of rarity in digital assets for the first time in history, it makes sense for this rarity to apply to tickets as well. Similar to Charlie and the Chocolate Factory, a handful of the tickets on sale could be "golden tickets" that grant additional rights. For example, out of 500 concert seats, the distribution could be as follows:

1 Unique	4 Ultra rares	45 Rares	150 Limited
- Life time access	- Backstage Access	- Exclusive Merch	- Discounts for the Next Album

Event organizers would even have the option to integrate a "reveal" function into the NFT. It would be possible to purchase the NFT well before the concert, but its level of rarity would only be unveiled a few days before the event. This would allow customers to buy or sell unrevealed NFTs, adding a new dimension to the ticket purchasing experience.

ACCESS TO A COMMUNITY OF SUPER FANS

Imagine that you're attending a Justin Bieber concert for the first time. You're excited to see your favorite idol, but none of your friends are willing to accompany you. Undeterred, you search for other people who share your interest. However, as a super fan, you've purchased the Limited version of Justin Bieber's NFT ticket. This gives you priority access to a Discord group exclusively reserved for NFT ticket holders. You join the Discord and start interacting with members of this exclusive club. Two weeks later, you attend the famous concert and meet some fellow club members. You have an amazing time with them and experience one of the best concerts of your life, all thanks to the NFT.

RESALE OF TICKETS WITH JUST TWO CLICKS ON THE SECONDARY MARKET

It's worth noting that for sold-out events, where all tickets have been sold, approximately 25% of tickets are resold. Reasons for resale can vary, ranging from illness, injury, speculation, waning interest in the artist, financial issues, to even pony lessons. However, when you have a concert ticket that you want to resell, it can sometimes be challenging to find a buyer, especially if neither your friends nor family are Justin Bieber fans (yes, that can happen). With NFTs, it will be possible to resell your ticket with just two clicks on a dedicated marketplace. You'll make someone happy, and you won't have to worry about finding someone to sell your ticket to!

EXAMPLE OF APEFEST

Apefest is a highly popular annual festival organized by Yuga Labs (the team behind Bored Ape Yacht Club) exclusively for owners of Bored Ape and Mutant Ape NFTs. The first event took place in October 2021 and was a huge success. Renowned influencers and celebrities, including Justin Bieber, Paris Hilton, Snoop Dogg, and Eminem, attended the festival. A wide range of activities were offered, such as an immersive gallery exhibition, a costume contest, and even a mutant Halloween party on a yacht! Yuga Labs used the TokenProof application to manage ticketing, which operates on a "token-gated access" system, meaning only NFT holders had access to the event.

THE NFT TICKET DOESN'T HAVE TO BE A TICKET...

For many years, we have been accustomed to using tickets (paper or digital) with QR codes to access various events. However, the advantage of NFTs lies in their ability to support multimedia formats, opening up a multitude of digital possibilities. Therefore, event access could be granted through an audio NFT, a video NFT, a book NFT, and more. The possibilities are endless! Similarly, NFTs could be directly integrated into bracelets used during events through NFC chips. Entry security personnel would simply scan the bracelet to verify that you possess the NFT that allows entry. Once scanned, the bracelet could change color to indicate that you are authorized to enter.

EXAMPLES

 **Billy** is a ticketing platform founded by Robin Champseix and Etienne Vaast in 2022. Its aim is to enable artists and organizers to better engage with their communities.

Ticket Master is a company that has been in existence since 1976 and is currently the global leader in the ticketing industry. The company has ventured into NFTs with the Flow blockchain.

II. VOTING

THE RELATIVE PROGRESS OF ELECTRONIC VOTING...

ADVANTAGES OF ELECTRONIC VOTING

The economy we live in today is largely virtual, where the money we handle is not tangible, and we no longer rely heavily on physical cash in the form of bills or coins. We have become accustomed to digital transactions. So why shouldn't voting be the same? Electronic voting offers numerous advantages over traditional voting methods. It facilitates electoral participation by providing easier access, allowing voters to cast their votes from home or from electronic voting centers. It is fast and efficient, reducing the risks of human errors or lost ballots, with results that can be instantly compiled and communicated. It also eliminates the costs associated with printing and distributing paper ballots, as well as the expenses related to their collection and counting.

ISSUES OF VOTE HACKING IN THE UNITED STATES

Although electronic voting is advancing, it is still far from infallible. In recent years, suspicions of fraud or hacking have been reported worldwide. Particularly after the 2016 US elections, several lawyers and scientists alleged that some electronic voting machines had been hacked to ensure Donald Trump's victory. It is believed that certain electronic voting machines used in the United States are riddled with security vulnerabilities, making it easy for hackers to manipulate the results in favor of a particular candidate. Hackers could focus on polling stations where the race is tight, exploiting security vulnerabilities by using USB drives or smartphones to spread malware, even without the voting machines being connected to the internet. While no conclusive evidence has proven successful attacks on the electoral system, doubts persist regarding its integrity.

ISSUES WITH BUGS DURING VOTING

Sometimes electronic voting systems are prone to bugs and technical issues. In Norway, a small minority of voters (0.75%) were able to vote twice in 2011 and 2013, leading to the abandon of electronic voting experiments[63]. Following these malfunctions, the Norwegian government decided to temporarily suspend internet-based remote voting. Belgium has also experienced bugs in several elections, leading to the discontinuation of electronic voting. Many Belgian civil rights organizations consider automated voting as a serious threat to democracy. In some cases, voter identities were revealed, which is particularly concerning.

THE CAMBRIDGE ANALYTICA SCANDAL

Cambridge Analytica was a political consulting firm based in the United Kingdom. It gained notoriety in 2018 due to a scandal involving the misuse of personal data obtained from Facebook. The incident revealed how Cambridge Analytica illegally obtained and used data from millions of Facebook users for manipulation and political targeting purposes. The collected data was used to create detailed psychological profiles of voters, enabling the creation of personalized political advertisements and messages aimed at influencing opinions and electoral behavior. This abusive use of data raised significant concerns about user privacy protection and the integrity of democratic processes.

VOTING WITH NFTS: A GOOD IDEA!

THE 3 ESSENTIAL CHARACTERISTICS OF VOTING

UNIQUE	SECRET	TRANSPARENT
A vote should represent the choice of one individual who has the right to vote. The conditions for having the right to vote may vary in different cases, and during a vote, voters must be able to prove their eligibility to vote through documents (e.g., voter ID cards) and/or identification.	The content of the vote must be anonymous, ensuring that each voter is free to make their choice without any identification. In physical polling stations, this is achieved through the use of voting booths and envelopes to conceal the ballot. Each ballot is placed in a closed transparent ballot box, preventing any association between a ballot and an individual. This system helps prevent corruption and external pressures on voters.	The results of a vote should be verifiable by everyone. This principle is crucial to prevent fraud and vote manipulation. In elections in France, for example, all citizens have the right to witness the ballot counting process, known as citizen oversight. Transparent ballot boxes are used to symbolize the public and transparent nature of the vote, and to ensure that they are empty at the start of the election.

THE POWER OF TRANSPARENCY IN VOTING

The blockchain functions as a transparent ballot box. Instead of placing the ballot in an ordinary ballot box, it is placed in a transparent one. To better illustrate this, imagine being at a polling station, with the transparent ballot box placed in the middle of a table around which several people are present. Each person could attempt to add extra votes, remove votes, or modify what is written on a ballot. However, no one would do so because any tampering would be immediately noticeable. Applying this concept to online voting, the blockchain ensures a high level of security by emphasizing the transparency of the process. Since everything is transparent and public, it becomes much easier to identify and verify any irregularities. The subtlety, of course, lies in maintaining the pseudonymity of the data to prevent coercion. There is no need to know that it is Mrs. Smith who voted for a specific candidate; the blockchain would only reveal that candidate number 35,182 voted for a particular candidate.

COST-EFFECTIVE, LESS POLLUTING, AND FASTER

Voting in traditional elections can be costly in terms of time and money. You have to drive to the polling station, fill up your vehicle if needed, find parking, wait in line at the polling station if it's crowded, and so on. These constraints could be circumvented with blockchain technology. With blockchain, voting can be done in two clicks without leaving your home, as simple as ordering Uber Eats or shopping online! It can also significantly reduce costs. Currently, for a city with 20,000 residents, a single day of traditional voting averages around 15,000 euros in expenses for the local government[64] (venue rental, personnel, etc.). With blockchain, these costs could be significantly reduced.

A SOLUTION FOR NON-VOTERS?

Many eligible voters who do not participate in traditional elections cite difficulties related to time, distance, or mobility. Blockchain-based voting can help overcome these barriers by allowing voters to cast their votes from home or any location with an internet connection, securely. According to a 2015 *Harris Interactive* survey[65], 56% of French citizens expressed support for implementing internet voting, enabling citizens to vote without having to travel to a physical polling station.

FOR EXPATRIATES, SIMPLIFIED PROXY VOTING

Today, if you are an expatriate and wish to vote by proxy from abroad, the procedures are lengthy and tedious. First, you must use the appropriate online service. After receiving the email indicating the reference of your request, you must then personally go to an embassy or consulate, presenting an identification document along with the reference of your request. After a waiting period, you will receive an email confirming the validity (or invalidity) of your proxy. By using Blockchain technology, this process could be greatly simplified. You would no longer need to go to the embassy, as your identity and voting rights would be automatically verified, as well as the identity of the person you have granted proxy to vote on your behalf. A smart contract would allow you to define the specific conditions of this proxy, including the authorized person to vote on your behalf (such as a family member) and the duration of the proxy.

IMMUTABLE, INCORRUPTIBLE, AND RESILIENT THROUGH DECENTRALIZATION

One of the fundamental principles of Blockchain is its incorruptibility. Or at least (in the case of Proof of Stake), it would be ineffective to try to corrupt it because it would immediately be known who did it. The perpetrator would be "slashed" (meaning they would lose a portion of the money they staked to secure the network), and their action would be nullified. It is important to note that Blockchain is also immutable, meaning that once something is recorded on the Blockchain, it cannot be erased, much like writing with a permanent marker on a whiteboard. When it comes to voting, this characteristic is valuable because it ensures there is no way to alter the vote.

AUTHENTICATING VOTES AND REAL-TIME RESULTS

NFTs can be used to authenticate voters' identities, ensuring that only authorized voters can vote and that they can vote only once. This can help prevent electoral fraud and strengthen the legitimacy of election results. With voting on the Blockchain, there would be no need for hours of manual vote counting. This would eliminate counting errors and allow for faster result announcements.

THE CASE OF ESTONIA: AN EFFICIENT ONLINE VOTING SYSTEM

In Estonia, nearly all public services are available online, 24/7, except for marriages, divorces, and real estate transactions, which must be done in person. Estonia's implementation of a secure, flexible, and user-friendly digital environment has improved administrative processes, including voting. Nearly half of Estonians use i-Voting, which relies on the national ID card issued to all Estonian citizens. The ID card contains encrypted files that verify the owner's identity and enables various administrative tasks, including voting by mail, electronically signing documents, and accessing public data.

CURRENT LIMITATIONS OF VOTING WITH BLOCKCHAIN

EXPERIMENTATION NOT YET MATURE

Several countries have started using Blockchain for online voting, but these are still experimental initiatives with varying degrees of success. For example, Russia uses the Polys Blockchain in collaboration with Kaspersky[66]. Switzerland is also considering implementing a Blockchain solution[67] after abandoning one of its e-voting platforms in 2018. The United States has used Blockchain for voting through the Voatz application[68]. While these initiatives are commendable, they are still small-scale tests, and there is still a long way to go before Blockchain voting becomes a mainstream solution.

ISSUES WITH HACKING

One of the concerns associated with Blockchain voting is the potential for data hacking. Hackers may attempt to disrupt the voting process for ideological, political, or personal reasons (such as vengeance or financial extortion). Cryptography experts have identified vulnerabilities in some Blockchain voting systems. For example, in August 2019, Pierrick Gaudry, a researcher at INRIA, discovered a critical flaw in the Exonum blockchain-based voting system a month before its planned use in Russia[69]. This vulnerability allowed an attacker to retrieve the system's private keys using the public keys, thereby gaining access to voters' identities. However, it's worth noting that some Blockchains have never been hacked. Bitcoin, for example, has remained intact since its creation in 2009, despite constant attacks due to the significant financial stakes involved.

BLOCKCHAIN SCALABILITY ISSUES

Blockchain voting is often praised for its security, transparency, and resistance to fraud. However, a major challenge remains: scalability. Current Blockchains are not yet capable of handling a large number of transactions simultaneously. It's akin to an overcrowded highway unable to accommodate a significant influx of cars[70]. The current Blockchains would struggle to process a large number of votes within a short period. Registering votes on the Blockchain requires transactions to be processed by network validators or miners. This process can be time-consuming, especially when dealing with a large volume of votes in a short timeframe. It can lead to delays in announcing vote results or even a complete system collapse if the load becomes too overwhelming. For instance, if there were 40 million votes within 10 hours, it would require processing over 1,000 transactions per second. Considering that Ethereum, one of the most decentralized and secure Blockchains, can handle an average of 15 transactions per second, it becomes clear that scalability is a challenge. One solution would be to use a more scalable Blockchain, but it would come at the expense of security (referencing the Blockchain trilemma). Another approach would be to extend the election period, but implementing this would also be complicated.

DATA CONFIDENTIALITY (KYC)

If voting on the Blockchain were to become a reality, it would raise concerns about data confidentiality. How would voter authentication occur? Would it be centralized, and if so, who would ensure the accuracy of voter identities? What would happen in the event of a change in government? Privacy of data is a fundamental question, and currently, there is no clear answer to these issues. However, there are solutions for decentralized, anonymous identification (such as Zero-Knowledge Proofs or ZKPs), but they are still highly experimental technologies.

EXAMPLE

Electis ensures the anonymity of voters as well as the verifiability of a ballot through ballots hosted on a decentralized ledger.

12. GAMING

NFTS IN VIDEO GAMES: LET'S GO!

PLAY TO EARN BEFORE PLAY TO EARN

The ability to resell items or characters in a game existed long before Play to Earn, but this practice was poorly perceived by players and publishers. For example, the game World of Warcraft (WoW) saw the emergence of "gold farms" where players spent 12 hours a day farming monsters to quickly level up their characters. These farmers would then sell them to third parties like IGE.com (Internet Gaming Entertainment) who would buy the items and characters at twice the negotiated price! However, these "gold farmers" were seen as a scourge by players. Blizzard, the game's publisher, began to delete tens of thousands of accounts and even filed a lawsuit against IGE.com because their practice violated the game's regulations.

THE BIRTH OF PLAY TO EARN (2017)

Everything changed in 2017 with CryptoKitties. This game launched by Dapper Labs involved buying/selling virtual cats with the possibility of breeding them. Since each cat had a unique DNA, breeding could result in billions of possibilities. As you can imagine, these unique cats were represented by NFTs. The game was a huge success (for example, on November 4, 2018, Kitty #896775 nicknamed Dragon was sold for 600 ETH, which was equivalent to $172,794 at that time[71]). The game gave birth to NFTs and provided an early glimpse of what Play to Earn could be. Other Play to Earn games followed, including Axie Infinity, which draws inspiration from Pokémon and Tamagotchi games. This game also made headlines with record-breaking sales. In April 2022, a creature from Axie Infinity (Dragon Axie) was sold for 750 ETH, equivalent to 2 million dollars[72].

TRULY OWNING THE GAME AND ITS ASSETS...

Using NFTs in video games allows players to fully own their digital assets, which is one of the main advantages. The current problem is that the digital assets purchased in video games are not truly owned by the buyer. For example, the skins purchased to customize your character in Fortnite do not really belong to you. The game's publisher can decide to remove the skins you purchased overnight if, for example, you fail to meet certain conditions. If you have spent hundreds of hours in your favorite game to acquire the best items for your character, unfortunately, they do not belong to you. You simply have the right to see and use these items in the game, but you are not the owner.

...AND ALSO EASILY SELLING THEM

With NFTs, you will have the ability to truly own your in-game items. But you can also easily sell them to other players. This was already possible in some games where players could find ways to sell their items for real money, such as in World of Warcraft, but it required various tricks to accomplish. With NFTs directly integrated into the game, a tangible economy can develop, one that is not just virtual. You will be able to sell your items directly to other players for dollars by simply putting your NFT up for sale. You will receive the game's cryptocurrency in exchange, which you can then convert into dollars.

A BOON FOR UNDERDEVELOPED COUNTRIES: THE CASE OF AXIE INFINITY

In the case of Axie Infinity mentioned earlier, some players were actually earning a living from reselling the NFTs they earned in the game! The game developed by the Vietnamese studio Sky Mavis was particularly popular in the Philippines. In a country where the average monthly salary is around $308[73], players were earning an average of $450 per month! It became a financial boon for many Filipinos who preferred to earn money by playing (albeit a risky game) rather than working. In 2021, the Philippines became the hub of Axie Infinity, with 40% of players residing in the country[74]. Some players even became wealthy overnight, inspiring other players to invest in the game in hopes of similar success.

EARNING MONEY BY RENTING YOUR NFT

Now, you don't have to play to earn money through NFTs. If you own a rare NFT in a game but no longer play for any reason (vacation, lack of interest, etc.), you can still rent it out on a marketplace. Other players would be willing to pay you money in exchange for renting your NFT for a limited period. This rental feature was conceived by some Play to Earn games, such as Stepn[75], where players could run with your virtual shoes. This rental functionality is made possible through ERC-4907[76].

IN THE WORLD OF ESPORTS

In the world of esports, NFTs can be used in various ways to offer richer and more engaging gaming experiences for players and fans. They can be used to provide exclusive rewards to competition winners (such as an honorary title or a unique weapon created specifically for the occasion). They can also serve as tickets for events: fans must possess the associated NFT to access the tournament, whether physically or virtually. Similarly, all fans present at the final of a tournament could be rewarded with an exclusive NFT that grants them benefits such as price discounts or access to a special video.

NFT CARD GAMES

NFTs are increasingly being used in online card games, offering new possibilities for players and collectors. Thanks to NFTs, cards are now unique, making them much more interesting to collect. Players can also trade their cards with other players, creating a market for NFT card trading. Furthermore, game developers can create more advanced cards with unique features, offering new ways to play and interact with other players. Games like *Cross the Ages*[77] are moving in this direction, combining NFT cards, literature, and science fiction.

A NEW SOURCE OF INCOME FOR CREATORS

The use of NFTs in video games provides a new opportunity for game creators to better monetize their work. NFTs allow them to create exclusive and unique elements in their games that can be sold to players for digital or real currency. This monetization method enables creators to receive direct compensation for their work, rather than relying solely on game sales. Additionally, since NFTs can be sold on the secondary market, creators can continue to earn revenue from their creations even after the initial sale, thanks to royalties.

GAMIFYING THE USER EXPERIENCE WITH NFTs

Even if you don't play video games regularly, it's always enjoyable when there is a form of gamification behind obtaining something. For example, in everyday life, you can participate in loyalty programs at stores to earn rewards or discounts, or strive to reach a higher level on your language learning app. Companies entering the Web3 space are increasingly adopting this kind of strategy to attract more people to their universe. Louis Vuitton, for example, recently released its own NFT game to celebrate the 200th anniversary of the company's founder. The game, titled "Louis: The Game," follows the main character Vivienne as she travels through six different kingdoms to reach Paris. Players must acquire all 30 NFTs throughout the game[78].

NFTS IN GAMING: NOT ALWAYS A PIECE OF FUN...

NFTs AND PLAY TO EARN FACE CRITICISMS

Critics of Play-To-Earn will start by telling you that there are already numerous games that offer the same features without the need for NFTs. We are familiar with these clichés: "Unique items with diverse properties? Team Fortress 2 has been doing it for over 10 years, with possible exchanges within the Steam platform. Items that can be exchanged for real money? Counter-Strike: Global Offensive has proven that it's possible, as well as WoW." NFTs also spark debates among game publishers. While Steam explained why they banned NFTs from their platform[79], Ubisoft faced some backlash from the community (and employees) when announcing Quartz, a game platform using NFTs[80]. Similarly, Team17, the publisher of the game Worms, had to abandon its NFT project just 48 hours after its announcement[81]. On the other hand, other companies were massively raising funds for Blockchain game development, like Forte[82].

DO NFTs TRULY BELONG TO YOU?

Some of these criticisms are entirely legitimate. In certain games, you won't have control over your NFTs. The "Digits" (meaning NFTs) in Ubisoft Quartz[83] are a glaring example. The terms of use[84] are clear on this matter: "We grant you a limited, non-exclusive, worldwide, and revocable license to access, represent, and display the Visual Representation of your Digit." In other words, you only have a license and not actual ownership rights. If you have already been frustrated by "games sold in pieces" with dozens of DLCs and season passes, don't expect these same companies to offer NFTs for free. If you want more control over the NFTs in your game, you'll need to turn to more decentralized solutions like The Sandbox or Decentraland.

THE MAJORITY OF PLAY TO EARN GAMES IN 2021-2022 WERE PONZI SCHEMES

A (very) large portion of Play-To-Earn games that emerged in 2021 were built on pyramid schemes (Ponzis), where early players could make money at the expense of latecomers. These scams were made possible due to the lack of regulation in the Blockchain gaming industry, allowing developers to create games with no real utility but promising significant gains. FOMO* played a role as well. The early Play-To-Earn games lacked distinctive gameplay mechanics, other than performing simple and repetitive actions to earn tokens for resale. As long as the system worked, everything was fine, but once the house of cards collapsed, prices also plummeted.

AN UNACKNOWLEDGED FINANCIALIZATION

In a more general sense, and as many players criticize, Play-To-Earn games lead to an unacknowledged financialization. This money-driven race can undermine the fun aspect of the game, as everything revolves around money. People no longer play for enjoyment but solely to earn money. The game is no longer a leisure activity but an obligation. For some, Play-To-Earn symbolizes an economy so driven by profit that it seeks to monetize elements that should not be.

THE LIMITS OF INTEROPERABILITY

Have you ever thought about importing your favorite weapon from Call of Duty to have fun with the birds in Angry Birds? Neither have I, to be honest... And it's not possible anyway. Unfortunately, the same applies to NFTs in Blockchain games. They are not yet interoperable. For example, you cannot import your favorite CryptoKitty to use it in Axie Infinity. Not to mention the technical limitations associated with the famous Blockchain trilemma*, the reason is quite simple: each game has its own rules and gameplay mechanics that determine the value and usefulness of NFTs in that specific game. Overcoming this limitation will be challenging, except for purely honorary NFTs that have no direct impact on gameplay mechanics.

EXAMPLES

 Ultra aims to revolutionize the gaming industry through Blockchain and take a portion of the market from major platforms like Steam. The Ultra ecosystem is rapidly expanding.

Gala Games was launched in 2020. It offers players real control over the platform through a node system on the protocol.

13. DIGITAL ART

THE FIRST INDUSTRY TO USE NFTS

A BIT OF HISTORY: FROM MCCOY (2014) TO BEEPLE (2021)

Contrary to popular belief, artistic NFTs did not originate with Bored Ape Yacht Club (BAYC) (2021) or even Cryptopunks (2017). The very first known artistic NFT was created in 2014 by Kevin McCoy with "Quantum." At that time, the Blockchain was not as developed as it is now: Bitcoin was only 5 years old, and Ethereum was still in its early stages. McCoy created his artwork to irrefutably prove its provenance. He came up with the brilliant idea of creating an NFT, a term that did not yet exist. Since then, numerous artistic NFTs have been created, including the famous collections of 10,000 NFTs like Cryptopunks and Bored Ape Yacht Club. However, it was in 2021 that artistic NFTs experienced an unprecedented hype with the sale of Beeple's artwork titled "Everydays: The First 5000 Days" for a whopping $69 million[85]. For comparison, the most expensive painting in history is currently "Salvator Mundi," sold for $450 million. As an anecdote, it seems that this painting is not actually a work by Leonardo da Vinci[86], but since NFTs did not exist at the time, it's impossible to know for sure!

AN EXPLOSIVE MARKET IN 2021 (A MULTIPLE OF 214.5!)

The NFT market experienced rapid growth in 2021: 21,350%. Yes, you read that right! The market multiplied by 214.5 that year[87]. Let's look at some significant figures. According to a study by NonFungible.com[88], the total volume of the NFT market in art reached $18 billion in 2021. Out of the 71 million active Ethereum wallets, over 2.5 million conducted NFT transactions in 2021, compared to 89,000 in 2020. The number of buyers increased from 75,144 in 2020 to 2.3 million in 2021. As for sellers, there were 1.2 million in 2021, compared to 31,774 the previous year.

ENTRY OF NEW PLAYERS IN THE MARKET

New players have entered this highly promising market, including previously unknown artists, marketplaces that skyrocketed overnight, and collectors who became wealthy by investing in the right NFTs. New artists have emerged, such as FEWOCiOUS, an 18-year-old crypto artist whose sale of 5 NFTs at Christie's generated $2.16 million[89]. Similarly, collectors of artistic NFTs have become more diverse and increasingly belong to the millennial generation: young, connected individuals who may not be familiar with traditional art or frequent galleries.

NFTS: THE STATE OF THE ART FOR ARTISTS

TRUE DIGITAL OWNERSHIP FOR (DIGITAL) ARTISTS

For the first time in history, NFTs have allowed digital artists to create digital scarcity. This is a major change. Before the advent of the Blockchain, it was impossible for artists to make their digital works unique. These works had virtually no intrinsic value. It was as simple as copying and pasting the artwork for personal use without compensating the artist accordingly. Similarly, in traditional art, since certificates of authenticity are signed by the artists themselves on physical media, experienced forgers can still falsify them. NFTs change the game by enabling the identification of digital files with tamper-proof ownership certificates. In other words, if you claim to own an original work by an artist, you must possess the associated NFT to prove it. With NFTs, it is now possible to know with certainty who created a particular artwork and to track its ownership.

BETTER ROYALTY MANAGEMENT THROUGH NFTs

The use of NFTs in digital art has facilitated the automatic and secure implementation of royalties. In the past, artists only earned money from the initial sale; they received nothing thereafter. With NFTs, artists can now continue to earn money from their works even after the initial sale. For example, an artist can decide to include a 5% royalty in the smart contract of one of their digital artworks. The artist will then earn 5% of the proceeds from each subsequent sale. This can sometimes amount to a significant sum. It's a new way to monetize artists' works in a fairer manner. Payments are made automatically (thanks to the smart contract) throughout the lifecycle of the artwork.

THE METAVERSE: PRESERVATION OF ARTWORKS AND ACCESSIBILITY

Traditional artworks have the unfortunate disadvantage of deteriorating over time (wear, scratches, stains, marks, etc.). Works that are over 500 years old, like the Salvator Mundi, have suffered the damages of time and have required restoration work multiple times. Digital artworks, on the other hand, are perfectly preserved over time because they are entirely digital. The only drawback was that, until now, they were easily duplicable. It was as simple as copying and pasting without easily determining the true origin of the artwork. However, with NFTs, this is no longer the case: each artwork possesses a unique ownership certificate. NFTs, therefore, allow the combination of the advantages of the traditional art world (authentic artwork) with the digital realm (timeless preservation). Moreover, the Blockchain eliminates the need to worry about transporting traditional artworks since they can have their digital counterpart in the form of an NFT, which can be displayed in the metaverse.

PFPs: A NEW SOCIAL DIMENSION

It's impossible to talk about artistic NFTs without mentioning PFPs, which stands for "Profile Picture." They are essentially avatars but in the form of NFTs. They are very popular on social media platforms like Twitter. They serve as a way to stand out and show support for a particular project. World-renowned celebrities have adopted PFPs as their profile pictures, such as Eminem with his Bored Ape Yacht Club #9055[90], purchased for a modest sum of 123 ETH ($460,000)[91]. NFT influencers in the Twittersphere were increasingly using PFPs of projects they supported as their profile pictures in 2021-2022.

A NEW MARKETING STRATEGY: AIRDROPS

Airdrops are at the forefront of this new type of digital artwork. The term "Airdrop" refers to the distribution of digital assets (cryptocurrency or NFTs) in exchange for retweets, likes, comments, shares, etc. By completing the required actions (some of which carry more "points" than others), you can become eligible for an Airdrop. This method allows information to spread rapidly, and projects gain publicity at low costs. Some NFT collections also require community participation on platforms like Discord to be eligible. Similarly, holding a particular NFT in your wallet may be the sole condition for receiving an Airdrop. For example, Bored Ape Yacht Club owners had the pleasure of receiving Airdrops of Mutant Ape Yacht Club or Ape Coin[92].

BRUSHING OFF NFTS: NOT SO GOOD FOR DIGITAL ART?

A HIGHLY SPECULATIVE MARKET

Artistic NFTs experienced a great frenzy in 2021-2022, but it mainly reflected excessive speculation, with many buyers seeking to resell their NFTs at higher prices to make a profit. This strategy worked for a few, especially early adopters who entered the market before prices skyrocketed. However, the majority of investors who entered during the late bull market cycle ended up losing money. It is important to remember that like any investment, there are risks involved, and one should only invest what they are willing to lose.

ROYALTIES: LESS PROMINENT IN 2023?

Royalties, which allowed artists to have additional income, no longer seem to be a priority in 2023. They were popularized by the marketplace Opensea, which also benefited from them. However, new marketplaces like blur.io found a way to avoid paying royalties to artists. In a bearish market context, it is understandable why owners of artistic NFTs turned to such platforms. Imagine buying a Bored Ape Yacht Club (BAYC) for $100,000, and it now being worth only $30,000, and on top of that, having to pay 5% or even 10% royalties to the artist if you want to resell it. These kinds of marketplaces quickly gained market share, and gradually, other marketplaces started to eliminate royalties.

BUYING AN ARTISTIC NFT DOES NOT NECESSARILY MEAN OWNING THE ASSOCIATED IMAGE...

It is important to note that when you buy an NFT, you are not buying the image itself. You are buying what is written in the smart contract of the NFT. Most artistic NFTs do not directly include the images in the smart contract, except for rare exceptions like Cryptopunks. What you are buying is often a link that redirects to the image, but it is not the image itself. Why, you may ask? Simply because an NFT, to exist, needs to take up a portion of the Blockchain network. And the heavier the smart contract of the NFT, the more space it occupies, and the more expensive it becomes. In other words, when you directly put your image in the smart contract, it becomes much heavier than a simple text file. For economic reasons, most NFT collections have chosen to store their images on IPFS (which operates on a peer-to-peer and decentralized system) rather than directly on the Blockchain. Therefore, there is nothing "tangible" about it. You are not buying an image, but rather a kind of digital archive, a sequence of numbers and letters. To use a more relatable metaphor, an NFT would be like the papers of a house. The papers are there to show that you own the house, but they are not the house itself. Similarly, the NFT shows that you own the file, but you do not own the file itself. What is recorded on the Blockchain is proof that the transaction took place. Okay, but what's the problem? I still have access to the image, right? Well, not necessarily, for two reasons. First, the link that redirects to the file can break. If that happens, you technically remain the owner of the NFT, but it will no longer lead to the image. Second, if the file is stored directly on one of the servers of the creators of the collection, they can decide to change the images as they please. This was the case with the Bull NFT collection[93].

...AND YOU DO NOT HAVE INTELLECTUAL PROPERTY RIGHTS!

The question of intellectual property rights for NFT-based artworks is a recurring issue. The answer depends on each NFT collection. Owning an NFT does not grant you any additional rights in terms of licensing or intellectual property. The artist who created the NFT still retains their copyright. For example, in the case of Cryptopunks, no clause regarding intellectual property was written in the smart contract because the concept was still too new at the time (2017). And since NFTs are immutable, it is impossible to go back. However, there are exceptions, such as the Bored Ape Yacht Club collection, where NFT owners also receive a commercial license, allowing them, for example, to open a restaurant inspired by the Bored Apes in the United States[94].

AUCTION HOUSES ENTERING THE NFT SPACE (AND THE DELAY OF THE FRENCH)

NFT, *Not the French Time*?[95] One may legitimately ask this question. Faced with the dominance of the English-speaking market in the NFT space, French galleries have remained cautious. There are two reasons for this. The first reason is the skepticism towards new technologies. The second reason, and perhaps the most important one, is the legal barrier: French legislation prohibits the public auction of "incorporeal" objects. Only tangible movable property is eligible. This effectively excludes the entire French market. This has led some French galleries to resort to various subterfuges to bypass these restrictions, such as conducting public auctions abroad or organizing private invitation-only sales. It's ironic for the country of the "startup nation"...!

EXAMPLES

Opensea was founded in 2017 by Devin Finzer and Alex Atallah. The platform took advantage of the NFT boom in 2021 to become the leading NFT marketplace.

Kalart is a French startup co-founded by Stanislas Mako in 2021. He was previously the CEO of uTip, which was founded in 2017.

14. INSURANCES

A HUGE MARKET TO DEAL WITH

$5 TRILLION MARKET CAP

As the famous saying goes, "where there are multiple zeros behind a product, there are usually insurers." And insurers are not mistaken: the insurance industry was worth over $5.3 trillion in 2021[96]. This market continues to grow and is projected to reach over $8 trillion by 2026. In this gigantic market and to remain competitive in the face of competition, some insurance companies have started exploring the use of blockchain and NFTs, albeit cautiously.

LARGE COMPANIES STILL HESITANT TO EMBRACE BLOCKCHAIN...

Large companies are still hesitant to embrace blockchain. Some have tried but quickly retreated. For example, as early as 2017, the Axa Group launched an insurance product called *Fizzy* on the Ethereum blockchain[97]. The insurance was connected in real-time to flight traffic data and automatically reimbursed policyholders in case of a flight delay of two hours or more. However, the project didn't gain traction, likely because Axa realized it would generate less profit compared to their existing products. If customers don't need to spend as much time dealing with insurance, it translates to less revenue for the company.

...UNLESS THEY USE A PRIVATE BLOCKCHAIN!

When insurance companies consider adopting blockchain, they often tend to prefer a private blockchain, which gives them greater control. However, this choice goes against the very founding principle of blockchain, which is decentralization. Unlike public blockchains that operate on consensus mechanisms like Proof of Work or Proof of Stake, private blockchains typically rely on a Proof of Authority consensus, which grants control of the blockchain to a limited number of actors. How can we build trust on the blockchain if we still have to trust these trusted third parties? The only real solution lies in a public blockchain controlled by a multitude of independent actors.

THE DOMINO EFFECT OF BLOCKCHAIN

Once a major company adopts blockchain as an insurance solution, and customers realize it is more convenient and cost-effective (we'll see why below), other companies will be compelled to adapt. Customers will demand that insurance companies integrate blockchain technology because it simply becomes more efficient for them. Otherwise, they will turn to competitors already using blockchain. Insurance companies that refuse to follow this trend will eventually decline, just as Kodak, once a leader in the photography world, fell by resting on its laurels. It is quite possible that the future leaders in blockchain insurance haven't even been created yet.

AUTOMATED INSURANCE AND MORE WITH NFTS

IMMEDIATE REIMBURSEMENT WITHOUT HAVING TO DO ANYTHING

Getting reimbursed by an insurance company can sometimes be a challenge. To illustrate this, let's consider the case of a flight delay. To get reimbursed, you need to fill out a form, contact the airline, gather proof of the delay, contact the insurance company, and provide all the necessary documents. The insurance company then has 30 business days to verify everything and decide whether to reimburse the delay. After 30 days, you receive the response. If it's positive, you need to provide your bank account details for the insurance company to make a transfer, which takes a few more days. In summary, it can be a real hassle to get a $40 refund. Blockchain enables simpler and faster handling of flight delay compensations. It is connected to the airport and identifies delayed flights. It then collects the list of insured clients with an insurance company like Axa and automatically reimburses clients who have purchased delay insurance. It's simple, quick, and efficient.

WHAT IF WE STARTED OUR OWN INSURANCE?

The business model of an insurance company is quite simple. Let's take an example to understand it better. Suppose an insurance company gathers 100 people, each paying 1$. At the end of the year, the company assesses the reported losses. Imagine there were accidents amounting to $30. Out of the $100 collected, the insurance company uses $30 to cover the losses and keeps the remaining $70 for itself. Now, let's imagine a similar situation but using blockchain. Suppose we create a smart contract with 99 other individuals. In this smart contract, we agree not to pay insurance premiums but instead deposit a 1$ security deposit. At the end of the year, we evaluate all the losses that occurred (let's say they amount to $30). We use the $30 to cover the losses, but the remaining $70 are refunded to the insured individuals!

FIGHTING INSURANCE FRAUD

Not reporting an incident, staging a car accident, simulating a house fire—these are practices that can cost insurance companies a significant amount of money. In the automobile sector alone, fraud is estimated to have cost around $2.5 billion in 2021[98]. For certain types of fraud (especially those involving any type of digital document), blockchain could help solve these issues. It would no longer be possible to provide false documents or proofs, as their validity could be quickly verified on the blockchain within seconds.

INSURANCE IN THE AGRICULTURAL WORLD

Now, let's imagine you are a farmer in the depths of Arizona. You had the foresight to take out blockchain-based insurance with contract terms directly embedded in a smart contract. Among these terms, you are covered in the event of an extreme drought for one month. Since this clause is directly written in the smart contract, it automatically executes if the conditions are met. This month, it has been exceptionally hot, and it didn't rain for a month! The blockchain will verify the weather conditions for the past 30 days and confirm that indeed, there was no rain. You will be automatically reimbursed without having to undertake any further steps.

HEALTH AND LIFE INSURANCE CONTRACTS

Some insurance companies offer programs that reward customers with vouchers based on their physical activities. It would be possible to integrate NFTs into this process to add a layer of security and transparency. An insurance company could offer a reward system with various partners by presenting an NFT certifying the regular physical activity of the policyholder. Projects like Stepn have already promoted this kind of healthier lifestyle by allowing users to earn cryptocurrency while running.

HEALTH INSURANCE

Privacy laws related to sharing medical data between hospitals and insurers can complicate and make the health insurance claims process costly. Additionally, a lack of data can lead to claim denials. By utilizing blockchain technology, these issues can be addressed. With patient records encrypted and stored on a blockchain, healthcare providers and insurers could access a patient's medical data without compromising their privacy (by storing cryptographic signatures for each medical record).

FACILITATING DATA SHARING AND REDUCING DUPLICATE WORK

Let's take the example of automobile insurance to illustrate the situation. Suppose you were involved in a car accident where the other driver is at fault. You submit a claim to your insurance company to recover your losses. This claim prompts your insurance company to initiate an investigation into the accident to recover funds from the other driver's insurance company. However, the other company has its own claims procedures, leading to duplicated work, delays, and even human errors. The entire process can be time-consuming, and you may be compensated much later than expected. However, all of this could be expedited if the claims were recorded on a blockchain where different insurers, reinsurers, brokers, and other relevant parties could access the same shared data. The blockchain would reduce repetitive tasks performed by different parties involved.

EXAMPLES

R☠**SKEX**   **Ryskex** helps provide insurers with an easier way to accurately assess and manage risks through the use of blockchain technology.

Etherisc operates on a decentralized insurance protocol. This protocol enables the collective construction of insurance products.

15. DONATIONS AND ASSOCIATIONS

DONATIONS ON THE BLOCKCHAIN: THE USE CASE APPEARED WITH CRYPTO...

INSTITUTIONS ACCEPTING CRYPTO DONATIONS FOR A WHILE NOW

Important organizations have been accepting cryptocurrency donations for some time now. The American Red Cross has been accepting Bitcoin since 2014. UNICEF launched its CryptoFund in 2019 to enable the acceptance of cryptocurrencies (9 in total). The *Food for Life Foundation* accepts 7 cryptocurrencies. The same goes for *Save the Children* and *The Water Project*. Even *Asmae Association* (founded by Sister Emmanuelle in 1980 to assist the most vulnerable) has joined in!

AN INCREASE IN CRYPTO DONATIONS WITH COVID-19

In its annual report, *The Giving Block*[99] reveals a 1,558% increase in the total volume of crypto donations on its platform in 2021 compared to 2020. The average crypto donation per transaction was $10,455. In comparison, cash donations averaged $128, which is 82 times less. This rise is partly attributed to the COVID-19 pandemic, as in-person charitable events became impossible, and crypto donations emerged as an alternative. Currently, crypto donations for associations worldwide are estimated to exceed $300 million annually. Even influential figures in the ecosystem make cryptocurrency donations. For example, Vitalik Buterin donated approximately $1 billion worth of $SHIB tokens to the COVID-19 relief fund in India[100].

UNCENSORABLE DONATIONS

Censorship of donations can be a problem as it restricts freedom of speech, association, and individuals' ability to support causes close to their hearts. However, donors always find ways to bypass censorship. The example of Julian Assange (WikiLeaks) is significant in this regard. Since the WikiLeaks scandal in 2010, Julian Assange has been receiving crypto donations as early as the 2010s when other donation channels were inaccessible. In February 2022, the AssangeDAO platform raised 17,422 ETH (equivalent to $55 million) in 6 days to aid in the release of the WikiLeaks founder[101].

ENHANCED TRANSPARENCY AND TRACEABILITY FOR YOUR DONATIONS

When making a donation today, you typically receive a confirmation email and gratitude but aren't certain where your donations actually go. You can't know precisely how your donation is utilized. For instance, when you send $100 to an organization aiding Syrian refugees, how can you be certain of the final amount reaching the association? With crypto donations, transparency is ensured as everything is traceable. You know exactly to whom you are sending your donation and how it is being used.

A RISE IN NFT DONATIONS

NFT donations have become the new method of fundraising for charitable organizations. Unlike cryptocurrencies, NFTs offer more than just a monetary donation. Charities, celebrities, and individuals can auction off their NFTs and donate the entire proceeds to the charity of their choice. According to The Giving Block's report, NFTs may be the most significant development in fundraising in 2021. In 2021, NFT projects generated over $12.3 million in donations.

NFTS AND DONATIONS: GIVE ME FIVE!

1. DONATIONS WITH EMOTIONAL VALUE

Donating in the form of NFTs goes beyond monetary value; it adds an emotional connection to the donation. If you donate an NFT that you've held for years, struggled to obtain, or has appreciated in value, you're giving something much more personal than just a cryptocurrency. Similarly, when you purchase an NFT to support a cause, you have the opportunity to choose an NFT that directly represents or evokes emotions related to that cause. For example, you could acquire an NFT of socially conscious artwork or a photograph symbolizing the issue you wish to support.

2. THE SPECIAL CASE OF UKRAINE

Through Ukraine's official crypto fund[102], "Aid for Ukraine," individuals can donate either cryptocurrency or NFTs. Several NFTs from significant collections have been donated to Ukraine to aid the country. One notable example is CryptoPunk #5364, valued at approximately $200,000[103]. Alex Bornyakov, a deputy at the Ministry of Digital Transformation in Ukraine, states, *"I believe this type of NFT is even more impactful than a simple crypto donation. You have the option to store this token, which will accompany you until you decide to sell it. Regardless of what happens, it will always be there and remind people of what happened."*[104]

3. ARTISTS ARE GETTING INVOLVED TOO!

More and more celebrities and artists are making donations in the form of NFTs or participating as ambassadors in charity projects involving NFTs. Imagine having the opportunity to meet the celebrity ambassador of a project in person by owning the NFT associated with the organization. Some celebrities have even made direct NFT donations. For example, Beeple auctioned an NFT that sold for $6 million, with the proceeds going to the Open Earth Foundation. Ellen DeGeneres also raised $33,495 for the World Central Kitchen through the sale of her NFT[105]. Similarly, in March 2021, Jack Dorsey, who sold an NFT of his first tweet for $2.9 million, donated 50 bitcoins to the *Give Directly's Africa Response fund*[106].

4. CELEBRITIES AS EXCELLENT COMMUNICATION TOOLS

Imagine that by owning the NFT received through your donation, you have a chance to be selected to meet your favorite celebrity. While Adriana Karembeu doesn't offer this option yet, other celebrities have already launched initiatives. This is an excellent communication tool for associations to leverage the visibility of their ambassadors, thereby raising more funds. It is possible that in the near future, telethon-style shows may also utilize this communication leverage.

5. ORGAN DONATION

NFTs offer a solution to the issue of organ donation by facilitating communication between donors and their loved ones. Currently, the lack of communication leads to a constant increase in organ donation refusals, despite only 15 to 20% of people opposing donation[107]. In France, 33% of potential organ donations are refused each year due to this problem. The process of expressing one's organ donor status is also lengthy and complex. NFTs could reverse this trend and simplify the process. The principle is simple: you create an NFT and embed your choice with a video recording stating either "I am an organ donor" or "I am not an organ donor." The digital file is stored on the blockchain as a certificate of authenticity, and that's it! You are the sole owner of this digital file and can automatically pass it on to your loved ones if something happens to you. Of course, this choice can be modified later. Simple, fast, and effective. A simple gesture that can save thousands of lives each year.

EXAMPLES

 The Giving Block was co-founded in 2018 by Alex Wilson and Pat Duffy. The startup aims to make crypto and NFT donations easier. They publish an annual report on cryptocurrency donations.

Giveth is a DAO (Decentralized Autonomous Organization) that facilitates fundraising by directly rewarding donors through the GIVbacks program, using their cryptocurrency called GIV.

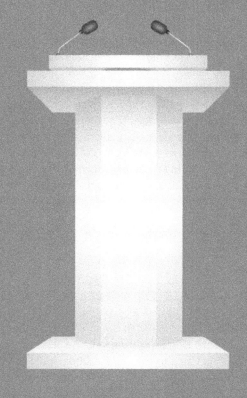

16. POLITICS

HOW CAN NFTS BE USED IN POLITICS?

THE INTRUSION OF NFTs IN THE FRENCH POLITICAL LANDSCAPE

Politicians can no longer afford to ignore the growing importance of blockchain technology in our society. While Emmanuel Macron positioned himself as the candidate of the "startup nation" during his 2017 campaign, his digital program for the 2022 campaign was somewhat lacking. However, he did grant an interview to The Big Whale on April 21, 2022[108], in which he discussed his vision of Web3 and his decisions in the event of re-election. This interview aimed to show that he was aware of the importance of this technology and that he wanted to position himself in favor of its development. Other candidates for the 2022 election had announced some measures regarding NFTs in their programs. Anne Hidalgo, for example, proposed subjecting them to a special legal classification[109]. Eric Zemmour, on the other hand, proposed implementing a tax[110]. More recently, on October 18, 2022, Jean-Noël Barrot (Minister Delegate for Digital Transition), during the inauguration of the NFT Factory, reaffirmed France's ambition to be at the forefront of blockchain technology[111].

FINANCING POLITICAL PARTIES: SOUTH KOREA TAKES THE LEAD

During the 2022 presidential campaign in South Korea, the Democratic Party (DPK) utilized NFTs to raise funds. Donors could exchange cryptocurrencies (BTC or ETH) for an NFT featuring Lee Jae-myung, the Democratic candidate, along with a presentation of his political program. Although this may seem highly innovative, it is a legal practice in South Korea, which became the first country to allow the use of NFTs for political campaign financing. Interestingly, the conservative Korean party led by Yoon Suk-yeol, who was elected president on 09/03, responded by creating over 22,000 NFTs themselves!

APPEALING TO THE UNDER 30 GENERATION

During an election campaign, NFTs can be an effective means to attract young, less politically engaged voters who are sensitive to new technologies. By offering NFTs related to political themes, candidates can generate interest and engagement from this specific audience. Attracting individuals under 30 years old was indeed the primary objective of the financing project conducted by the Democratic Party of Korea.

CREATING A MORE ENGAGED COMMUNITY

NFTs provide an effective means for politicians to strengthen their personal branding and foster increased engagement from their community. By creating exclusive NFTs representing their message, image, or personal history, they can establish a strong and unique brand image that sets them apart from their competitors. Moreover, NFTs can offer a new way to communicate with their community, such as enabling NFT holders to have direct contact with the politician through applications like Discord. One can also imagine the possibility that by owning a particular NFT, individuals could be entered into a drawing to attend a more exclusive meeting (which would be broadcasted for those who are not selected).

POLITICAL EVENTS IN THE METAVERSE?

Political rallies in the metaverse? The idea doesn't seem so unrealistic, considering, for example, the success of Jean-Luc Mélenchon's dual meeting in Lyon and Paris on February 5, 2017, during the presidential campaign, which featured his hologram[112]. In the case of blockchain utilization, NFTs could serve as entry tickets to this entirely new type of virtual gathering. The use of this technology would overcome geographical barriers and enable people from around the world to participate in real-time. While it would not replicate the experience of an in-person event, it would open up new possibilities for political engagement and citizen participation.

THE CASE OF DONALD TRUMP (CARDS) AND MELANIA (BE BEST)

In February 2021, one month after Donald Trump's defeat in the U.S. presidential election, Beeple's artwork depicting a naked Donald Trump covered in insults sold for $6.6 million[113]. It was a blow to Donald Trump's image. However, in December 2022, he got his revenge with the sale of a collection of 45,000 NFTs, each priced at a modest $99. The collection, named Donald Trump Digital Trading Card, sold out in less than 24 hours, fetching nearly $4.5 million[114]. And the former president's fans didn't "trump" this one... or almost: within a month, the NFTs had lost 99% of their value[115]. It's worth noting that in December 2021, Melania Trump had already put an NFT up for sale—a watercolor titled "Melania's Gaze"[116], created by Marc-Antoine Coulon. In April 2023, Trump made a comeback with a second series of NFT cards featuring his image!

BLOCKCHAIN AND NFTS: THE RETURN OF POLITICS? HISTORY AND OUTLOOK

THE BIRTH OF THE CRYPTO-ANARCHIST MOVEMENT

The history of blockchain is intimately linked to the history of Bitcoin, originally created with a cypherpunk mindset (as a side note, the first NFTs were created on the Bitcoin blockchain as early as 2012 with BitDNS[117]). Cypherpunks are primarily "people who write code"[118] to protect freedoms. This movement did not emerge overnight; it is the result of 40 years of technological discoveries, particularly in cryptography[119]. In the 1970s, asymmetric cryptography[120] emerged alongside the field of computer science. Initially funded by the military, computer scientists recognized the potential and risks of these technologies. They viewed them through a civilian lens, leading to the birth of crypto-anarchism in the 1980s, with notable publications such as the _Crypto-Anarchist Manifesto_ in 1988[121]. In 1993, Eric Hughes and Timothy C. May published _A Cypherpunk's Manifesto_[122], outlining the conditions for ensuring privacy in the digital age, point by point.

THE 3 INGREDIENTS: ASYMMETRIC CRYPTOGRAPHY, PROOF OF WORK, AND PEER-TO-PEER

With the advent of email (see dedicated chapter), a community formed in the 1990s through mailing lists as the Internet entered households. Concurrently, proof of work (PoW) emerged as a means to combat spam (email senders had to provide proof of work, making spam economically unviable due to the electricity costs associated with providing proof). Shortly after, the first peer-to-peer implementations such as the BitTorrent protocol appeared in the 2000s. This protocol quickly gained popularity as it enabled free movie streaming.

In summary, three technical innovations...

1980s	1990s	2000s
Asymmetric cryptography	Proof of work for emails	Peer-to-peer

...The ingredients for creating Bitcoin were gathered!

BITCOIN, "THE ULTIMATE DEMOCRATIC TOOL[123]" ?

The ingredients for creating Bitcoin were indeed gathered. Only the trigger was needed. And that trigger came with the bankruptcy of Lehman Brothers on September 15, 2008, which led to the 2008 subprime crisis. On that day, the global financial system panicked, with $700 billion disappearing in the following days and thousands of employees being laid off. This crisis was largely due to the complete opacity of the financial system and the toxic assets held by banks. The crisis expedited the finalization of Bitcoin by the famous Satoshi Nakamoto. On January 3, 2009, the first block was created. Bitcoin was inherently political, as evidenced by the message included in that first block: *"Chancellor on brink of second bailout for banks"*[124]. The parallel whitepaper explaining the functioning of Bitcoin was only 9 pages long[125], but the protocol has never been hacked.

The goal of this chapter is not to explain the workings of Bitcoin. The essential point is to understand the context in which Bitcoin was born (cypherpunk ideology + global financial crisis) and why it is profoundly political: for the first time, it was possible to exchange value without intermediaries, in a peer-to-peer and uncensorable manner. With Bitcoin, individuals regained monetary sovereignty, making it, for some, the "ultimate democratic tool"[126]. However, as we will see, NFTs are also making their mark!

DAOs, THE RETURN OF POLITICS? A NEW MODEL OF GOVERNANCE

In 2014/2015, the creation of Ethereum by Vitalik Buterin went beyond Bitcoin by introducing programmable money through smart contracts. This programmability opened up new possibilities, including the creation of DAOs (Decentralized Autonomous Organizations) shortly thereafter. DAOs are primarily a political tool. They offer a new model of governance because they are designed to operate autonomously and decentralized, without the need for a central governing body or authority to make decisions. This powerful new governance model has led some English-speaking thinkers to believe that it could eventually replace the current mode of governance known as the nation-state, as mentioned in Balaji Srinivasan's book, *The Network State*[127].

TURNING THE TABLES ON POLITICIANS? BLOCKCHAIN DOESN'T LIE

As the French comedian Coluche once said, *"Journalists don't believe the lies of politicians, but they repeat them! That's worse!"* We are well aware of the close relationship between some journalists, media, and those in power[128]. We also know how politicians can conveniently change their stance when necessary. However, thanks to the blockchain, it would be possible to hold politicians accountable for their own contradictions. Why not use NFTs to record their campaign promises, statements, and various speeches on the blockchain? The advantage of the blockchain is that it doesn't lie. These NFTs would serve as constant reminders to politicians of everything they promised without ever delivering.

17. SPORT

NFTS IN SPORT: A NEW PLAYING FIELD

FOR THE BETTER... AND FOR THE WORSE!

In January 2022, the Australian Open sold a collection of 6,776 NFTs that gained attention for its innovative approach. Each NFT represented a 19 cm² space on the tennis court (with the exact position on the court unknown to the buyer). After the tournament, each ball impact was analyzed, allowing the NFT holder to receive a reward based on the number of ball impacts on their location. However, the world of sports has gone even further, as seen with the example of tennis player Oleksandra Oliynykova. She claims to be the world's first tokenized tennis player according to her Twitter bio. Ranked 619th in the WTA, she sold a part of her arm through NFTs[129], allowing the buyer to display, for example, a tattoo representing a brand. Fans who purchased NFTs from her created game, "OliCrypto," can even make decisions in her career. Beyond the amusing or grotesque aspect, this raises ethical questions about the extent to which tokenization can go.

MAJOR SPORTS BRANDS INVEST IN NFTs...

Nike is undoubtedly one of the major sports brands that has heavily invested in the world of NFTs. The sportswear giant patented a method for authenticating sports shoes using NFT technology called CryptoKicks[130]. When a customer purchases a pair of CryptoKicks, they also receive an NFT that guarantees the authenticity of the shoes, even if they are sold to other buyers. In late 2021, Nike also acquired RTFKT[131] (pronounced "artefact"), an NFT-focused company. This acquisition allowed Nike to strengthen its presence in the Web3 space. On February 27, 2021, RTFKT had already sold 621 limited-edition pairs of sneakers (in collaboration with artist Fewocious), generating a net profit of $3.1 million[132].

...AS DO THE BIGGEST STARS

Antoine Griezmann, Gerard Piqué, Ronaldinho, Giorgio Chiellini, David Trezeguet, Pelé, Romelu Lukaku, Zinédine Zidane, and many other famous names have ventured into the world of NFTs to some extent. For instance, Lionel Messi made headlines after announcing his partnership with the fan token platform socios.com in March 2022[133], signing a deal worth $20 million. Similarly, Binance secured a partnership with Cristiano Ronaldo in June 2022 for an NFT collection, released as Mystery boxes[134].

THE NBA CASE

The NBA quickly got involved in NFTs with a platform called NBA Top Shot, allowing fans to collect and trade NFT video clips of memorable NBA moments. By March 2022, the platform had reached a market capitalization of $1.1 billion[135]. The best moments in NBA history were sold in limited editions, and their rarity increased their value in the market. The platform became very popular among basketball fans and NFT collectors, offering a new way to connect with their favorite teams and relive exciting NBA moments. One of the most expensive moments on the platform is a clip of LeBron James dunking against the Houston Rockets in February 2020, a few days after the passing of Lakers legend Kobe Bryant. The clip was sold for $387,000[136].

ONLINE TICKETS

NFTs can be used in event ticketing in various ways. Firstly, they can authenticate tickets and prevent counterfeiting. Due to their unique nature, NFTs can be associated with physical or digital tickets to ensure they cannot be duplicated or falsified. NFTs can also be used to track ticket ownership transfers, helping organizers prevent illegal resale and ensure tickets are used by their legitimate owners. An entire chapter is dedicated to this topic in the book.

ONLINE SPORTS BETTING

In the case of online sports betting, NFTs can be used to verify a person's age. NFTs can be associated with a verifiable identification document like a passport or ID card, and this information can be stored on the blockchain. When a person wants to place a sports bet, they can provide their NFT associated with their identity, allowing for instant age verification. If the person is underage, they will not be allowed to place a bet as their NFT will not be accepted by the verification system. This way, NFTs can enable quick and efficient age verification for bettors, preventing minors from placing bets.

NFTs FOR REWARDS: THE BALLON D'OR 2022

NFTs offer numerous possibilities for rewarding athletes. Medals and other trophies can be represented as NFTs and distributed to winners of sports competitions, who can store them in their wallets as proof of their sporting success. For example, for the Ballon d'Or 2022, a collection of 5 NFTs was created to reward the 5 winners of the competition (Men's Ballon d'Or, Women's Ballon d'Or, Kopa Trophy, Yachine Trophy, Gerd Müller Trophy)[137]. These NFTs were not for sale and could not be transferred to anyone else. Other NFTs (2022 "common" and 3 "rare") created for the occasion were available for purchase on the dedicated marketplace.

SPORTS AND NFT CARDS: THE UNICORN SORARE

Sports go beyond players sweating on the field and hordes of spectators cheering in the stadium, as exemplified by Sorare. Sorare is a fantasy football platform based on blockchain technology, allowing users to collect, trade, and play with digital player cards. Since its launch in 2018, Sorare has experienced rapid growth, attracting football fans from around the world. Initially focused on football, the game has gradually expanded to other sports, including baseball and basketball.

THE REVOLUTION OF FAN TOKENS

NEW REVENUE STREAMS FOR CLUBS

Sports teams will soon be able to generate additional revenue through the issuance of NFTs. Traditionally, sports enterprises derived revenue from ticket sales, merchandise, media rights, and partnerships. With NFTs, teams will have the opportunity to tokenize match tickets (selling them at a higher price) or organize exclusive events for NFT holders in the metaverse. This allows them to offer additional experiences through NFTs. Fans would be willing to purchase these NFTs at a premium to access these experiences.

EXCLUSIVE RIGHTS FOR FANS

NFTs can offer exclusive rights to sports fans, granting them access to unique content and experiences. For example, fans can unlock exclusive videos of certain players, vote for the next slogan, contribute to the design of the new jersey, or help choose the players' entrance music. Additionally, NFTs can be used to sponsor their favorite players, providing fans with a way to financially support their beloved athletes while accessing exclusive benefits.

FAN BADGES: NFTs THAT ARE NOT FOR SALE, BUT FANS WILL DESIRE

Just like in sports, the Web 3 is centered around communities, and we know how passionate fans are about their teams. It is conceivable for clubs to reward the most engaged fans with "fan badges." These badges cannot be sold or traded; they simply serve as proof of a certain level of involvement. This involvement can be measured based on various criteria such as the number of matches the fan has attended, their engagement on social media, and more. The more involved the fan is, the more access they can have to rare badges, granting them exclusive rights such as loyalty programs, private meet-ups, access to private Discord groups, and more.

BRAND IMAGE FOR PLAYERS

By issuing NFTs, players have the opportunity to offer exclusive experiences to token holders. For example, they can offer autograph sessions, privileged access to their Discord community, or even the chance to attend a private training session. These experiences are directly linked to the ownership of NFTs. By establishing a direct connection with their fans through these exclusive experiences, players can strengthen their relationship and create a more engaged and loyal community. For athletes who are not yet widely known, NFTs can serve as proof of their status, representing their performances or sporting achievements.

AN EXAMPLE: PSG FAN TOKEN (SOCIOS)

In January 2020, the football club Paris Saint Germain became the first football club to issue fan tokens through the Socios platform. According to the platform, these tokens allow fans to influence certain decisions of their favorite team, unlock VIP rewards such as match tickets, access exclusive promotions, participate in a chat, and receive recognition as a "superfan." A crypto "PSG Fan Token" was even created in December 2020[138] on the Chiliz blockchain (the blockchain used by socios.com). When Lionel Messi signed with PSG in August 2021 and it was rumored that a portion of his signing bonus was paid in this cryptocurrency, the price skyrocketed, peaking at almost $50. This demonstrates the enthusiasm this new type of asset can generate within the fan community.

NFTS IN SPORTS: YELLOW CARD?

CONTRACTS ENTERED INTO TOO QUICKLY

While the use of NFTs in the sports world is a commendable development, cases of fraud have also been reported. Several contracts between NFT-related companies and football clubs have ended badly due to suspicions of fraud surrounding these companies. For example, in November 2021, FC Barcelona canceled a marketing agreement with Ownix, an NFT marketplace, following the arrest of Moshe Hogeg, a person involved with the company, on allegations of fraud[139]. Similarly, Manchester City suspended its sponsorship agreement with 3Key Technologies[140] after discovering that no one in the company's management team had an online presence, raising doubts about the legitimacy of the company. Since then, 3Key Technologies has ceased communication on social media. These clubs did not conduct the necessary due diligence before engaging with these companies.

CONCENTRATION OF WEALTH AND CONFLICTS OF INTEREST

In October 2021, an investigation revealed that only 1% of players on Sorare held 45% of the total value of cards issued by the platform[141], creating an asset concentration that is susceptible to market manipulation by the wealthiest participants. However, this is not the only issue raised by the investigation. When active players like Gerard Piqué invest in Sorare and participate in the game, significant conflicts of interest arise. Since the game is based on the real-life performances of players in matches, it is possible for a footballer to intentionally lower their performance to serve their own interests or those of an accomplice. Socios.com also raises many questions. For example, it would be easy for a player to buy a club's fan token shortly before accepting a transfer offer from that club to take advantage of the price increase resulting from the announcement of their signing.

EXAMPLES

 Socios.com is a platform that allows sports clubs and teams to increase fan engagement and monetize it more effectively. The concept of the platform is inspired by the "socios" (supporters in Spanish football) who participate in their club's decision-making process.

Sorare is a blockchain platform for fantasy football. It enables players to buy, sell, and trade digital cards of real-life players across various sports, including football, basketball, and baseball.

18. PRECIOUS METALS

PRECIOUS METALS: A MARKET THAT'S WORTH ITS WEIGHT IN GOLD

A MARKET THAT WEIGHS $200 BILLION AND KEEPS GROWING

The precious metals market was worth nearly $200 billion in 2022[142] and is expected to reach over $260 billion by 2028. This market has been growing continuously for decades. One reason for this growth is that when the value of the dollar, which remains one of the most important reserve currencies, declines compared to other currencies, people flock to the safety of gold, driving up metal prices. Between 1973 and 2023, the price of an ounce of gold increased twentyfold, from $100 to $2000, during a period marked by several financial crises[143]. If there were to be another economic crisis in the coming years, history suggests that the price of precious metals would rise even further.

GOLD: A HEDGE AGAINST INFLATION[144]...

Gold is considered a hedge against inflation for several reasons:
- The supply of gold is limited, which means there is not enough gold to meet growing demand. This can lead to a price increase in response to increased demand.
- Gold is a tangible asset with intrinsic value, making it less prone to economic and financial fluctuations compared to financial assets like stocks and bonds.
- Gold has been used as currency in the past and is still considered a safe haven by many during periods of economic and financial uncertainty, which helps maintain its value during inflationary times.

...BUT NOT ONLY THAT!

The role of gold, however, is not limited to protecting against rising prices due to inflation. Among its many qualities are its electrical conductivity, high resistance to oxidation and corrosion, and chemical inertness (making it a safe material for implants). Gold is used in mobile phones, computers, communication equipment, spacecraft, the medical industry for prosthetic manufacturing, jet engines, and many other fields. According to the World Gold Council, demand in all these industries remains strong, contributing to its scarcity. However, it is worth noting that silver is increasingly being used in electronic components at the expense of gold.

BETTER TO SELL SHOVELS IN A GOLD RUSH...

THE METAPHOR OF SELLING SHOVELS APPLIED TO NFTs

This metaphor comes from a story that recounts how a shovel salesman profited from the gold rush in the United States during the 19th century by selling his shovels to gold miners in search of wealth. Contrary to what one might think, the shovel salesman is the one who comes out on top: instead of wasting time searching for the next nugget (which they probably wouldn't have found), they offer others the opportunity to embark on that quest. This metaphor also applies to NFTs associated with the gold markets. Those who will truly gain are likely to be those who utilize the use cases of NFTs linked to gold, rather than those who try to make money by directly speculating on the price of gold.

FROM DIGITAL GOLD (BITCOIN) TO PHYGITAL GOLD (NFTs)

We experienced digital gold with Bitcoin, created in 2009. This marked a turning point in the history of gold, similar to the gold rush in the 19th century. However, Bitcoin represents purely digital gold that cannot be physically touched. Nevertheless, the blockchain can also be used for physical gold through the use of NFTs. When you combine the advantages of the digital realm with the physical world, it is referred to as "phygital." This concept applies well to gold, which can have a "phygital" counterpart through non-fungible tokens, for example, associating each gold bar with an NFT.

COMBATING COUNTERFEITING

There is currently more gold in circulation than actually exists in the world. Counterfeiting is the main reason for this. However, the primary use case of NFTs is to guarantee the authenticity of goods without the need for a trusted third party. Using NFTs in the field of gold would help combat counterfeiting. There will be no need to bite gold coins to ensure they are genuine. There won't even be a need to physically possess them to be certain of their authenticity. All the necessary information will be available on the blockchain, including details such as where the gold was mined, when, by whom, using which methods, how it was transported, and more. It is even conceivable that in the near future, the purchase of gold will be mandatory through an NFT registered on the blockchain, similar to the verification code used to send money from a bank.

TOKENIZATION: A MEANS FOR POOR COUNTRIES TO FINANCE THEMSELVES

Tokenization can be applied at both an individual and national level. Particularly, some poor countries may find it beneficial to tokenize a portion of their commodities, such as gold or silver. This tokenization would allow them to raise funds by issuing NFTs representing their resources, offering an alternative to bank loans or government aid to finance their development projects. However, this approach comes with risks and challenges in terms of regulation and investor protection, which must be taken into account.

BRINGING MORE LIQUIDITY TO THE MARKET

The gold market is considered relatively liquid, meaning it is relatively easy to buy and sell gold at any time. However, in specific markets such as numismatics, this may not always be the case. The number of rare coins or collectible items available on the market is often limited, and price can be a limiting factor. With NFTs, it will be possible to tokenize (i.e., split into multiple NFTs) coins or collectible items, facilitating their purchase and resale. For example, it will be possible to buy 1/10th of a gold Louis without needing to trust the other nine buyers since trust will be certified by the blockchain.

THE ADVANTAGES OF NO LONGER WORRYING ABOUT TRANSPORTATION

Using NFTs to invest in gold means you may not necessarily need to physically possess the object while being 100% sure that you truly own it, such as a gold Louis mentioned earlier. This presents two significant advantages. Firstly, it eliminates the need to go through customs to import the coin, greatly simplifying the purchasing and holding process. If you buy your gold Louis from a collector in Turkey, there will be no need to physically bring the coin to be certain that you are the sole owner. The other advantage, resulting from this, is that it makes collecting such objects more environmentally friendly as there is no need to transport the coin to one's location.

EXAMPLES

 Aurus was founded in 2018 and enables investment in gold, silver, and platinum bars through the use of blockchain. They have also developed a mobile application.

Artorus is a platform that allows the purchase of ancient coins, focusing more on the aspect of numismatics and collecting.

19.
ADMINISTRATION

ADMINISTRATIVE SLOWNESS, A FRENCH SPECIALTY

THE FRENCH « ADMINISTRATIVE MILLEFEUILLE »

I hope not to offend anyone by writing these lines, but it must be admitted: France excels in its administrative complexity, commonly known as the "administrative millefeuille" (referring to a layered pastry). As of 2022, France had a staggering 34,955 municipalities, 332 arrondissements, 101 departments, and 13 regions (previously 27). That's quite a lot! Not to mention all the internal subdivisions within each municipality. With so much to manage, it's not surprising that the system sometimes gets clogged up.

A LOSS OF 150 BILLION EUROS IN 2021

Of course, all these intermediaries generate management costs. In 2021, according to INSEE[145] (National Institute of Statistics and Economic Studies), public administration expenses amounted to 1,475 billion euros, while revenues amounted to 1,314 billion euros. That's a loss of 160 billion euros for the year 2021 alone! These losses are due to the administrative millefeuille, but not solely. There are also simply poorly managed expenses, whether in France or at the European Union level. Here's a recent example related to our topic: in November 2022, the EU had the bright idea of organizing a gala to celebrate the launch of its metaverse for 18-25 year-olds. The gala cost the modest sum of 387,000 euros and brought together... 6 people[146]. Yes, you read that right, only six unfortunate individuals!

THE USE OF DIGITAL TECHNOLOGY IN ADMINISTRATION: THE CASE OF ESTONIA

Estonia (or rather e-Estonia), a small country with 1.3 million inhabitants, has become a global reference in digital matters. Since gaining independence in 1991 following the fall of the USSR, Estonian leaders have focused on the use of digital technology, particularly in administration. Estonians can carry out numerous administrative procedures simply by using their electronic identity card, adopted by 98% of the population. They can vote, access public transportation, pay taxes, track their children's academic results, apply for agricultural subsidies, and even receive digital medical prescriptions that can be retrieved from pharmacies by presenting their electronic identity card. For Estonians, this means less paperwork, less bureaucracy, and significant time savings.

NFTS TO STREAMLINE ALL OF THIS!

REDUCING UNNECESSARY PAPERWORK

It is common to see offices cluttered with client mail, invoices, notes, and requests that will eventually be stored in folders, drawers, and files, or even colorful sticky notes for the more creative ones, only to be lost in the abyss. Employees sometimes waste a tremendous amount of time searching for these documents: did you know that an office worker spends an average of 5 hours per week looking for lost papers? Fortunately, more and more administrations are opting for document digitization to be more efficient and avoid unnecessary paper waste. The use of NFTs would take it a step further by providing a decentralized storage solution for these documents. Thanks to the blockchain, digitized documents would be stored transparently and accessible to all, making them easy to retrieve in case of technical issues. Moreover, the use of NFTs would guarantee the security and authenticity of the documents, facilitating their management and sharing.

PREVENTING FRAUD (PASSPORTS, ID CARDS,...)

Fraud can cause significant financial damage to individuals or companies, and it can also lead to a loss of trust and commitment from customers, employees, and partners. For example, it is estimated that social welfare fraud accounts for between 100 and 120 million euros (14% of fraud cases). Housing benefits represent 25% of fraud, and the RSA (income support) goes up to 60%. The use of NFTs could create a permanent and immutable record of transactions, helping to limit fraud by providing irrefutable proof of the authenticity and origin of a document.

FACILITATING COMMUNICATION BETWEEN ADMINISTRATIONS

Each administration has its own procedures and protocols, which can complicate coordination and exchanges between different services. Bureaucracy often makes processes cumbersome and complex, with hierarchical levels to navigate before obtaining clear answers. Different administrations have different priorities and objectives, which can sometimes hinder collaboration. Additionally, technical limitations associated with the use of outdated or non-existent computer systems can add to the difficulties. Blockchain could help simplify these processes by offering a unique, immutable, and transparent registry shared by all administrations.

COMPLETING ADMINISTRATIVE PROCEDURES IN TWO CLICKS

In France, we have all heard of Jérôme Cahuzac or Thomas Thévenoud and their "administrative phobia" (note the use of quotation marks). The former Secretary of State was fined 20,000 euros for not declaring his income in 2012[147]. Such a situation would likely not have occurred if NFTs had been employed at that time: the procedures would have been completed in two clicks, or even without any clicks at all. The administration would already have all the necessary information and could be sure of its veracity. No more room for cheating.

COVID-19: SOME LESSONS TO LEARN

THE DANGERS OF DIGITAL PASSPORTS

In some aspects, the digital pass could represent a threat to democracy. It could lead to a restriction of individual liberties and increased polarization in society by excluding individuals who choose not to be vaccinated. Moreover, governments have realized how easy it was to confine an entire population under the guise of protecting them. With blockchain, this mass control could be automated through a kind of 3.0 digital pass, potentially applied to all administrative matters. That's why it's crucial to have safeguards in place, such as the protection of privacy, in a society.

A SOCIETY WITHOUT DEVIANCE = A SOCIETY OF TRUST?

Would we live in the "Brave New World" if we lived in a society without deviance? Not so sure. A society without deviance is not a society of trust; quite the opposite. Small deviations are necessary for a democratic society worthy of its name. Have you ever lied? I have. And I imagine that is the case for many of us. Once again, I insist on this point: I am not saying in this book that everything about blockchain and NFTs should be embraced and that everything is wonderful. It is simply a tool. This tool is faster and more efficient than the ones currently in use. But it all depends on how we use it... Food for thought.

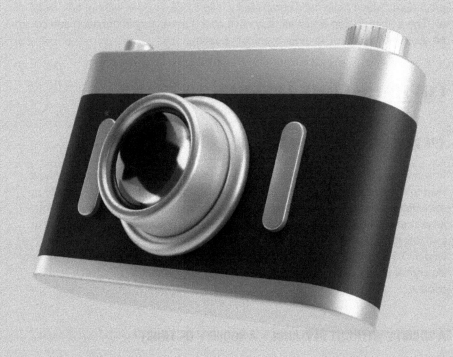

20.
PHOTOGRAPHY

NFTS AND PHOTOGRAPHY: FAR FROM CLICHÉS

AUTHENTICATION AND ANTI-COUNTERFEITING

In the 20th century, photographers started printing their photographs in limited editions. Today, art galleries around the world sell these limited edition prints. However, it is challenging for them to keep track of all the prints produced, which requires time and resources. NFTs provide a solution to this problem. They allow for the creation of unique and traceable certificates of authenticity. These NFTs record all relevant information such as the artist, creation date, and the number of limited edition photographs.

When a collector decides to purchase a limited edition print, the gallery also provides them with the associated authenticity NFT (e.g., "print 3/50"). The NFT is transferred to the collector's digital wallet and becomes their proof of ownership for the artwork. Through the blockchain, all transactions related to this NFT are transparently and immutably recorded, ensuring the authenticity and traceability of the artwork. The NFT enables the gallery to maintain an accurate record of all copies sold in that limited edition.

BETTER REMUNERATION FOR PHOTOGRAPHERS

In addition to providing proof of authenticity, NFTs can allow photographers to earn better compensation for their limited editions. Due to the novelty of NFTs, some NFT photographs have sold for record prices. To date, the most expensive NFT photograph in history comes from Justin Aversano's *Twin Flames* series[148], where he portrays 200 twins from around the world. The 100 physical prints of the series were initially sold by Christie's for $1.11 million. Twin Flames #49 was later sold for 871 ETH (equivalent to $2.4 million at the time). Other individuals have also taken advantage of the opportunities offered by NFTs, such as Zoë Roth, the girl in the famous "Disaster Girl" meme, who sold the photo for $400,000[149].

APPLICATION OF ROYALTIES

These record-breaking sales are, of course, exceptions. Beyond speculation, inherent to the youth of any innovation, NFTs are a powerful tool to enable photographers to apply royalties to their limited editions. These royalties are paid to them each time their artwork is resold. This means that even after the initial sale of the limited edition, the photographer can continue to receive compensation whenever the artwork is resold in the secondary market.

Here's an example: a photographer releases a limited edition of their photographs using NFTs. When a collector purchases one of these limited editions, an NFT is minted and associated with the artwork. In the smart contract of this NFT, a 5% royalty is applied for each subsequent resale. If the collector decides to resell their NFT, the blockchain automatically records the transaction, and the photographer can benefit from a share of the profits through royalties.

PHOTOGRAPH EXHIBITION IN THE METAVERSE

NFT photographs have a prominent place in the metaverse as digital artworks. In the metaverse, photographers can go beyond the limits of traditional exhibitions. They can create realistic virtual environments to showcase their photos and bring them to life in a unique way. For example, a landscape photographer can create a virtual exhibition where visitors can wander through breathtaking landscapes, hear the sounds of nature, and feel the immensity of each photo. Similarly, a portrait photographer can design a space where visitors can interact with the subjects photographed, getting a close look and discovering the stories behind each face. The metaverse offers photographers the opportunity to push the boundaries of creativity and artistic experience. They can incorporate interactive elements such as animations, sounds, or even videos to enrich the visual and emotional experience of visitors.

NFTS AND PHOTOGRAPHY: SAY CHEESE.. !

A WAY TO PROVE "WE WERE HERE": THE SOUVENIR PHOTO

Photography is the witness of our fleeting moments, the art of capturing our memories and freezing them in time. And in this quest for timelessness, what could be better than using Blockchain technology? For example, it would be possible to encapsulate a photo using an NFT and only reveal it after a certain period of time. Imagine taking a photograph of your newborn, the very first evidence of their existence on Earth. You could encapsulate it in a smart contract that will only reveal the photo 18 years later, to celebrate your child's coming of age. This way, you can be sure that you won't be tempted to reveal the photo before your child reaches adulthood, as the smart contract won't allow it.

PROOF OF GEOLOCATION

Another interesting use case is using NFTs to certify that a photograph was taken at a specific location and time. This can be very useful in various situations. For example, let's say you had a car accident. You make an amicable report to provide evidence to the insurance company about what actually happened. However, this is not always entirely reliable. With geolocation proof through NFT photos, both parties can take photos of the damages separately, and thanks to the geolocation proof, the insurance company can be assured that both parties were indeed present at that location and time, thus trusting the photos.

Another scenario: imagine a journalist sent to a war-torn country. In such circumstances, it is crucial to be able to prove the authenticity of the photographs taken on the ground. NFTs offer the possibility to certify that each image is the one captured by the journalist at a specific moment, with the exact geographic location. NFTs can provide indisputable evidence that the photographs were taken on the ground and reflect the reality of the events taking place. This enhances public trust in the media and their ability to provide authentic information.

SECURE TRANSMISSION OF PHOTOGRAPHS

In addition to their artistic aspect, photographs can also have strategic implications, particularly in the military domain. Military-related photographs are often highly confidential and may contain sensitive information about locations, installations, or military operations. Their disclosure can compromise national security, endanger lives, or allow the enemy to obtain valuable intelligence. Unfortunately, leaks of such photographs have occurred, such as the leakage of classified US documents concerning Ukraine in April 2023[150]. To prevent such incidents, it would be possible to assign an NFT to each photograph, thus restricting access to that image only to holders of the corresponding NFT. The NFT would act as a digital key to decrypt and view the photograph.

NFTS AND PHOTOGRAPHY: STILL SOME GREY AREAS...

LEGAL AND TAX STATUS TO BE CLARIFIED

Although NFTs are experiencing growing popularity, they are currently not subject to clear regulation in terms of legal and tax matters. Legally, NFTs raise several questions due to their unique digital nature. Currently, there is no specific legal framework for NFTs in many countries, which can lead to legal uncertainties and gaps in terms of liability and protection of the rights of the parties involved. For example, the intellectual property associated with a digital work sold as an NFT may be subject to disputes in cases of infringement or copyright violation.

On the tax side, the same ambiguity surrounds NFTs. Since they are often bought and sold using cryptocurrencies, questions of taxation and reporting transactions can be complex. Tax authorities still need to provide clear guidance on how to treat NFT transactions, including determining taxable value and the tax obligations of the parties involved.

THE NFT CREATOR IS NOT ALWAYS THE ORIGINAL PHOTOGRAPHER

The NFT allows the person who minted it for the first time to have a kind of ownership title on the blockchain. However, it does not certify the authenticity of the underlying object. By itself, the NFT does not authenticate a photograph. It also does not certify whether the person who created the NFT had the rights to do so. The case of the Metabirkins is a good example in this regard[151]. Currently, NFT platforms simply state in their terms of use that it is the buyer's responsibility to verify if the NFT they are purchasing is associated with a work whose creator holds the rights. To address this issue, some marketplaces impose a curation principle. For example, on SuperRare, a photographer wishing to sell their images must be invited by other collectors to join the platform.

WILL WE USE NFTs FOR ALL OUR PHOTOS?

Nowadays, anyone can be a photographer thanks to the improvement in photo quality on new smartphones and cameras. It is highly likely that you yourself already have hundreds or even thousands of photos taken with your own smartphone. According to *WorldStream*, 95 million photos and videos are shared on Instagram every day[152]. The question is whether we will need to use NFTs for this countless number of photos. Considering the current state of NFT technology, the answer is clearly no. Only photos that have true intrinsic value will be stored in a decentralized manner on the Blockchain.

EXAMPLES

 Keeex was founded in 2014 by Laurent Henocque. In addition to securing documents and data, the company also develops an innovative solution for using blockchain in photography.

Rhaspody is a French startup specialized in using NFTs for photography. It offers photos from famous artists such as Yann Arthus-Bertrand.

21. MARKETING

THE BORED APE YACHT CLUB (BAYC): A CASE STUDY

A BRIEF HISTORY

Valued at $5 billion after just one year of creation, that's the achievement of Yuga Labs with their BAYC. To understand this feat, let's go back a bit... It's April 2021, and it has been a month since Beeple sold his NFT for $69 million, which started generating a lot of buzz around NFTs. The founders of BAYC, Greg Solano and Wylie Aronow (also behind Yuga Labs), who were already active in the crypto world, decided to create a collection of NFTs that would stand out. For this, they chose to target people who had already made fortunes in crypto and were looking for new challenges. And thus, the Bored Ape Yacht Club, or BAYC, was born. The name comes from the expression "ape in," which means buying a crypto without thinking, and apes were chosen to represent this idea. The idea for the collection was there, but it still needed to be promoted. The best way to do that was through Twitter, with the target being Gary Vee, who had 3 million followers. And they succeeded!

WHY ARE BAYC UNIQUE?

There are three reasons why BAYC is a truly unique collection:
- **The roadmap**: Before BAYC, NFT projects that were released did not have a clearly defined roadmap. They were the first ones to do it. They promised to offer merchandise, create a radio station, and provide other benefits.
- **The community aspect**: It's no coincidence that the term "Club" is part of BAYC. The idea was there from the beginning: to generate a collection of 10,000 unique NFTs that would give access to a club of people who share the same values as you. But what made BAYC stand out was that they didn't settle for just a Discord community. They created events where only BAYC owners could gather. This was the case, for example, with the first Ape Fest in October 2021.
- **Commercial exploitation**: To bring all these people together around the project, a powerful "Why" was needed. That "Why" was to offer the NFT owners the opportunity to commercially exploit their BAYC. It was a way to completely disrupt the way marketing is done. And it worked. Some people launched restaurant chains. Well-known artists like Eminem and Snoop Dogg used the image of their BAYC in a song[153]. A trilogy was even planned![154]

A ROLE MODEL FOR ALL THE FOLLOWING

Numerous collections of 10,000 NFTs have emerged afterwards, drawing inspiration from the BAYC model (which itself drew inspiration from Cryptopunks). Some examples include World of Women, Moonbirds, Meebits, Azuki, Doodles, Clone X, Cool Cats, and more. You can find all the data associated with these collections on CoinMarketCap[155]. Each of these collections has unique traits and characteristics, as well as a community of owners who share a common interest and a sense of belonging to an exclusive group. These collections have created active and passionate communities around each NFT, organizing online events, contests, and exclusive activities for the NFT owners.

YOU'RE NOT THE PRODUCT, YOU'RE CREATING IT

BEING CO-OWNERS OF THE BRAND

In Web2, big brands that want to advertise their products pay influencers to promote their brand. In contrast, Web3 companies don't give money; they offer influencers the opportunity to invest in their brand (via NFTs) so that the influencers advertise for them (like BAYC with Eminem and Snoop Dogg). This advertising model is radically different because it allows influencers to be somewhat co-owners of the brand. But the most interesting part is that this model is not only for big influencers; it's for everyone. Many unknown individuals bought BAYC simply because they believed in the project and vision. Some still hold their BAYC since the beginning, and they can be considered as co-owners of the brand.

NOT SO EASY FOR WEB2 COMPANIES TO JOIN THE GAME...

Many big Web2 companies are afraid of missing the train. That's why some of them heavily invested in Web3 in 2021-2023, particularly in the metaverse. However, most of them failed in their strategy, such as Meta, which spent billions of dollars without achieving the expected results. It's not that easy for Web2 companies to enter Web3, even when they have the community and the budget... They simply lack the Web3 mindset. They lack something they can never have, which is the fact that investors (unlike shareholders) will co-build the company and have an interest in making it grow.

HOW TO ENSURE THE EFFECTIVENESS OF A MARKETING CAMPAIGN?

One of the current problems for brands using traditional advertising channels is that they don't have accurate and verifiable statistics on the effectiveness of their marketing campaigns. With the proliferation of intermediaries and data, measuring campaign performance has become very complex. Similarly, recent controversies over ad fraud on the internet have eroded advertisers' trust in advertising. Blockchain could help clean up the advertising market by ensuring that it is humans, not robots, who view the ads, and by providing better traceability of money usage. Advertisers could verify precisely what their expenses correspond to, allowing for better cost analysis. Similarly, with smart contracts, it becomes possible to condition the payment made by the advertiser on the guarantee that the advertisements they are paying for have actually been viewed. If visibility standards are not met for a given impression, the payment doesn't trigger.

NIKE, RTFKT, AND THE "PHYGITIALS"

"Phygitials" (a combination of physical and digital) are one of the new gateways to this new marketing. Nike understood this and acquired the studio RTFKT (pronounced "Artefact") in December 2021, a studio that was founded just in 2020. With this acquisition, Nike truly enters the Web3 with the legitimacy of a company that is already successful. It was crucial for Nike to partner with another company instead of trying to internalize everything themselves. Too many risks. Nike has thus launched a collection of "phygitials" with a range of shoes integrated with NFC chips. These chips establish a connection between the physical object and NFT technology.

22.
PORNOGRAPHY

THE PORN INDUSTRY: A JUICY MARKET

THE PORN INDUSTRY IN NUMBERS

According to a report from SimilarWeb, the website Xvideos alone generated 3.1 billion visits in April 2021, almost as much as Amazon.com and Netflix combined (2.45 billion and 1.23 billion) during the same period[156]. For Pornhub, there are 1.3 billion monthly visits, with over 30,000 unique visitors every day. 25% of all search engine queries are estimated to be related to pornography. Considering that Google processes an average of over 40,000 search queries per second, this would translate to over 3.5 billion searches per day. You can imagine the economic stakes behind this. On the internet, pornography already generated $5 billion per year and accounted for 35% of worldwide downloads in 2016, with over 4 million adult websites[157].

WHAT PORNHUB TEACHES US ABOUT PORN WITHOUT CRYPTO

In 2019, Paypal blocked Pornhub due to suspicions of hosting child pornography and non-consensual videos. This forced the platform to gradually add crypto payment options, including Bitcoin, for premium services. In late 2020, Visa and MasterCard also exerted pressure. As a result of the sanctions imposed by Visa and MasterCard, users could no longer use their credit cards to pay for premium content on Pornhub. In response, the site decided to accept only cryptocurrency payments in certain regions, such as North America, the United Kingdom, and Singapore. Up to 13 cryptocurrencies were added for purchasing content, including Monero, a crypto known for providing fully anonymous transactions.

NFTs: JUST ANOTHER TECHNOLOGICAL BRICK

It is undeniable that the pornographic industry has capitalized on technological advancements throughout the decades. Over the years, this industry has contributed to popularizing several technological innovations such as Minitel and VCRs, credit card payments and online commerce, as well as streaming. More recently, the porn industry has embraced cryptocurrency technology. For example, Pornhub has accepted payment in multiple cryptocurrencies for years, and many other sites have allowed users to spend their bitcoins, some since 2014. It is evident that in the years to come, the porn industry will also adopt NFTs.

NFTS AND PORN: A NATURAL FIT

THE FAMOUS 18+ BUTTON

Ah, the famous 18+ button. I think we all (at least men under 40!) have clicked "Yes" when we were not yet 18. But the ease of access to adult content by minors is still a concern, especially for parents. Adult websites are theoretically required to verify that their users are of legal age. However, in practice, this remains challenging to implement. This problem could be solved with blockchain technology. NFTs could be used so that each time a user logs in, and in a 100% anonymous manner, they can prove that they are indeed over 18 years old. Zero-Knowledge Proof (ZKP) technology allows users to maintain their privacy while generating proof of legal age. No need to know that you are named John Smith and live at 123 Main Street—the essential part is to know that you are indeed over 18.

EXCLUSIVE RIGHTS FOR LOYAL USERS

NFT owners could have rights on the platform, which is not the case currently. One can imagine that they would have governance rights over the platform. If you hold a specific NFT, you would have the right to decide the next logo for the site or propose new categories, for example. You would have more direct access to those who manage the platform, such as access to their private Discord. The longer you hold the NFTs you acquired on a platform, the more you demonstrate your support for it. This loyalty can be rewarded with various benefits at the discretion of the platform's managers.

A NEW WAY TO ENTER THE X MARKET

At first glance, one might think that pornographic platforms don't invest much in marketing. All you need is a camera, two actors or actresses (or more), some elbow grease, and you're good to go. Well, think again! There is fierce competition among platforms, and they strive to offer things that their competitors do not. NFTs can enable the development of services that we haven't even thought of yet. It will be up to the platforms to create this new kind of utility. For example, imagine that by owning one of the 10 exclusive and super rare NFTs from a platform, you could meet your favorite actress at a convention! (*Yes, we all have our favorite actress, no need to lie.. !*)

A NEW SOURCE OF INCOME FOR ACTORS

Like any good intermediary, porn platforms (especially streaming platforms) take a significant percentage of actors' and actresses' earnings. However, blockchain technology is designed to eliminate intermediaries and enable users to exchange services peer-to-peer, similar to how Uber disrupted the taxi industry or Tinder disrupted matchmaking agencies. The blockchain could increase existing revenues by allowing actors to retain a larger share. But it could also create new income streams! With the creativity offered by NFTs, the possibilities are endless. For example, the first NFP (Non-Fungible Porn) from Rareporn was sold for 2.5 ETH, equivalent to $10,000 at the time of sale. The NFT holder would have the privilege of receiving the panties worn by the actress Cléa Gaultier, one of Marc Dorcel's muses[158].

RESTORING VALUE TO CONTENT

Nephael, an actress and ambassador for the Pokmi platform, explains how NFTs can restore value to pornographic content: *"When I discovered NFTs and understood what they were, a vast world opened up to me... I'm not usually particularly into new tech, but I wanted to offer content to my audience differently. It can be photos, videos, or secret content visible only after purchasing the NFT. The advantage of NFTs is that they ensure the authenticity of the media, its tracking, and thus restore value to our content that is too often stolen"*[159].

NFTS AND PORNO : HUMMM... NO THANKS?

WHAT ABOUT WOMEN IN ALL OF THIS?

The porn industry is often criticized for the treatment of women and the gender inequalities it involves. The use of NFTs in this industry does not seem capable of changing this situation. Although they may potentially offer women greater control over their work and a better source of income, it does not address the broader issues of gender inequality. Sexual violence, harassment, and discrimination are still prevalent in this industry. Furthermore, the use of NFTs in the pornographic context raises ethical concerns due to the increased financialization of women's bodies.

SCAM ALERT: LANA RHOADES, §1.5 MILLION VANISHED

Have you ever considered investing in an NFT project promoted by an adult film actress? Probably not. However, there are many NFT projects in the pornographic industry, with promises of significant financial gains for investors. One of them was promoted by Lana Rhoades. With her fame in the adult industry, she attracted nearly 140,000 followers on her Instagram account (which is still active[160]) and hundreds of thousands on her TikTok account (which has been deleted), all to invest in her NFT project called "CryptosisNFT." Seduced by the beauty's promises, many investors acquired CryptoSis NFTs. But fans had the unfortunate surprise of realizing (too late, of course) that it was actually a scam, as the influencer ran off with the $1.5 million collected from the NFT sales. This scam caused a lot of uproar at the time, to the extent that Coffeezilla (a crypto YouTuber with over 2.5 million subscribers) made a video about it[161].

EXAMPLES

 Pokmi was created in May 2021 by two entrepreneurs, Nils Lataillade and Marco Garniga, along with Fred Coppula, a legend in the adult content industry.

Jimizz is a project launched by the famous duo Jacquie and Michel. Their slogan perfectly summarizes the spirit of the platform: *"Grab the bull by the balls."*

23. LOYALTY PROGRAMS

LOYALTY PROGRAMS TODAY

IT'S BETTER TO RETAIN A CUSTOMER THAN TO ACQUIRE A NEW ONE

According to Dawkins and Reichheld (1990), *"retaining a customer can cost up to five times less than acquiring new ones."* Customer loyalty has always been a key question in marketing, but it continues to generate debates. Over 75 years after the introduction of the first loyalty card by a major retailer (the FNAC card in 1954), the value of loyalty remains important, but consumer expectations in terms of rewards have evolved. In the current digital era, brands need to constantly reinvent themselves and offer new things to revive customer interest.

TRIVIALIZATION OF LOYALTY CARDS = WASTE

In recent years, there has been a proliferation of loyalty programs, contributing to the trivialization of loyalty cards. In 2018, the average number of loyalty cards held by French consumers was 6.7, compared to 4.7 in 2010[162]. However, consumers consider them less and less useful: according to a study conducted by Forrester in 2008 and 2011, loyalty cards have less influence on purchasing decisions (-30%), and more consumers perceive them as lacking value (+50%). Take a look at your wallet and see how many loyalty cards you have, then ask yourself how many you actually use. It's likely that you only use half of them, not to mention all the ones you have thrown away!

FROM TRANSACTIONAL TO RELATIONAL LOGIC

Loyalty programs were initially based on a transactional logic, with loyalty points exchangeable for complementary products or services. Later, a new type of loyalty, relational loyalty, introduced notions of trust and commitment to establish a more stable relationship with the customer. This type of loyalty focuses more on personalizing the relationship, providing access to offered or exclusive services, and taking into account customer interactions with the brand, particularly through customer service. NFTs fit perfectly into this new dimension.

USE CASES OF NFTS

MORE PERSONALIZED AND FLEXIBLE OFFERS

The current loyalty system is starting to show its limitations as most rewards have limited validity and lack flexibility and transferability. Consumers expect loyalty programs to be more adaptive to their needs. To meet this demand, brands must innovate by offering more innovative loyalty programs that take into account the needs and preferences of their customers. NFTs provide a solution as they allow brands to create more personalized and flexible loyalty programs by offering unique rewards that can be securely exchanged or sold. NFTs can also offer exclusive benefits such as early access to products, VIP experiences, or special events.

LIQUID AND EASY-TO-EXCHANGE VOUCHERS

NFTs offer numerous possibilities, including the digitization of vouchers. Unlike paper vouchers, they are more liquid and easier to exchange. Moreover, their traceability allows the development of an entire ecosystem of services around them. This provides greater flexibility for customers and better inventory management for brands. For example, let's say Emilie received a cosmetic treatment voucher at a renowned beauty institute. Suppose she already has everything she needs at home and doesn't need to purchase new cosmetic products. She tries to give her voucher to her friends, but none of them are interested. With NFTs, she could easily list it for sale on a marketplace and exchange it for dollars.

INCREASED CUSTOMER ENGAGEMENT

NFTs offer a new way to engage customers by offering unique benefits to those who purchase and hold these tokens. This can incentivize customers to buy NFTs to gain exclusive access to events or products they couldn't otherwise obtain. Additionally, NFTs can enable direct interaction with creators or artists, providing a more personalized and engaging experience. Customers can interact with creators via chats, video calls, or even participate in the creation of the artwork itself. NFTs can be shared on social media, allowing customers to show their support for the brand or community and generate interest from others. NFTs can also be used as rewards for contests or challenges on social media, further increasing customer engagement and brand reach.

LOOT BOXES: THE COCA-COLA EXAMPLE

On July 30, 2022, Coca-Cola launched its first collection of virtual collectibles in the form of NFTs on International Friendship Day[163]. This "loot box" was auctioned off and raised 137 ETH (approximately $285,000 at that time). The proceeds were donated to the Special Olympics International association. The virtual items in this collection can be used in Decentraland. In addition to NFTs, the lot included a real vintage Coca-Cola fridge filled with soda bottles. This loyalty strategy allowed Coca-Cola to reach new target audiences and portray a more "modern" image of the brand.

STARBUCKS ODYSSEY: A SUCCESSFUL NFT STRATEGY

Starbucks is known for its ability to leverage emerging technologies and make them accessible and easy for its customers. In the past, the company introduced WiFi in its stores to encourage customers to spend more time there. Additionally, it also adopted the concept of mobile wallets long before the advent of Apple Pay. The company was also one of the first to adopt mobile ordering systems, even before the COVID-19 pandemic. It's no surprise to see Starbucks venture into the world of NFTs with its Starbucks Odyssey program. On their web application, users can participate in different activities called "journeys." They can play interactive games or take on challenges. As they complete the "journeys," members can collect NFTs called "journey stamps." Odyssey points can be exchanged for experiences and other benefits, unlike the stars in the Starbucks Rewards program, which can earn free coffees or gifts.

BECOMING BRAND AMBASSADORS

Large brands' loyalty strategies are increasingly focused on transforming customers into brand ambassadors. These ambassadors can play an essential role, especially if they have the ability to influence the brand's development. By distributing special NFTs, voting rights can be granted to NFT holders, allowing them to participate in decision-making processes, such as choosing the next brand logo or selecting new product features. This level of participation would further strengthen their engagement and sense of belonging, encouraging them to promote the brand even more.

AN ADDITIONAL SOURCE OF REVENUE (ROYALTIES)

NFTs associated with loyalty programs represent a new source of revenue for brands through royalties. Whenever a customer transfers or sells their NFT on a marketplace, the issuing company can receive royalties, for example, 5%. In the NFT's smart contract, these 5% royalties would be automatically transferred to the company with each transaction. This royalty mechanism is already applied in many sectors of the blockchain, particularly in digital artwork with platforms like Opensea.

GROWING TOGETHER AS A COMPANY

NFTs can be used to allow customers to become investors in the brand. Companies can issue NFTs representing a stake in the company, and loyal customers can purchase these NFTs to become investors. Customers will be much more involved in the brand's success because they can benefit from the NFTs they own. The customer and the brand will share a common interest: the growth of the company. If the company expands, the value of the NFT also increases. The customer becomes more invested in the brand, laying a solid foundation for a strong brand-customer relationship.

NFTS: A NEW WAY TO GAMIFY CUSTOMER LOYALTY

Gamification through NFTs can also drive growth for companies. They can be used as rewards for loyal customers. Customers who make regular purchases or reach certain spending thresholds can receive unique NFTs as rewards. NFTs can have intrinsic value, such as access to exclusive products or VIP benefits, or they can simply be unique collectible items that showcase customers' commitment to the brand. For example, companies can launch a contest, and the winner receives a unique NFT. Starbucks, mentioned earlier, is a perfect example of this approach.

EXAMPLE

 Metacard is a plug & play solution that enables brands and e-commerce businesses to create loyalty programs using NFT technology.

24. CINEMA

NFTS IN THE FILM INDUSTRY

A NEW FORM OF FINANCING FOR A STRUGGLING SECTOR

Although we are still far from the $100 billion spent in 2022 by American streamers like Netflix and Disney+ on films and series, initiatives involving NFTs are multiplying and exploring new territory. One current area of exploration is financing films through NFTs. NFTs can be used not only to generate additional revenue but also as a means of funding a film. In exchange for financing, NFTs can provide access to profit sharing, membership in a fan club, or even exclusive premiere screenings.

THE POSSIBILITIES OF THE METAVERSE

The film industry is no stranger to the metaverse. Films like *Tron* (1982), *The Matrix* (1999), and *Ready Player One* (2018) have each explored the concept in their own ways. Watching a film in the metaverse would be a logical evolution of our current viewing experiences. The internet has made it easy to watch films from the comfort of our homes through streaming services. The metaverse could take the at-home film viewing experience to the next level. Imagine being able to recreate the feeling of being in a movie theater in your own living room by being in a virtual cinema. The possibilities that arise from the convergence of film and the metaverse are fascinating.

A POWERFUL MARKETING TOOL

Marketing plays a crucial role in the success of a film. NFTs have the potential to add a new dimension to marketing by providing special rights to NFT holders. Some blockbusters have already experimented with this approach, such as the film Spiderman: No Way Home, which offered 86,000 NFTs for the film's premiere[164]. The objective of this marketing strategy was to create a buzz around the film's release.

YOUR FILM: BECOME A CO-PRODUCER AND HELP FINANCE CINEMA

Becoming a (co-)producer of a film is currently difficult unless you have your own production company or substantial funds. NFTs could significantly reduce the entry barrier to becoming a co-producer, with maximum investments in the range of a few thousand dollars. Similar to crowdfunding, films could come to life thanks to community support, making each NFT holder a co-producer. NFTs could provide the right to have a say in the film's roadmap or even influence its development through a voting system. NFT holders could also share a significant portion of the film's profits. This is good news considering the film industry has faced significant financing challenges in recent years.

INFLUENCING THE COURSE OF THE FILM

How would you like to have your own character in a film? With NFTs, this could soon become a reality. Several initiatives have already been launched in this regard. For example, the Bored Ape Yacht Club (BAYC) announced in April 2022 that they were planning to release a trilogy with the first trailer scheduled for July of the same year[165]. The film was supposed to be produced by Coinbase but is currently on hold. BAYC NFT holders have complete rights over their images, suggesting that one of the 10,000 NFTs in the collection could be randomly selected to appear in the film, allowing the lucky owner to influence the story's development.

NFTS IN THE SPOTLIGHT

HOLLYWOOD, THE FIRST NFT FILM WITH "A WING AND A PRAYER"

In May 2022, during the Cannes Film Festival, Niels Juul (executive producer of Martin Scorsese's film "The Irishman") promoted the financing of their upcoming film, "A Wing and a Prayer," through the sale of NFTs (all information in their whitepaper[166]). The goal is to raise over $8 million from the general public by selling 10,000 NFTs through their company, NFT Studios. Juul sees this as a way to "democratize" film financing in the face of Hollywood's "archaic" system. The film will tell the story of Brian Milton, the first person to fly around the world in an ultralight aircraft. The studio subsidiary, KinoDAO, will offer fans the opportunity to purchase NFTs to finance the production. By buying these NFTs, fans will have the privilege of exclusive merchandise, access to premieres, as well as parties organized around the film at the Cannes, Berlin, and Sundance festivals. The biggest investors will receive silver and gold tickets from KinoDAO.

STONER CATS, THE FIRST MAJOR NFT ANIMATED SERIES

Stoner Cats is an animated series launched by actors Mila Kunis and her husband Ashton Kutcher in July 2021. The series raised around $8 million in just 35 minutes by selling 10,000 NFTs for 0.35 ETH (approximately $800 at that time)[167] ! Mila Kunis explained in an interview[168] the reasons for using NFTs to access the series, reflecting the artists' desire to take control of the rights previously controlled by studios: "I produce content for television, and I had to make an animated series for a channel. There is so much content, and I have so little control once it's sold that I wanted to bring ownership of the content back to the artist. I want a transparent system. So, I thought I would do it with NFTs."

NUMEROUS OTHER EXAMPLES

In 2022, film studios have been experimenting with NFTs in various ways. On October 20, 2022, Warner Bros. announced that the iconic film *The Lord of the Rings: The Fellowship of the Ring* would be distributed in the form of NFTs[169]. In July 2022, Netflix launched a collection of NFTs for its hit series *Stranger Things*[170]. It featured 17 limited-edition posters of characters from the series, all sold via Mystery Box. In the independent film realm, the most prominent example so far is *Zero Contact*[171], a thriller featuring Anthony Hopkins, which was used to launch Vuele, a platform for viewing NFT-based content.

THE FINAL CUT? SOME LEGAL ISSUES...

THE CASE OF TARANTINO

Quentin Tarantino recently decided to sell script pages and deleted scenes from his film *Pulp Fiction* as NFTs (raising $1.1 million)[172]. However, as intellectual property is a separate entity from the blockchain, the film's production studio, Miramax (currently owned by beIN Media Group and ViacomCBS), argued that Tarantino's contract prohibited him from commercializing these specific elements of the film. This led to a lawsuit filed in November 2021 in a California court. However, since the production contract dates back to the 1990s, there was no mention of possible commercial use of NFTs. This legal ambiguity allowed the director to make some NFT sales related to his iconic film, despite protests from the rights holder. An amicable agreement was eventually reached on September 8, 2022[173].

INTELLECTUAL PROPERTY AND THE WORK

The application of NFT technology in the audiovisual domain raises questions, particularly from a legal standpoint. The issue of intellectual property arises when considering the representation of NFTs, which can be an image from an existing work, a representation of TV series characters, or even "rushes" (unused scenes) as in Tarantino's case. Each situation requires a different legal framework, depending on the contracts signed for the work's exploitation. On the other hand, there is another type of NFT that grants a share of the film's revenues. These NFTs are called "security tokens" and are subject to highly restrictive regulatory frameworks. Their distribution requires agreements or registrations with financial institutions such as the AMF in France. Creating such an asset often requires a long-term collaboration with these institutions. Operating outside this regulatory framework can lead to criminal prosecution.

THE ISSUE OF FUNDING MOVIES THROUGH NFTS: THE TROUBLES OF PLUSH

On April 23, 2023, the French media *Mediapart* published an article revealing how *"700 investors lost over a million euros in the animated film project Plush, promoted by the star Kev Adams"*[174]. The case made a big splash and even became a topic of discussion outside the blockchain ecosystem, such as on HugoDécrypte[175]. The concept was unprecedented: financing an animated film through NFTs, with participation allowing investors to receive up to 80% of the global box office profits. The project had a prestigious cast including Kev Adams, Gérard Darmon, Éric Judor, Audrey Lamy, Gims, Camille Lellouche, among others. The idea seemed promising on paper, but unfortunately, it did not succeed. The project is now at a standstill, and it is no longer possible to purchase NFTs. This failure clearly demonstrates that NFTs are not yet mature enough to be used as a reliable source of financing in the film industry.

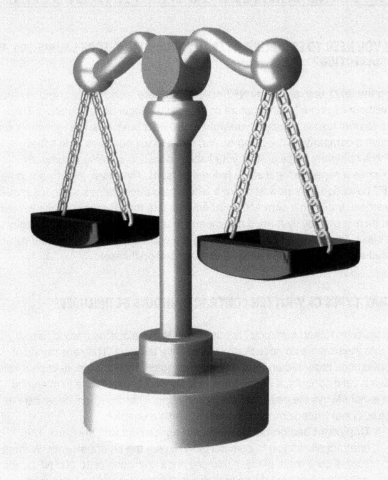

25. JUSTICE

QUESTIONS RELATED TO NFTS AND JUSTICE

1. DO YOU NEED TO ESTABLISH A LEGAL STRUCTURE BEFORE LAUNCHING AN NFT COLLECTION?

During the 2021 bull run, many NFT collections were launched and sold in record time without having a legal structure or established legal documentation. This poses several issues. Firstly, if you want to create a business, it is recommended to establish a company as not doing so can result in tax penalties. Additionally, forming a company helps protect your liability because creating a company establishes a separate legal entity (a legal person). Therefore, if you want to launch an NFT collection tomorrow and hire a blockchain developer as a service provider, for example, you sign a contract. If, for any reason, the developer wants to hold you liable, having previously formed a company means that the company's liability will be at stake. In case of conviction, it will be the company that is liable, and its financial assets will be used rather than your personal assets.

2. WHAT TYPES OF WRITTEN CONTRACTS SHOULD BE INCLUDED?

While the term "smart contracts" is often used in the blockchain world, smart contracts themselves do not actually represent a contract. They are pieces of computer code recorded on a blockchain that automatically execute certain actions. To have a valid contract, it needs to be clear and understandable to everyone, which is not always the case with smart contracts. Therefore, it is necessary to have traditional written contracts. Here are some examples:

- **Copyright assignment** or licensing agreement with the artist: This contract allows you to commercially exploit the artist's artwork. Without such a contract in place, if you sell out a collection of 10,000 NFTs, the artist may legitimately claim a share of the proceeds from the mint.
- **Service agreement**: Depending on your project, you may need contracts with a blockchain developer, marketing team, NFT influencer, etc.
- **Shareholders' agreement**: If you have partners or shareholders in the project, this contract clarifies the relationships and avoids future conflicts. It covers aspects such as the management of crypto funds (e.g., how ETH funds will be handled, given its volatility), conditions for a shareholder to exit the company, and the sale of shares.

3. WHAT LEGAL DOCUMENTS SHOULD BE INCLUDED ON THE COLLECTION'S WEBSITE?

During the 2021 bull run, many NFT collections had websites that lacked legal documents, which posed obvious problems. The essential legal documents to include are:

- **Legal notices**: These documents identify the company behind the project.
- **Privacy policy**: As NFT use cases become more complex, collecting certain personal data from customers, such as KYC (know your customer) information to prevent money laundering, may become necessary.
- **Terms and conditions** of sale (and service): It's important to clarify the terms of sale, especially considering that NFT ownership can provide access to various services (e.g., event access, discounts). This helps prevent customers from claiming more rights and benefits than those outlined in the contract.

4. IS THERE ANY SPECIFIC REGULATION FOR NFTs?

Regulating NFTs is complex because they have various functions. Some are collectibles, others can generate passive income, and some offer regular airdrops. NFTs are challenging to define legally, and the law is struggling to keep up, as evidenced by the ongoing regulatory developments such as MICA.

HOW CAN NFTS BE USED IN THE LEGAL FIELD?

WHAT DOES THE LAW SAY?

Under Article L 122-4 of the French Intellectual Property Code, *"Any representation or reproduction, in whole or in part, made without the consent of the author or his/her beneficiaries or assigns is unlawful. This also applies to translation, adaptation, transformation, arrangement, or reproduction by any means or process"*[176]. Therefore, downloading the file associated with an NFT could be considered an act of reproduction, requiring the author's permission. Additionally, when an NFT is sold on a platform, the display of the image, video, or music constitutes an act of representation, which is punishable if not authorized by the author or their rights holders.

RETURN TO THE FUTURE

Those who experienced the early days of the internet and attempted to start a business remember how challenging it was due to regulations. In the United Kingdom, for example, opening a website required a legal entity. Today, in 2023, this seems absurd, but it was the market reality a few years ago. A similar situation exists now with NFTs.

IMMUTABLE PROOFS OF AUTHENTICITY

NFTs could be used as evidence in legal proceedings due to their unique and non-modifiable nature. For example, they could be used to prove the authenticity of a document or object, or to demonstrate ownership of an artwork. Thus, if someone is sued over the authorship of a work, they could use an NFT as proof of their ownership. This could expedite the handling of judicial cases.

THE FIRST SUMMONS IN THE UNITED KINGDOM (2022)

According to press releases from *Giambrone & Partners LLP*[177], in July 2022, a British judge validated a summons sent via an NFT, marking a global first. This followed a complaint filed by Fabrizio D'Aloia, an Italian engineer and founder of Microgame, against five exchanges (Binance, Poloniex, Gate.io, OKX, and Bitkub) that held funds stolen from him by a criminal through a clone trading site. The judge authorized the sending of the summons to the two wallets used by the fraudster. Subsequently, NFTs were also issued to the five exchanges.

NFTs AS A SOURCE OF DISPUTES?

In an article dated January 4, 2022[178], *Le Monde* stated the following: "*Crypto-counterfeiting is causing tension in the art world. Numerous works of art are illegally reproduced as digital tokens, the famous NFTs. This process, which violates intellectual property rights, is proving very difficult to contain.*" It is true that NFTs can sometimes be at the center of legal disputes (for example, the case of Metabirkins, which we will detail shortly). That is why platforms like OpenSea specify in their Terms of Service that NFT creators must guarantee that they do not infringe on copyright.

HERMÈS AND THE METABIRKINS BAGS

Hermès took legal action against "digital artist" Mason Rothschild and the platform OpenSea. Mason Rothschild had drawn inspiration from the Birkin bag to create "MetaBirkins," a series of 100 NFT interpretations of the famous Hermès bag, which were listed for sale on OpenSea in December 2022. OpenSea had removed the MetaBirkins from its interface, likely due to Hermès' request, but the artist, invoking artistic freedom of expression, continued promoting them on Discord and Rarible. Mason Rothschild had also filed a domain name request related to the project on November 7, 2022. As a result, Hermès reportedly filed a lawsuit in a New York court, emphasizing the deceptive nature of the project. The luxury brand sought the termination of the project, the recovery of the domain name, and payment of damages, partly related to the NFT sales. So far, the court has ruled in favor of Hermès[179].

EXAMPLE

Kleros (founded in France in 2017) is a protocol based on Ethereum that enables decentralized resolution of legal disputes through smart contracts.

26. CARS

THE CARS WILL SOON BE ALL ELECTRIC...

THE POLLUTION PROBLEM IN NUMBERS

According to a report from the European Environment Agency, transportation was responsible for about 25% of the EU's total CO_2 emissions in 2019, of which 71.7% came from road transport[180]. Cars accounted for about half of the pollution from road transport. These figures highlight the importance of reducing greenhouse gas emissions in the transportation sector, particularly by promoting more sustainable modes of transportation and facilitating the transition to electric vehicles. In this context, the European Green Deal was established in 2021.

NO MORE POLLUTING VEHICLES BY 2035

In line with the roadmap of the European Green Deal[181] and efforts to reduce CO_2 emissions and achieve climate neutrality by 2050, a 90% reduction in transport-related greenhouse gas emissions is necessary by 2050 compared to 1990 levels. The EU plans to achieve zero CO_2 emissions from new cars by 2035, effectively phasing out the sale of internal combustion engine vehicles in favor of 100% electric vehicles. With this announcement, several manufacturers have taken the lead by announcing their transition to a fully electric vehicle lineup by 2030. Brands such as Peugeot, Alpine, Volvo, Mini, Citroën, Fiat, Audi, Ford, DS, and Mercedes have all planned to switch to an entirely electric range by 2030.

USING NFTS? OK, LET'S GO!

AVOIDING SCANDALS LIKE VOLKSWAGEN IN 2015

On September 20, 2015, Volkswagen admitted to massively deceiving US regulators about the polluting emissions of its diesel vehicles since 2009[182]. The company acknowledged using prohibited software to circumvent regulations and reduce the emission levels of its vehicles. *The International Council for Clean Transportation*, an NGO specializing in clean transportation, had tested the emissions of certain diesel vehicles. In May 2014, the organization published a report revealing that the emission levels of certain vehicles, including the Jetta and Passat, were up to 35 times higher than regulatory standards. If the Blockchain had been used to produce emission data, such a scandal may not have occurred or would have been detected more quickly.

REDUCING INSURANCE COSTS

In the near future, all cars will be electric, that's a fact. It is highly likely that data from these cars, such as mileage, repairs, and technical inspections, will be recorded directly in the vehicle's system, which will be connected to the Blockchain. Insurance companies can be certain of the accuracy of the information they have access to. This will allow them to more easily provide bonuses or penalties for policyholders and offer more personalized insurance options.

MASTERING THE SUPPLY CHAIN

The supply chain is a fundamental element to be mastered in any industry, particularly in the automotive industry where car components are numerous and come from all over the world. It is necessary to ensure traceability at every step of the process. Solutions already exist, such as the transfer of responsibility. A link in the supply chain will only accept responsibility for the goods if they are in compliance. All of this is recorded on the blockchain, which allows for process automation. Furthermore, it promotes a more responsible approach, especially in the context of electric vehicles whose raw materials (cobalt, lithium, copper, nickel, etc.) can come from polluting extraction. With blockchain technology, companies can prove the responsible origin of their raw materials from environmentally friendly mines.

USED CAR MARKET AND MAINTENANCE LOG 3.0

When buying a used vehicle, you are never 100% sure of what the owner tells you or the documents they provide. Documents can be easily forged, and few people meticulously verify the provided documents as it requires time and attention to detail. With NFTs, all the necessary documents can be verified with a few clicks. When the owner sells their car, they can also transfer the corresponding NFT, which will contain all the vehicle information (maintenance, repairs, parts purchases, etc.). It will be like a 3.0 passport for the car. The same principle could apply to car rentals as well.

DIGITAL TWINS IN THE METAVERSE: THE MORE EXPENSIVE, THE BETTER!

In his book *The Theory of the Leisure Class* (1899), sociologist Thorstein Veblen highlighted what is now known as the "Veblen effect", which suggests that an increase in the price of a luxury product can make it more desirable. This effect, also known as the "snob effect", can very well apply to luxury cars: the more expensive a car is, the more I want to buy it because it shows that I have the financial means to afford it. It is likely that in the coming years, luxury car brands like Ferrari or Lamborghini will offer their customers a digital version of their car in the form of an NFT (digital twin) at the time of purchase. For example, for a highly coveted VIP event in the metaverse, the owner of a Ferrari digital twin can make a strong impression by arriving at the event. Of course, all of this may seem fanciful, but it is a possibility that should not be overlooked.

HACKS AND DATA MANAGEMENT

Electric vehicles will become true "computers on wheels." And where there are computers, there are...hacks. The need for blockchain (and NFTs) will increasingly be felt in this industry for this reason as well. For example, did you know that in 2015, the hacking of the brakes of a Jeep led to the recall of 1.4 million vehicles[183]? Let's also consider vehicle theft: it is now enough to copy the signal from a key to unlock the vehicle. It costs only a few tens of dollars. To minimize this risk, one can imagine a unlocking system accessible only with the NFT of the car. Similarly, with the advent of connected and autonomous vehicles, new risks will arise as they produce and exchange large amounts of data with other machines. This opens the door to data theft, sometimes very sensitive, such as the owner's address or payment information. In the future, this data transfer could be done via the blockchain to ensure the protection of these sensitive data. Each car would be a node* in the blockchain. From there, one can imagine that network effects will take shape, allowing for the decentralization of data across a multitude of nodes, limiting the risk of hacking. Consensus and immutability mechanisms will ensure that the transferred data is reliable.

BETTER DOUBLE CHECK YOUR MIRRORS...

AN ACCESSIBILITY ISSUE

100% electric cars are often seen as the future solution for more environmentally friendly mobility, but their adoption remains limited due to their high cost. Who can actually afford a new electric vehicle priced over 30,000 dollars? The high price of electric cars is attributed to several factors, including the development and production costs of batteries, which constitute a significant portion of the total cost of the vehicle. Since the electric car market is still relatively restricted, it limits the ability of automakers to benefit from economies of scale and reduce production costs.

ENVIRONMENTAL ISSUES WITH BATTERIES

Electric vehicles are often presented as a more environmentally friendly alternative to gasoline or diesel cars because they do not produce direct exhaust emissions. However, they are not without environmental impacts. The manufacturing of electric vehicle batteries requires the use of raw materials such as lithium, cobalt, and nickel, the extraction of which can have significant consequences on the environment (deforestation, water and air pollution, etc.). It should also be noted that the environmental impact of electric vehicles is linked to the source of energy used to recharge them, particularly if it comes from fossil fuel sources such as coal or oil.

DYNAMIC NFTS, NOT YET READY

Similar to how dynamic content complements simple HTML on websites, dynamic NFTs could be used in the automotive sector to create more sophisticated models of ownership and data management than traditional NFTs. For example, dynamic NFTs could be used to record the mileage history of the car, all maintenance and repairs. Unfortunately, the technology is not quite ready yet. Currently, to record any modification to the vehicle, a new NFT would need to be created each time instead of being able to modify a single NFT associated with the vehicle.

PORSCHE HITS A WALL WITH NFTS

On January 23, 2023, Porsche released a collection of 7,500 NFTs for sale, priced at 0.911 ETH (a nod to the iconic Porsche 911 model), which was approximately $1,400. However, two days after the minting started, only 25% of the 7,500 NFTs had been sold. Realizing the failure, the automotive company announced on Twitter that the minting would be halted[184]. This launch can undoubtedly be considered a misstep in the Web3 space for such a renowned entity. How can this crash be explained? Firstly, the minting price was simply too high: in January 2023, during a bear market*, $1,400 for an NFT was exorbitant. Secondly, the communication was poor: the roadmap was unclear, and specific use cases associated with the NFTs were not announced. Lastly, the community was not at the core of the project: the Discord* server was solely used for announcements and not for allowing investors to ask their questions.

27. FASHION

PHYGITALS WILL BECOME FASHIONABLE IN THE FASHION INDUSTRY

FIGHTING COUNTERFEITING WITH CERTIFICATES OF AUTHENTICITY

You have probably already heard of fake Nike sneakers or counterfeit Louis Vuitton handbags. The fashion industry has been struggling to eliminate these counterfeits. According to *Red Points*, the global counterfeit industry is expected to reach $4.2 billion this year[185]. NFTs offer fashion brands new ways to combat counterfeiting by allowing users to verify the authenticity of products. It will essentially be a "product sheet" with all relevant information (place of manufacture, materials used, etc.). Currently, when you want to verify if a brand truly uses recycled materials for its clothing, you have to trust the brand. In the future, you won't need to rely on trust anymore; you will be able to verify ("Don't Trust, Verify").

EARLY USE CASES IN THE FASHION INDUSTRY

By issuing NFTs, brands will provide consumers with both proof of purchase and proof of authenticity for their products. Several players have already positioned themselves in this area. For example, in April 2021, the fashion brand Overpriced introduced the concept of a hoodie linked to an NFT. Each hoodie had a scannable code that allowed anyone to view the complete history of the NFT, including previous owners and the value of the hoodie. In case of theft or damage, the buyer receives a new hoodie with a different code, thereby canceling the old one.

ETHICS IN FASHION

The fashion industry is often associated with glamour and style, but behind this image lie numerous ethical challenges. From clothing production to distribution, many questions arise regarding sustainability and social responsibility. Child labor, the use of hazardous chemicals in dyes, and the pollution caused by the globalization of fashion are all significant issues in this industry. NFTs could be used to encourage transparency and sustainability in fashion. For example, brands could create NFTs for clothing made from recycled or sustainable materials, and consumers could purchase these NFTs to show their support for ethical fashion.

A NEW WAY OF STORYTELLING

Storytelling is a crucial element in a brand's marketing strategy. It helps create an emotional connection with consumers, convey values, and differentiate the brand from its competitors. Some brands have started using NFTs for storytelling. For example, Rimowa offered a storytelling experience about an infected space station to announce its NFTs linked to physical suitcases. In addition to marketing, with digital ownership certificates, it is possible to authenticate and tell the story of the product, its brand, and thus strengthen customer trust. By purchasing NFTs, collectors also want to be part of the story told by the brands.

THE SECONDHAND MARKET

The use of NFTs could be particularly useful in the fashion world, especially for the secondhand market. One of the main challenges when buying secondhand fashion items is authenticity. Counterfeits are a common problem, making it difficult for buyers to verify if an item is genuinely branded. NFTs can solve this problem by providing an immutable proof of ownership and authenticity. Each item can be associated with a unique NFT that attests to its authenticity, history, and origin, thereby giving buyers increased confidence in their secondhand purchases. This traceability also allows brands to have more visibility into buying behavior on the secondary market.

NFTs IN FASHION: TELLING YOUR OWN STORY

The clothes and objects we wear are a form of communication. What we wear can be a symbol of wealth or belonging to a group. This is especially true in the luxury sector (such as luxury watches), where a new generation of buyers is more than ever interested in secondhand items with a "story." NFTs will enable the telling of the product's story: when was it created, by whom, where, has it been repaired, when, by whom, has it been resold, belonged to a celebrity? In this way, NFTs can digitally translate the evolving behaviors and expectations of consumers.

ROYALTIES FOR BUSINESSES (AND CREATORS): THE NIKE EXAMPLE

In the luxury sector, Nike surpassed all its competitors in 2022. According to Dyne Analytics, the company generated $186 million in revenue and $93 million in royalties through NFTs[186]. It's no wonder that Nike spent several hundred million dollars to acquire RTFKT (a company specialized in NFT creation) in December 2021[187]. This figure illustrates the importance of royalties for a brand, as they accounted for half of Nike's total revenue in 2022! With NFTs, it becomes possible to track transactions and automatically receive royalties each time a garment or

163

object associated with an NFT is resold. Whether for brands or artists, royalties will generate additional income and create new economic opportunities.

THE QUESTION OF CONNECTED WEARABLES

Connected devices are currently trending, and the fashion world is gradually joining in, particularly by leveraging blockchain technology. This was the case with Nike's CryptoKicks[188], where shoes were sold with integrated NFC chips, similar to those found in contactless payment cards. These NFC chips allow the physical shoe to be associated with the digital NFT of the collection. One can envision a system in which the possession of the NFT is conditioned upon actual ownership of the physical object, connected via the NFC chip.

RECOVERING LOST LUXURY ITEMS

Let's take the example of a luxury watch once again. Imagine you bought it at a high price because it belonged to a celebrity or your grandfather. In any case, you value it greatly. But one day, for some reason, you lose the watch. In today's world, there's very little chance of finding it again. However, in the future, these luxury items will have NFC chips integrated inside them that can be scanned to access the complete history: the current owner, previous owner(s), etc. The person who finds the watch can simply scan it to know who it belongs to and return it. They cannot claim ownership unless the previous owner validates the transaction. However, in the NFT's smart contract, there will be a function that allows the finder of the watch to send a message to the owner (anonymously) to agree on the terms of returning the watch.

IMPLEMENTING COMMUNITY CONTESTS

Fashion brands could organize community contests using NFTs to reward the community. Participants would be invited to create unique designs or illustrations inspired by the brand. The selected works could be transformed into NFTs, offering creators increased visibility and potentially monetization opportunities. Contest winners could receive special rewards, such as limited editions of clothing or accessories associated with the NFTs. Brands would find this an interesting lever to promote their image, encourage fan engagement, and stimulate creativity within their community.

NFT, FASHION, AND THE METAVERSE

AN INCREASINGLY BLURRED LINE BETWEEN DIGITAL AND REALITY

In an increasingly connected world, the boundary between digital and reality is becoming more and more blurred, creating new opportunities and challenges for the fashion industry. Technological advancements will soon lead to the emergence of the metaverse. This revolution will have a significant impact on the fashion industry by offering even more immersive and personalized shopping and self-expression experiences.

MAKING YOUR DIGITAL IDENTITY UNIQUE

In this context, clothing becomes an essential means for individuals to make their digital identity unique. The metaverse offers unparalleled creativity and the ability for users to push the boundaries of personal expression through clothing. Users can explore extravagant designs, experimental shapes, and vibrant colors, creating outfits that embody their unique vision of self and distinctive style. The absence of material limitations allows individuals to break free from the conventions of physical fashion and fully express their creativity.

CLOTHING STORES IN THE METAVERSE

The metaverse would offer the possibility for major brands to establish their clothing stores in the metaverse. Brands could faithfully recreate the ambiance and aesthetics of their physical stores while providing users with an immersive and authentic shopping experience. This presence in the metaverse would allow them to reach a global audience without the geographical limitations of physical stores. Users from around the world could visit virtual stores, discover collections, and purchase products. Additionally, clothing stores in the metaverse would offer remarkable flexibility and scalability. Brands could easily update their collections, offer metaverse-exclusive limited editions, and organize special events more easily.

REAL-TIME VIRTUAL TRY-ON

When purchasing clothing online, the current challenge lies in the uncertainty of fit. The return process can be tedious and time-consuming. However, the introduction of NFTs and augmented reality offers a solution to this problem. By using a personalized avatar that reflects the user's measurements, it becomes possible to virtually try on clothing in the metaverse or through augmented reality, ensuring a perfect fit. Features like zooming or 360-degree visualization would provide a smoother and more immersive shopping experience.

WATCHING FASHION SHOWS AS IF YOU WERE THERE

Imagine being able to participate in the Paris Fashion Week from the comfort of your own living room instead of taking a plane to attend. This possibility will become a reality thanks to the metaverse. Major brands have a vested interest in taking advantage of this opportunity. By using virtual reality and augmented reality, users can virtually immerse themselves in the heart of the event, admire the creations up close, observe fabric details, and even interact with virtual models. It would even be possible to acquire, for example, one of the dresses from the runway as an NFT and receive it custom-made at home two months later.

GAMERS: A NEW MARKET?

Gamers could open up a promising new market for the fashion industry in the metaverse. A concrete example of this trend is illustrated by the phenomenon of Fortnite, where the purchase of skins has gained considerable traction. These skins go beyond purely aesthetic aspects, as they allow players to stand out, express themselves, and create a unique identity within the gaming community. Players are willing to spend real money to acquire exclusive, rare skins or those associated with renowned brands like *Louis Vuitton* or *Balenciaga*[189]. NFTs could play a crucial role in this new trend. NFTs provide gamers with verifiable digital ownership and guaranteed rarity, adding additional value to the skins and other virtual items they acquire. The market is substantial, considering that gaming encompasses 3.2 billion people worldwide[190].

THE FOMO OF BIG BUSINESSES

Just like brands rushed into online sales about fifteen years ago, major luxury brands are afraid of missing out on the metaverse. This is the famous Fear of Missing Out (FOMO) effect. By the end of 2021, there was a frenzy surrounding the metaverse, and the topic was making headlines in the media. Not a week would go by without a brand entering the metaverse or launching an NFT airdrop. However, according to Gartner's "Hype Cycle," the metaverse is not expected to become mainstream for another decade[191].

EXAMPLES

 Aura is is a private blockchain created in 2021 by a consortium formed by LVMH, Prada Group, and Cartier. OTB Group and Mercedes-Benz joined the project shortly after.

Arianee is a French startup that has been using blockchain since 2017 to guarantee the authenticity of luxury products while enhancing their traceability. It also aims to improve customer engagement through NFTs.

28. LUXURY WATCHES

THE LUXURY WATCH MARKET

THE SECONDARY MARKET FOR LUXURY WATCHES

The secondary market for luxury watches is currently valued at $20 Billion and is expected to exceed $35 billion by 2030, accounting for over half of the primary market[192]. The market is dominated by the Swiss-French watch industry, which employs over 15,000 people. However, behind these numbers, there are significant disparities: 99% of watches sold are valued at less than $1,000, but the remaining 1% represents 42% of the market value. Rolex watches are widely in the lead and clearly dominate the market.

A MARKET VULNERABLE TO FRAUD

The luxury watch market is a substantial market, but it also attracts fraudulent activities. According to the Federation of the Swiss Watch Industry (FHS), over 40 million fake watches are distributed each year, while the annual production of genuine Swiss watches is only 30 million[193]. It is also estimated that one-third of Rolex watches worldwide are counterfeit. Asia, particularly China, is a hub for luxury watch counterfeiting, with 85% of counterfeit products originating from the region and being exported to Dubai, according to industry insiders.

LUXURY WATCHES AND NFTS: IT'S ABOUT TIME!

CERTIFICATES OF AUTHENTICITY

With approximately 40 million fake watches circulating worldwide each year[194], it is inconceivable to purchase a luxury watch without its associated certificate of authenticity. However, the process of authenticating a luxury watch remains archaic. For example, how can it be that many buyers still rely on a paper certificate to test the authenticity of a Rolex Daytona? Unless one is an expert or consults an expert, it is impossible to self-authenticate an official watch. So why not leverage blockchain technology? For luxury brands, incorporating the certificate of authenticity onto the blockchain and making it accessible only through an NFT embedded directly in the watch would provide buyers with a trust guarantee. Unlike paper certificates, blockchain certificates cannot be altered, duplicated, or modified. The watch can be traced back to its origin with complete transparency.

REDUCING THE CIRCULATION OF FAKE REPLICA WATCHES WITH THE SAME SERIAL NUMBER

By utilizing blockchain technology, it would also become more difficult for counterfeiters to produce large quantities of fake watches. Currently, it is possible to create multiple replicas of a watch produced by a watchmaker since the serial number can be replicated infinitely. For instance, a counterfeiter could create an unlimited number of replicas bearing the serial number 2R35F965 simply by engraving it on the watch. However, with blockchain technology, it would only be possible to manufacture a single replica watch at a time because the associated non-fungible token (NFT) is not replicable, unlike an engraving. Such innovation would significantly reduce the number of fake watches in circulation.

LIMITING SNATCH THEFTS AND FACILITATING RECOVERY

Implementing NFTs would not only limit the number of fake watches in circulation but also reduce the incidence of snatch thefts (which have increased by 31% in the Île-de-France region since 2022). Without access to the digital certificate recorded on the blockchain, attempting to steal and resell such a watch would be futile. Unlike paper certificates that can be forged, it is impossible to create a counterfeit authenticity NFT for a watch. Consequently, no one would want to buy a watch from a seller who cannot prove ownership of the associated NFT. Similarly, with NFTs, it would be much easier for a customer who has lost their watch to locate it and prove their rightful ownership with just a few clicks.

IDEAL FOR THE SECOND-HAND WATCH MARKET

Due to their prestige and longevity, it is rare for luxury watches to have only one owner throughout their lifespan. As exemplified by the brand embodied by the spirit of Gérald Genta, "You never actually own a Patek Philippe. You merely look after it for the next generation." Therefore, it is common for these watches to end up on the second-hand market. NFTs appear to be the ideal solution for luxury houses in this regard. They enable knowledge of the successive owners and provide much better traceability for the watch. For example, imagine owning THE watch that belonged to Leonardo DiCaprio (and having the NFT to prove it). The value of pre-owned luxury watches has also increased significantly in recent years.

BUYERS ENJOY KNOWING THE HISTORY OF A COLLECTIBLE WATCH

It is well known that all watch collectors enjoy knowing the history of their timepieces. A watch is not merely an item worn on the wrist; it is also an artwork imbued with emotions and memories. Having a watch that belonged to someone important to you (whether it's a family member or a celebrity) adds significant value to your watch. Using NFTs would be a way to preserve its history over time. Similarly, even without considering emotions, it is always useful for the customer to know all relevant information about the watch, such as the place of manufacture, manufacturer, date of production, any repairs, and maintenance history. With NFTs, the customer could securely verify all this information.

THE IMPORTANCE OF NFC CHIPS FOR THE BUSINESS MODEL

For practical reasons, it is highly likely that luxury watches utilizing NFT technology will incorporate NFC chips within them for security purposes. Solutions already exist, such as *Watch Certificate*, which uses a metal card affixed with a QR code linked to the certificate of authenticity recorded on the blockchain. However, this solution remains susceptible to duplication since it relies on a simple QR code. In contrast, an NFC chip cannot be copied or transferred to someone else through a simple photograph. This offers the advantage of enhanced security and an assurance of the watch's authenticity once the NFC chip has been scanned and verified to link to an official NFT issued by the brand. Of course, integrating a chip inside a mechanical watch may not be appealing to everyone.

ACCESSING EVENTS WITH YOUR NFT WATCH

The possibilities offered by luxury watches incorporating NFT and NFC technologies are immense. Let's consider an example to illustrate this. Imagine a major luxury watch brand decides to organize an event and restricts access to only watch owners of that brand. All one would need to do is scan their watch containing the NFC chip. It would directly link to the watch's NFT recorded on the blockchain, proving it is an authentic watch of which they are the legitimate owner. Consequently, they would gain access to the event. Thus, the watch would transcend being a mere collectible item and become a gateway to unique experiences.

LUXURY BRANDS AND NFTS: A RACE AGAINST TIME?

JANUARY 2021: MURAKAMI WATCHES WITH HUBLOT

Hublot was one of the first luxury watch brands to venture into NFTs in January 2021 by collaborating with Japanese artist Takashi Murakami[195] to create a limited edition watch called the "Classic Fusion Takashi Murakami All Black". This watch sold out in just a few days. Following its success, a second version was offered (the "Classic Fusion Takashi Murakami Sapphire Rainbow"), this time featuring colorful designs. This limited edition also sold out in a few days. Both collections incorporate the artist's iconic flower theme.

APRIL 2021: JACOB AND CO

On April 4, 2021, the renowned brand Jacob and Co auctioned an NFT watch called Jacob and Co. SF24 NFT[196]. The digital watch (listed for sale on the NFT platform ArtGrails) had a starting price of $1,000 and ended up selling for $100,000, with the anonymous buyer paying in cryptocurrency[197]. The watch was based on the Jacob & Co. Epic SF24 model but instead of displaying cities, it showcased cryptocurrencies like Bitcoin, Ethereum, and Fantom. The watch brand didn't stop there. In August 2022, they introduced a range of limited edition luxury watches with a Bitcoin theme[198], offering 25 black titanium models priced at over $350,000. More recently, they launched an NFT watch collection called "Astronomie Metaverso," with each watch representing a planet[199].

MAY 2022: TAG HEUER ENTERS THE GAME

In May 2022, Tag Heuer (part of the LVMH group) introduced cryptocurrency payments for its products through BitPay[200]. This was a strategic move by the luxury brand, allowing its customers in the United States to purchase watches with cryptocurrencies, setting them apart from their competitors. They accepted over a dozen cryptocurrencies. A month later, in June 2022, during the Vivatech trade show, they unveiled a new feature for their Connected Calibre E4 smartwatch, allowing users to display their NFTs on the watch[201]. By connecting their wallet via a smartphone, users could showcase their NFTs on the watch's dial. Of course, the watch also tells the time… !

JESUS CALDERON AND HIS GENERATIVE WATCHES

Luxury watch brands are not the only ones selling watches in the form of NFTs. Jesus Calderon, a 3D designer and watch enthusiast, decided to do the same with his Generative Watches collection, available on Opensea[202]. He creatively parodied the famous Rolex brand with several variations, such as *Rødex Daitona*[203] or *Rødex Bitmariner*[204]. The prices reached up to $17,000, more expensive than an actual Rolex watch!

2022: BULGARI, THE WORLD'S THINNEST MECHANICAL WATCH... WITH AN NFT QR CODE AS A BONUS

Bulgari, known for its ultra-thin watches, unveiled a new version of its flagship model, the Octo, which was celebrating its 10th anniversary[205]. The watch, called the Octo Finissimo Ultra, measures only 1.8 mm thick, thinner than a 10-cent coin! As a bonus, it comes with an NFT in the form of a QR code displayed on the front of the watch. By scanning the QR code, the lucky owner of the watch gains access to a unique and exclusive digital artwork in the form of an NFT. This model is offered in a very limited edition of only 10 pieces worldwide, priced at $400,000. Many of us may have to wait a long time before being able to afford it.

OCTOBER 2022: ROLEX AND ITS PATENT APPLICATIONS

Rolex has also joined the race by filing a trademark application with serial number 97 655 284 on October 31, 2022[206]. Attorney Michael Kondoudis, specializing in trademarks, made a Twitter post about it a few days later[207]. Classes 9, 35, and 36 are included, specifically mentioning NFT marketplaces, virtual goods auctions, and more. The term NFT appears multiple times in the document, indicating that Rolex has a definite interest in this field.

29. DECENTRALIZED IDENTITY

OUR IDENTITY IS INCREASINGLY DIGITIZED

THE ARRIVAL OF THE INTERNET AND THE BIRTH OF DIGITAL IDENTITY

Since the advent of the Internet in households about twenty years ago, our identity has become heavily digitized. Using the Internet often requires authentication to access services. On every website where there is a user account, you need to authenticate yourself with an email address and password to prove that you have access. Try to think about how many times a day you need to identify yourself. Whether it's accessing your online banking, insurance, social media, emails, or even public services like healthcare or taxes, as long as there is an account, you need to authenticate yourself and use a digital identity. Identification shapes our daily lives, even without us realizing it.

TWO TYPES OF DIGITAL IDENTITIES

We distinguish two distinct types of digital identities:
- A **social identity**, created by ourselves, especially on social networks. It consists of the information we choose to share on our profiles, such as our name, profile picture, professional background, interests, opinions, and relationships with other users.
- A **product identity**, also created by us, but without our knowledge. This identity encompasses our consumption habits, purchases of goods and services, etc. In short, all the data we disseminate in our online behavior. **Companies love this identity!** They analyze it to offer targeted offers or sell the data to advertisers. It is the basis of e-marketing targeting, retargeting, and all the marketing techniques of the past 20 years.

THE MONOPOLY OF BIG TECH ON OUR DIGITAL IDENTITIES

The problem is that it is the big tech companies (GAFAM) that control this identification and thus our digital identities. Today, everyone has already logged into a website using their Facebook or Google account. It's the famous "Sign in with Google" button. It is true that for practical reasons, it is much easier to authenticate with your Google account than to remember dozens of different passwords with different email addresses. Revolutionary for the user experience, but also for the retrieval of our personal data... Collecting this data allows advertisers to offer an increasingly precise catalog to their prospects. A market that weighs several hundred billion per year! Sacrificing privacy for the ergonomics of a supposedly free service may seem tempting... Even though everyone knows that this "free" comes with a hidden cost: the cost of our freedom.

THE RELEVANCE OF NFTS FOR DIGITAL IDENTITY

ENSURING A DIGITAL IDENTITY FOR EVERYONE

According to a World Bank study[208], around 1.1 billion people worldwide cannot officially prove their identity. This worrying situation highlights the fact that many people do not have access to the identification documents necessary to enjoy their fundamental rights, such as access to healthcare, education, and employment. But the arrival of Web 3 could enable these individuals to obtain a digital identity in a decentralized manner.

NO NEED TO REMEMBER 30,000 PASSWORDS

A problem we all face is having to find a password for each site that requires a login with an identifier. In fact, one of the basic security measures on the Internet is to use a different password for each website we use (and preferably a complex password!). This requires remembering a lot of passwords or letting Google remember them for us. With NFTs, you will only need access to your wallet to then access all the sites that require identification. Identification via your wallet will be sufficient to prove your identity.

THE FAMOUS 18+ BUTTON (FOR ONLINE GAMBLING)

Let's discuss another example: online gambling. It is effortless nowadays for someone underage to pretend to be of legal age to participate in online gambling. In theory, online gambling platforms should verify that all their users are at least 18 years old. In practice, all it takes is clicking "OK" to affirm that you are of legal age to play. This poses a significant problem, especially for parents. This is where decentralized identity comes into play. Decentralized identity allows you to prove easily that you are of legal age without revealing your age or name. This is the magic of Zero Knowledge Proofs (ZKPs).

DATA CONFIDENTIALITY WITH ZERO KNOWLEDGE PROOFS

ZKP technology is a true revolution as it ensures privacy for decentralized digital identity. To understand this better, let's consider a concrete example:

The Cave of Ali Baba[209]

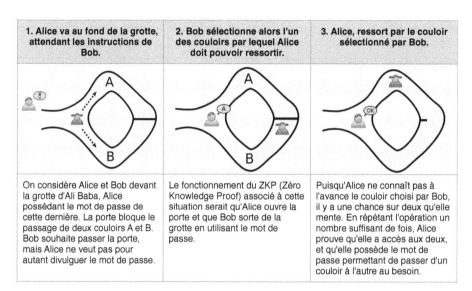

1. Alice va au fond de la grotte, attendant les instructions de Bob.	2. Bob sélectionne alors l'un des couloirs par lequel Alice doit pouvoir ressortir.	3. Alice, ressort par le couloir sélectionné par Bob.
On considère Alice et Bob devant la grotte d'Ali Baba, Alice possédant le mot de passe de cette dernière. La porte bloque le passage de deux couloirs A et B. Bob souhaite passer la porte, mais Alice ne veut pas pour autant divulguer le mot de passe.	Le fonctionnement du ZKP (Zéro Knowledge Proof) associé à cette situation serait qu'Alice ouvre la porte et que Bob sorte de la grotte en utilisant le mot de passe.	Puisqu'Alice ne connaît pas à l'avance le couloir choisi par Bob, il y a une chance sur deux qu'elle mente. En répétant l'opération un nombre suffisant de fois, Alice prouve qu'elle a accès aux deux, et qu'elle possède le mot de passe permettant de passer d'un couloir à l'autre au besoin.

Alice was able to prove that she possesses
the password without revealing it.

THE CASE OF ESTONIA: A HIGHLY ADVANCED DIGITAL IDENTITY...

Ranked as the most advanced digital society in the world by *Wired* magazine[210], Estonia has made considerable progress in digital identity since the 1990s. In this small republic of 1.3 million inhabitants, which was part of the Soviet bloc 30 years ago, all doctors use e-prescriptions. 95% of citizens pay their taxes online, and 30% of voters cast their votes online. Today, every Estonian is assigned an online national identity from birth, which allows them to obtain a digital identity card. In this context, the creation of the State Platform (X-Road) began in 2000 with the digital identity card and online tax declaration, followed by the implementation of electronic signatures in 2002. In 2015[211], Estonia partnered with a blockchain startup, Bitnation, to securely sign documents such as notarial acts, marriage contracts, birth certificates, and commercial contracts.

...BUT SOME TECHNICAL CHALLENGES REMAIN

Despite Estonia's technological advancement in digital identity, it has faced some technical vulnerabilities. In November 2017, 760,000 Estonian citizens (out of a total population of 1.3 million) were deprived of digital services for several days[212]. The vulnerability was related to the Infineon chips integrated into national identity cards, which contained citizens' personal data and helped secure identifiers and transactions. However, the vulnerability allowed the inexpensive retrieval of the private key from the public key. In response, the Estonian government decided to temporarily close access to digital services until the issue was resolved.

MONETIZING YOUR DATA

Data confidentiality will enable you to monetize your data. If someone wants to access your Decentralized Identity (DID) data, they will have to request your permission, and you will have the choice to say yes or no. If you agree, there will be a price for those who want to access your data. This will also apply to companies like Google or Apple. When they want to access your data, they will have to pay for it.

HAVING MORE CONTROL OVER OUR DATA

Becoming a full-fledged digital adult, taking full responsibility for our personal data, is not necessarily straightforward. We already see the challenges in achieving this with cryptocurrencies like Bitcoin. Not everyone will want to take full responsibility for their personal data, but blockchain will provide us with a choice. We will have the choice to leave our data with the big tech companies (GAFAM) for practical reasons or to take control by using the blockchain. Of course, decentralization (if it truly exists) will not solve all the problems related to managing personal data, but it will give users the freedom to choose, which is already a significant step forward.

1984... BUT IN 2023? THE CHALLENGES OF IDENTITY ON THE BLOCKCHAIN

WILL DECENTRALIZED IDENTITY TRULY BE DECENTRALIZED?

For decentralized identity to be genuinely decentralized, the underlying technology must be genuinely decentralized. However, this is not necessarily the case yet. For example, Ethereum, often regarded as the epitome of decentralization, is only decentralized to a certain extent. Since its transition to Proof of Stake (PoS), it is now necessary to lock up 32 ETH to participate in block validation. This has resulted in a greater centralization of the blockchain. Currently, block validation is predominantly controlled by a few actors, including Lido and Coinbase[213].

IN THE BEST OF WORLDS, A 100% BLOCKCHAIN IDENTITY?

At first glance, one might rejoice at a 100% blockchain identity due to decentralization and the protection of personal data. However, as we have just seen, it is unlikely (at least in the medium term) that our blockchain identity will be genuinely decentralized. A centrally controlled identity via blockchain would be the worst scenario, as it would grant significant power to the entity controlling identity management. For example, consider the current situation in China with social credit and their progress in CBDC*. Privacy is also a crucial issue.

EXAMPLES

 Sismo aims to restore individuals' sovereignty over their digital identity. The company utilizes Zero Knowledge Proofs to create badges anonymously.

Aztec, unlike most other zkRollups, focuses not on improving Ethereum's scalability but on the privacy of its users.

30. WINE

WINE ANS NFTS: A WINE-WINE SITUATION

COMBATING COUNTERFEITING

Counterfeiting is a significant problem affecting tens of thousands of wine bottles worldwide each year. According to the most pessimistic experts, around 20% of international wine trade is impacted, with that number rising to 50% in China[214], where valuable fine wines are particularly targeted. Deceptive blends, appellation falsifications, and fake labels are common occurrences in this industry. With increased global trade, detecting these frauds has become increasingly challenging.

Rudy Kurniawan is one of the most famous wine counterfeiters in history. Little is known about Rudy except that he possesses one of the finest palates in the world and an above-average memory. He can recognize any wine and decided to use his talent to mimic high-end wines by blending inexpensive ones.

He started participating in auctions, and his encounter with John Kapon (Owner of the auction house Acker Merrall & Condit) sealed his fate. The two partners decided to orchestrate the most illustrious wine auction in the world. Their October 2006 sale in New York was a triumph, with bids reaching a record-breaking $24.7 million.

However, one of his bottles, dated 1945, was auctioned despite the appellation only being established in 1982. Rudy's reputation was tarnished. Suspicions grew, and in September 2009, American billionaire Bill Koch filed a lawsuit against Rudy Kurniawan, alleging that he had sold him counterfeit wines.

In 2013, Rudy's house was raided, and what the FBI discovered was astonishing. The floor was littered with empty bottles, handwritten recipe books worthy of a three-star chef, complex rating systems, and tens of thousands of fake labels.

BOTTLE LABELING: A REAL CHALLENGE

One common method of wine counterfeiting involves intentionally labeling a cheap wine with a more expensive vintage to sell it as a high-end product. Wine counterfeiters use cheaper and lower-quality substances, passing them off as wine. These substances sometimes contain toxins and harmful chemicals like methanol. Blockchain can provide a solution to this labeling problem. With NFTs, once a bottle is certified, customers can scan the digital fingerprint with their phones. They will immediately receive proof of authentication and can verify on the blockchain that the certificate itself is authentic.

INVESTING IN WINE WITHOUT POLLUTION: REDUCING UNNECESSARY TRANSPORTATION

Some fine wines travel thousands of kilometers to reach investors' cellars, even if they have no intention of drinking them as they are solely investments. However, it is not necessary to physically store a fine wine to invest in it securely. Blockchain technology and NFTs offer an interesting alternative by enabling the transfer of ownership of the fine wine through a simple transfer of the associated NFT. This would also avoid temperature variations and bottle disturbances during transportation.

ACCESS TO A COMMUNITY OF ENTHUSIASTS

Companies selling NFT collections often offer NFT holders the opportunity to join a Discord server. In the case of wine-related NFTs, owning an NFT related to wine can grant you access to a community of wine enthusiasts. Being part of this community means more than just owning a unique digital artwork—it's about joining a community of like-minded individuals who share the same interests and are eager to discover and support talented winemakers. As a member of the community, you can engage in discussions with fellow enthusiasts, participate in events, and meet other members. You may even find potential business partners in the wine industry within this community!

WINE AND NFTS: CHEERS!

STRENGTHENING THE BRAND IMAGE THROUGH STORYTELLING

The reputation and quality of each wine bottle are guaranteed by the brand, and NFTs provide major wineries with an opportunity to showcase their emblems, stories, and create a connection with their customers by immersing them in their unique world. Every vineyard strives to cultivate its image, notoriety, and positioning to ensure the success of its brand. NFTs serve as a means to reinforce this marketing strategy. As a recent innovation that is still relatively uncommon in the industry, NFTs allow wineries to stand out from the competition. They can also enhance the brand image by utilizing storytelling. For example, a winery can offer an NFT collection that showcases their bottles as digital artworks, providing consumers with the opportunity to delve into the brand's universe and create a strong emotional bond.

INVESTING BEFORE BOTTLE COMMERCIALIZATION

NFTs offer a unique possibility of direct financing without intermediaries, which may not be immediately intuitive but can be highly interesting. By providing ownership titles, NFTs enable bidding before the commercialization of the bottles, in exchange for a share of potential profits. Once the harvest is complete, wines require a certain amount of time to mature before they can be commercialized. For instance, vintage Champagne wines often mature for 8 to 10 years in the cellar before hitting the market. In an industry where income can be unpredictable, this method can help producers secure funds to finance their future harvests and partially protect against weather-related risks.

THE BENEFITS OF NFC CHIP TECHNOLOGY

Near Field Communication (NFC) chips can be coupled with NFT technology to facilitate the traceability of physical products. By adding an NFC chip to each wine bottle, detailed information about the wine, such as its origin, grape varieties used, and year of harvest, can be easily accessed by consumers through their smartphones. These details are guaranteed by the blockchain, ensuring transparency and authenticity.

UNIQUE EXPERIENCES

While you can currently buy wine bottles online, the experience typically ends there. Through Web3 technology, this experience can be enhanced by offering customers unique experiences. For example, a winery may choose to offer those who have held their wine NFT for 10 years (without trading it and with the bottle still stored at the winery) access to an unprecedented experience, such as a vineyard tour or an hour-long conversation with a renowned winemaker from the estate. In this way, the NFT provides a far richer experience than simply acquiring a fine wine.

RESTORING AN ARTISTIC ASPECT TO WINE BOTTLES

The visual and artistic aspect of NFTs also extends the wine experience. Instead of purchasing a fine wine and leaving an empty bottle lying around or throwing it away, you can have a digital and stylized version of the bottle. Artists have already created unique designs for bottles that have never been seen before[215]. For example, before the harvest, the NFT could be represented by a wooden case, and once the harvest is complete, on a specific date, all the NFTs of the wine batch could be revealed simultaneously. The rarest NFTs (which provide access to rarer experiences) would have more elaborate designs.

EXAMPLES

 **Wine Bottle Club** is a French startup founded in 2022 by Florent Coulon, Maxime Garraud, and two Bordeaux wine merchants, Louis de Bonnecaze and Philippe Papillon. WBC allows you to join a community of wine enthusiasts.

Winechain was co-founded in Miami by four French entrepreneurs—Guillaume Jourdan, Marc Perrin, Xavier Garambois, and Nicolas Mendiharat—develops an NFT marketplace for fine wine enthusiasts.

31. DAOS

WHAT IS A DAO AND HOW DOES IT WORK?

THE CONCEPT OF DAO: WHAT IS IT?

A DAO, or Decentralized Autonomous Organization, is a term used to describe an autonomous and decentralized organization. The concept emerged with the idea of a "Decentralized Autonomous Corporation" introduced by Daniel Larimer in an article published by Vitalik Buterin in 2013[216]. They have different visions of what blockchain governance should look like[217]. Vitalik provides the following definition of a DAO: "*It is an entity that exists on the internet and operates autonomously, but also relies heavily on the collaboration of individuals to perform certain tasks that the automation itself cannot do*".

HOW DOES A DAO WORK?

A DAO operates using governance tokens. The rules, written on the blockchain through a smart contract, are visible to everyone. Unlike traditional organizations, DAO members are not bound by formal contracts. Instead, they are united by a common objective and network incentives defined by the consensus rules. DAOs use smart contracts to automatically execute actions when certain conditions are met. This mode of operation is particularly useful for organizations that aim to make decisions in a democratic manner. To have voting rights, one needs to possess a sufficient amount of governance tokens, which can be purchased or obtained through specific actions.

THE SMART CONTRACT, BACKBONE OF A DAO

The key component of a DAO's operation is its smart contract. It defines the organization's rules. Once the smart contract is deployed on a blockchain (such as Ethereum or others), it cannot be modified. It is also visible to everyone, ensuring that all participants agree on the same rules. DAOs are autonomous, meaning they do not require a central authority to function and do not have a vertical hierarchical structure. Only the rules specified in the smart contract allow a DAO to operate. Smart contracts are automatically executed when all the conditions within them are fulfilled. Each member of the organization can propose things that the organization decides to implement or not (typically requiring a 66% majority vote).

THE 5 PILLARS OF A DAO

1. A purpose	2. A voting system	3. A governance token
The purpose can be economic, social, or even artistic in nature. It is important for all DAO members to align with this common goal.	Decisions within a DAO are made collectively and in a decentralized manner. This voting system allows all members to participate in decision-making.	This token represents voting rights and can also be used to reward member participation and engagement.

4. A community	5. Fund Management
A community that shares common interests and values is essential for ensuring the smooth functioning of a DAO.	A transparent and decentralized fund management system is established to ensure proper utilization of resources.

A DISASTROUS BEGINNING (THE DAO, 2016)

The history of DAOs actually began in the worst possible way. It all started in 2016 with the birth of a project called TheDAO. The idea was simple: to raise enough funds to create a venture capital fund with the ETH cryptocurrency. The project was an immediate success, raising 12.7 million ETH, equivalent to around $150 million at that time. Each participant had a voting right to fund projects, and profits were distributed fairly. Everything was going well until a vulnerability in the smart contract was exploited in June 2016. The attacker was able to withdraw 3.6 million ETH, approximately $70 million at that time. It's important to note that the vulnerability was in the smart contract, not the blockchain itself. Unfortunately, TheDAO never fully recovered despite various attempts to find solutions. The event even led to a hard fork of Ethereum and the emergence of Ethereum Classic. The hacker was eventually identified by Chainalysis after several years of investigation[218].

A NEW MODE OF GOVERNANCE

COMMUNITY FIRST

DAOs are created by communities, for communities. This is an essential aspect to understand the value of DAOs. The community is the crucial pillar of DAOs as it drives decision-making and organization governance. In a DAO, the community is responsible for decision-making, validating proposals, and overseeing task execution. Community members also monitor the DAO's activities, ensuring transparency and integrity.

TRANSPARENT RULES, AUTOMATED TRUST

For the first time in human history, we have the ability to trust a group of people we don't know, on the other side of the planet, without any issues. Imagine that! Regardless of nationality, religion, or skin color, technology doesn't care. Only how DAO members want to organize and move forward together matters. And this happens automatically with minimal friction because the rules of the game have been predefined and cannot be changed unless the community decides to do so.

A HORIZONTAL ORGANIZATION (IN THEORY)

You might think, "DAOs are like companies with shares, where an NFT represents a share." Well, think again! Unlike traditional shareholder companies, DAOs operate in a horizontal manner. There are no general assemblies, and anyone is free to submit a proposal. Well, that's in theory. In practice, the more tokens you have, the more decision-making power you possess. However, some DAOs have implemented systems to obtain governance tokens through means other than purchasing. This philosophy represents a true paradigm shift and an evolution from the traditional model of "shareholders, company, and customers."

FOCUS ON AAVE PROTOCOL

Aave (pronounced "aah-vey," meaning "ghost" in Finnish) is a decentralized lending and borrowing protocol built as a DAO. Every holder of the Aave token can participate in the platform's governance by voting on proposals brought forward by other users. By visiting the governance forum, connecting their token-holding wallet, and selecting proposals to vote on, participants can engage in the governance process. These proposals can be made by any user and go through different phases before official voting. Once a proposal is verified and accepted by the community, the on-chain voting phase begins. Proposals can cover various aspects, such as adding new cryptocurrencies to the platform, adjusting revenue distribution, modifying stacking rewards, or even overhauling parts of the governance.

FROM NATION-STATE TO NETWORK-STATE?

THE CONCEPT OF NETWORK-STATE

In his book _The Network State_[219], Balaji Srinivasan explains how the current nation-state could eventually be replaced by the network-state. The author defines the network-state as "_an online community with shared values that acts together, crowdfunds territories worldwide, and eventually attains diplomatic recognition from pre-existing states._" An example of this is seen in El Salvador, which adopted Bitcoin as legal tender in September 2021[220].

POTENTIAL GEOPOLITICAL CONSEQUENCES?

With the rise of the internet, online communities have emerged and demonstrated a significant impact on the world, even leading to the overthrow of governments (e.g., the _Arab Spring_). The emergence of DAOs as a new governance model is a product of our society. The state has failed in its social contract mission. In a future, more or less distant, networks might replace states, and communities might supplant nations.

EXAMPLE

Cosmos ("The Internet of Blockchains") is one of the most advanced examples of on-chain governance. Decisions regarding the development of Cosmos are indeed subject to on-chain governance votes directly on the Blockchain using the ATOM token.

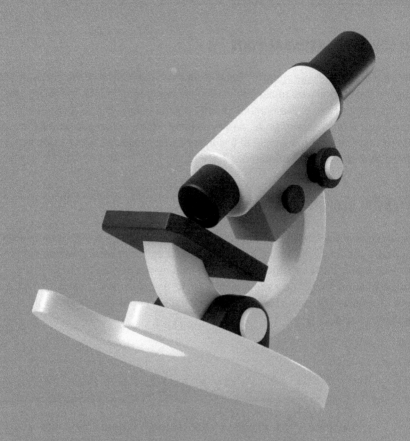

32. SCIENCE

NFTS IN SCIENCE: A PARADIGM SHIFT

DECENTRALIZED SCIENCE (DESCI): WHAT IS IT?

In December 2021, Sarah Hamburg, a neuroscientist and founder of a Web3 innovation consulting firm, made a call to join decentralized science in an article published in the renowned scientific journal *Nature*[221]. In this article, she briefly explains what decentralized science, or DeSci, entails. According to Hamburg, DeSci refers to the approach of conducting scientific research that relies on decentralized networks rather than traditional hierarchical structures. It is a radically different approach from traditional science, enabling new use cases.

A COMMUNITY THAT ORGANIZES ITSELF

DeSci forms a thriving ecosystem with a growing community since 2020. This flourishing ecosystem has given rise to the website DeSciWorld[222], created with the aim of "promoting and expanding the culture of decentralized science." In addition to online initiatives, the community also gathers at physical events like DeSci Berlin[223], which brings the community together for two days of around twenty conferences[224]. These physical events allow community members to meet in person, exchange ideas, and strengthen their commitment to DeSci.

THE CHALLENGE OF OBTAINING FUNDING IN THE TRADITIONAL MODEL...

In the traditional scientific model, funding is lengthy and difficult to acquire. For instance, in the United States, researchers spend more than four hours per week on administrative tasks to secure funding instead of utilizing that time for new discoveries[225]. Scientists must prepare and submit proposals to review committees that may have diverging personal interests to defend. Some may wait for years, often in vain, to secure funding as most applications are unsuccessful.

...AND THE EMERGENCE OF DAOs TO ADDRESS THIS PROBLEM

Conversely, in the decentralized model, funding is obtained directly from DAOs*, and the funds are entirely traceable through the blockchain. This enables the tracking of contributors, invested amounts, and transaction dates while preserving the anonymity of those involved. In this regard, the Sciencefund platform has developed blockchain protocols to pool scientific donations within DAOs. This platform has helped numerous DAOs gain visibility and funding, such as VitaDAO,

Ants-Review, and Blockchain for Science. Investors bet on early-stage research, and scientists can receive support for work that is not yet a product or patent. For example, the project Molecule successfully raised $12.7 million in funding in July 2022[226] using this financing method.

INTELLECTUAL PROPERTY (IP NFT)

In traditional science, researchers' intellectual property rights are not always recognized, particularly concerning the articles they publish. Through the decentralized model, intellectual property can be transformed into a digital asset using NFTs, also known as "IP-NFTs" in the English-speaking world. Scientists could publish their articles as NFTs on the blockchain, signing them with their names to prevent others from claiming their discoveries. The blockchain's timestamping would ensure the rightful ownership of the article or discovery. Experimentation has already taken place, such as in *The Longevity Molecule* research project[227].

CENSORSHIP-RESISTANT SCIENTIFIC ARTICLES

Scientific research is central to knowledge development and innovation, but it is often subjected to financial and political pressures. Currently, most scientific articles are hosted on centralized servers, making them susceptible to censorship by governments uncomfortable with particular articles. However, the blockchain offers a decentralized solution that makes censorship impossible. Similar to how no government can stop Bitcoin, no entity can censor articles registered directly on the blockchain.

REWARD SYSTEMS THROUGH TOKENS

DeSci aims to be the successor of "Open Science." Both approaches share the idea of making knowledge accessible to all. However, unlike "open science," DeSci provides economic incentives to encourage knowledge sharing. For example, scientists could receive rewards in the form of tokens for their contributions to scientific research, whether it be publishing articles or correcting existing ones. By offering such incentives, DeSci seeks to encourage scientists to share their knowledge and participate in building a more open, transparent, and collaborative scientific community.

SCIENCE AND NFTS: NOT NECESSARILY WHAT YOU THINK

EXAMPLE 1: THE BIRTH OF THE WORLD WIDE WEB FOR $5. 4 MILLION

From June 23 to 30, 2021, computer scientist Tim Berners-Lee, the founder of the World Wide Web, auctioned an NFT containing the source code of the first web browser, along with a silent video of the code being typed[228]. This NFT, which featured a video of the typed code and an animated signature by Berners-Lee himself, fetched $5,434,500. The source code of the first web browser is a historic object that played a crucial role in the history of the internet, which partly explains its exorbitant price.

EXAMPLE 2: SELLING GEORGE CHURCH'S GENOME

George Church, co-founder of Nebula Genomics and a genetics professor at Harvard Medical School, embarked on a one-year mission to turn his complete genome into an NFT. Although the NFT is not yet ready for auction, and no specific date has been set, once completed, Church's experiment will demonstrate the storage of complex scientific data on a decentralized server. The idea of selling George Church's genome as an NFT has generated divided opinions. However, for Nebula Genomics, this NFT serves a more serious purpose: a test run. The company already utilizes the blockchain to allow 15,000 individuals whose genomes have been sequenced to grant temporary access to their data to specific users, such as pharmaceutical laboratories.

EXAMPLE 3: GENERATIVE ART, A WAY TO REGENERATE SCIENCE

Generative art is an art form that uses computer algorithms and automated processes to create artworks. Generative artists establish rules and systems that dictate how the elements of the artwork are created, often leaving room for chance and unpredictability in the process. Generative art can be seen as a way to "regenerate" art through NFTs, as it enables artists to explore new creative territories through science. Conversely, scientists can engage artists to create generative art NFTs to fund their research. Scientists can provide scientific data or mathematical models to the artist, who can then use those elements to create unique generative artworks.

"SCIENCE WITHOUT CONSCIENCE IS BUT RUINATION OF THE SOUL"

SCIENCE, NFTS, AND SPECULATION

How can one promote the idea that the blockchain enables a more decentralized and democratic science when some NFTs are sold for hundreds of thousands of dollars? While it may offer short-term benefits for research funding, it can also raise concerns about ethics and transparency in decentralized science. Some NFT collections may be launched solely to generate money without a significant impact on scientific research, other than generating hype around the project.

ETHICAL QUESTIONS

This increased financialization of scientific research raises ethical issues. Firstly, it may foster a competitive approach rather than a collaborative one in scientific research, where the goal is to advance knowledge rather than maximize profits. Additionally, it may lead to inequalities in access to scientific research, where only the wealthy can afford to invest in NFTs to fund research projects. This could also result in a concentration of scientific research in specific areas that attract investors, rather than focusing on areas that may be more important for society as a whole.

EXAMPLE

Blockchain for Science was created in 2021 with the aim of promoting the development of DeSci worldwide. They organize events every year to bring the movement together and facilitate the exchange of ideas.

33. E-COMMERCE

E-COMMERCE HAS BECOME A GIVEN FOR US...

A BRIEF HISTORY OF E-COMMERCE

- **1979: Michael Aldrich invents electronic commerce**. His remote selling system uses a modified television connected to a computer via a telephone line. This setup allowed buyers and sellers to conduct transactions with secure data transmission.
- **1982: Launch of Minitel by French developers**. Minitel, a precursor to the Internet, used a Videotex terminal that users could access through their telephone lines. By the late 1990s, the service had around 25 million users. However, the service slowly declined as it couldn't compete with the introduction of the Internet in 1994.
- **1995: Launch of Amazon and eBay**. Although Amazon was initially designed as an online bookstore, it has become the largest online retail store for a wide range of products. eBay was created as an online auction site and remains one of the largest e-commerce platforms to this day.
- **1998: Creation of Confinity, renamed as PayPal in 2001**. The company was rebranded as PayPal in 2001 after merging with Elon Musk's online banking company, X.com. Today, there are over 100 million active PayPal accounts, and the platform handles 24 different currencies.
- **1999: Launch of Alibaba**. Jack Ma, a former English teacher, created Alibaba in 1999 with a $60,000 funding. Alibaba experienced rapid growth, even forcing eBay to withdraw from China a decade ago. "eBay may be a shark in the ocean, but we are a crocodile in the Yangtze River. If we fight in the ocean, we will lose. If it's in the river, we will win," Ma declared.
- **2006: Creation of Leboncoin**. The famous French website was launched by Spir Communication, a specialist in classified ads, and the Norwegian publisher Schibsted. The site disrupted the sector and facilitated peer-to-peer exchanges.
- **2011 : Facebook introduces sponsored content, Ads**. The giant used it as one of its earliest advertising channels.
- **2011 : Creation of Stripe (Apple Pay in 2014)**. It was truly from this moment that e-commerce really took off as these solutions greatly facilitated online payments.
- **2017: Instagram Shopping**. Instagram Shopping was introduced as a way for users to display product information directly on social media posts. Users can add product tags to their photos that include links to the website where subscribers can purchase the featured product.

E-COMMERCE TODAY

The global e-commerce market is estimated to be worth $5.7 trillion[229] and continues to grow exponentially. This expansion is driven by the high demand for fast delivery and competitive prices. Millions of online sellers offer their products, and commercial advertisements are ubiquitous on social media platforms. The e-commerce market continues to thrive as our society becomes increasingly reliant on the Internet. This market has experienced significant growth because it addresses a fundamental need: the desire for faster and more affordable products.

Furthermore, NFTs present a new opportunity to further optimize e-commerce by speeding up purchasing processes and offering innovative features.

...JUST LIKE THE USE OF NFTS IN A FEW YEARS

CERTIFYING AN ONLINE PURCHASE

A decade ago, buying a product online was not a given. Today, it is, thanks in part to confirmation emails. When you make an online purchase, receiving a confirmation email is expected to ensure that your order has been successfully processed. Nowadays, no one would consider making an online purchase without a confirmation email. In a few years, it will be inconceivable to make an online purchase without an NFT proving that transaction. The proof of purchase provided by an NFT will be more reliable than a simple email confirmation since it will be directly recorded on the blockchain.

AUTHENTICATING PRODUCTS AND PREVENTING FRAUD

Fraud has always been a significant challenge for e-commerce. For example, in the shoe industry, counterfeits represent hundreds of millions of dollars, accounting for 22% of the total value of seized counterfeits worldwide in 2016[230]. This is why Nike decided to stop selling its shoes on Amazon in 2019[231]. With the rapid advancement of technology, particularly AI, which can create incredibly realistic counterfeits, distinguishing genuine items from fakes can become challenging, even for experts. This is where NFTs come into play. They can provide certain authentication for products, ensuring they are not counterfeit. Some companies, like Nike with RTFKT and SUKU with INFINITE, have already begun experimenting with this technology by integrating NFC chips into shoes and linking them to specific NFTs through an application.

SECURE AND VERIFIED REVIEWS

Similarly to verifying the authenticity of a product, determining whether a review is genuinely from someone who purchased the product can be difficult. How can we be sure that a review is not from a competitor aiming to harm the product's reputation? This can pose a problem for buyers who seek to make informed purchasing decisions and gain an accurate understanding of a product's quality. E-commerce platforms have implemented strategies to minimize this risk, such as verifying purchases through confirmation codes sent via email or implementing a rating system based on the authenticity of the purchase. However, these measures are not always foolproof. Blockchain could provide an alternative model to guarantee the authenticity of reviews.

LOYALTY PROGRAMS

E-commerce websites now offer loyalty programs to reward their regular customers and encourage their continued purchases. However, according to RetailWire, nearly 40% of customers choose not to join loyalty programs because they perceive them as offering little value. Loyalty programs often only prove effective for a short period as customers are easily tempted by more enticing offers. To maintain long-term loyalty, it is crucial to provide unique and authentic value. NFTs are perfect for this purpose as they allow for the addition of emotional value. These NFTs can hold great sentimental value for customers, signifying their loyalty to the brand and creating a stronger sense of connection. Some customers may become brand ambassadors, and each action they perform could be certified on the blockchain with NFTs. These NFTs could appreciate in value, further engaging customers in the brand's success.

SHOPPING IN THE METAVERSE

E-commerce platforms will soon extend their presence into the metaverse to offer unprecedented experiences to their customers. In the metaverse, it will be possible to view products in 3D and interact with them before making a purchase. This will enhance interactivity and customer engagement. Additionally, certain NFT products will be entirely virtual, catering to customers interested in products solely for their virtual avatars. Although this may seem like a concept that is currently far from realization, the idea of offering products without shipping or storage costs is highly advantageous for e-commerce sites, as their business becomes even more scalable.

INVENTORY MANAGEMENT: REDUCING SHRINKAGE

Shrinkage refers to the difference between the theoretical accounting stock and the actual inventory. Its rate varies between 1% and 10% for sensitive items such as cosmetics, alcohol, and textiles. The higher the percentage, the more stock is missing. Several factors contribute to shrinkage, including fraudulent customer returns, cashier errors, inventory discrepancies, administrative losses, and internal employee theft. In France, theft accounts for over two-thirds of shrinkage and represents $3.5 billion in losses for businesses[232]. Blockchain could help reduce these losses. For example, if a customer attempts to defraud an online store by claiming they did not receive their package, the blockchain could associate the package with an NFT that can be automatically traced by all actors in the supply chain. This would make it easy to prove that the package was delivered and not lost.

A NEW MARKET EMERGES FOR EARLY ADOPTERS

Today, products within the same industry tend to be similar, making competition fierce. Having an associated NFT will provide a much easier way to stand out, especially if the platform highlights this with a distinctive mark (similar to verified accounts on Twitter). The use of NFTs will be a means for e-commerce brands to capture a new market by offering something truly unique and exclusive. Customers will feel like members of an exclusive club, having access to products and experiences not available to the general public. This differentiated approach can help brands distinguish themselves from their competitors and attract a wider customer base.

SHOPIFY NOW SELLS NFTs: THE EXAMPLE OF THE CHICAGO BULLS

Shopify has also entered the wonderful world of NFTs[233]. The platform aims to enable merchants to easily create and sell NFTs. In July 2021, Shopify partnered with the Chicago Bulls to create a limited edition collection. The NFT collection featured video clips inspired by the team's six NBA championship victories in the 1990s, each distributed across multiple levels of rarity (rare, iconic, legendary).

34. MUSEUMS

A JOURNEY THROUGH TIME: NFTS AND MUSEUMS

SOUVENIRS FROM THE VISIT

Most museum or exhibition visitors throw away their ticket once their visit is over, even if they enjoyed the experience. However, it would make a good souvenir. For example, it would be a shame to throw away the ticket from your first visit to the Louvre or the British Museum! With NFTs, you can keep museum tickets in your wallet, which will prove that you have indeed been to a particular museum (and show that you are culturally inclined!). You will have a record of the museums you have visited throughout your life, and you can enjoy sharing them with your family and loved ones.

EXCLUSIVE BENEFITS FOR VISITORS

Museums can leverage NFTs to offer benefits to visitors who support the institution by purchasing NFTs. These benefits could take various forms, including discounts at the museum shop, exclusive access to certain spaces and events, and priority in queues. Museums could also organize special events reserved for NFT holders, such as meetings with curators, artists, or domain experts. This approach would create a rich and personalized experience for art enthusiasts.

NFTS IN VIRTUAL MUSEUMS

A NEW WAY TO SHOWCASE ARTWORKS

Artists are always looking for new ways to disseminate their work. Museums that have the means can offer artists the opportunity to display their artworks in the museum's metaverse through NFTs. This would give artists more visibility and allow art lovers to admire the artworks, even from their own homes. Some startups specialize in immersive experiences in the metaverse. For example, Spatial[234] offers unique immersive experiences and even allows users to create their own universe.

TEMPORARILY TRANSFERRING RIGHTS (LENDING)

Museums could benefit from lending their artworks to other institutions for specific periods, as not all pieces are displayed simultaneously. For example, out of the 500,000 artworks held by the Louvre, only 7%, or approximately 35,000, are displayed at any given time[235]. Given the difficulty of transporting artworks, which are often very fragile and at risk of damage during transportation, some museums could consider virtually lending their artworks via NFTs to allow other institutions to project them in their premises. Thanks to new technologies, it is now possible to display highly realistic 3D reproductions.

VIRTUAL MUSEUMS FOR A GOOD CAUSE

Ukraine recently launched the *Meta History Museum*[236], an NFT museum aimed at tracing the history of the Russian invasion and raising funds. The initiative came from the Ukrainian Ministry of Digital Transformation, which inaugurated the museum on March 25, 2022. The platform is regularly fueled by illustrations from artists that depict each stage of the conflict and allow the purchase of digital artworks to acquire military and civilian equipment[237]. This innovative initiative shows how NFTs can be used for good causes, enabling artists to contribute to an important cause while allowing individuals to contribute financially.

EASIER EXHIBITIONS FOR YOUNG ARTISTS

Young artists often struggle to monetize their work and gain recognition in an art market that is often saturated. Artistic NFTs exhibited in the metaverse are a true revolution for aspiring artists who aspire to make a name for themselves in the art industry. Finally, they have the opportunity to benefit from global exposure for their work, reach a wider audience, and be able to generate enough income to support their passion. The exhibition of NFTs in the metaverse offers a unique opportunity for artists to connect with fans and buyers from around the world. Artists can directly interact with their audience, share their creative process, and build a loyal community of supporters for their artistic career.

WHAT IF WE SOLD THE MONA LISA? THE LIMITS OF THIS MODEL

What if the Louvre created an NFT representing the Mona Lisa? This would mean that there are two "official" Mona Lisa paintings: the real one and the virtual one. This would offer numerous use cases, as we have seen. But what if the Louvre decided to sell this NFT to finance other projects? Should they sell the Mona Lisa as an NFT? If so, at what price? Why that price? What would be the public's reaction? What would be the ethical and cultural impacts? Many questions remain unanswered... or almost, because other museums have already started selling artworks as NFTs.

MUSEUMS AND THE SALE OF NFTS: SOME EXAMPLES

In recent years, international museums have seized the opportunity offered by NFTs to find new sources of revenue. Among the notable examples, the Belvedere Palace in Vienna created a fractionalized version of Gustav Klimt's "The Kiss" into 10,000 NFTs[238]. These NFTs were put on sale on Valentine's Day for a unit price of 1,700 dollar. With approximately 2,400 sales, this operation raised over 4 million dollars. The British Museum sold two hundred NFTs representing Hokusai's artworks in 2021, as well as twenty NFTs representing Turner's watercolors in March 2022[239]. In May 2021, a digital copy of a Michelangelo painting was sold by the Uffizi Gallery in Florence for 140,000 dollars[240]. In the summer of 2021, the Hermitage Museum in St. Petersburg sold five digital reproductions of artworks, including paintings by Monet and da Vinci, which raised over $440,000[241].

SPECULATIVE PITFALLS

These few examples show that museums are starting to realize the financial advantages offered by NFTs... at the risk of falling into speculation and turning artworks into mere commodities. Should the value of an artwork be determined by its artistic quality or, failing that, by its price? Moreover, this practice raises questions about access to art and ownership of artworks. By selling NFTs, museums create exclusivity that goes against their primary mission, which is to enable as many people as possible to access art.

LACK OF CLEAR LEGAL FRAMEWORK

NFTs are a legal anomaly; there is currently no legal definition. Their hybrid nature positions them at the intersection of several different legal concepts, making them difficult to define. As we have seen, there are growing and significant issues that suggest classifying NFTs under a legal category. Having a clear legal structure would allow museums to more easily plan and project their use of this technology.

EXAMPLES

NFT Factory is a modular space of 400 square meters located in the heart of Paris, opposite the Centre Pompidou. This initiative, driven by 128 co-founders, aims to promote NFTs and build the Web3 ecosystem in France.

Le Seattle NFT Museum was co-founded by Jennifer Wong and Peter Hamilton. It opened its doors in January 2022. The museum's ambition is to establish crypto-art as a new artistic movement and open it to the general public.

35. FINANCE

THE FUNCTIONING OF TRADITIONAL FINANCE

DO NOT BELIEVE THAT YOUR MONEY IS SAFE IN BANKS

If you didn't know, I'm sorry to inform you: the money you deposit in a bank does not belong to you. It belongs to the bank. The balance in your account is only a promise from the bank to repay you; that's the key difference. Those who believe that the amount indicated in their account is stored in the bank's vaults are mistaken. A significant portion is used by the bank for speculation and profit generation. Additionally, due to the fractional reserve banking system, banks can create more money than they actually have in their vaults. This system is made possible because depositors, in theory, will not all withdraw their money at the same time (and if they did, it would lead to a bank run and immediate bank failure #Cantona). Thus, banks can inflate the money supply as they wish, leading to inflation and an increase in private debt.

WHAT HAPPENS TO MONEY WHEN A COUNTRY COLLAPSES: EXAMPLES OF ZIMBABWE AND AFGHANISTAN

It would be false to believe that your money is safe when it rests in a bank. We tend to think so because we live in a peaceful country with a stable currency. However, if things were to worsen (as was the case with Germany in the 1930s following the 1929 crisis), the bank will not be there to protect you. It will be impossible to withdraw your money because it does not belong to you.
When we change our perspective and look elsewhere, we can see what is happening in certain countries around the world. This is notably the case in Zimbabwe or Afghanistan, where inflation is skyrocketing. War doesn't help the situation either. In these countries, people cannot withdraw their money as they wish because the government makes it impossible (fearing that the country will collapse if everyone withdraws their money simultaneously).

THE CONTRIBUTION OF DEFI TO FINANCE

THE PROGRESSIVE EMERGENCE OF DEFI

Unlike traditional banking, in Decentralized Finance (DeFi), it is you (and not the banks) who truly own your money. DeFi truly emerged in 2019 and began attracting many users. The period from 2019 to 2022 was extremely fruitful for the decentralized finance ecosystem. The Total Value Locked (TVL) in different protocols rose to nearly $180 billion in November 2021[242], in less than three years since its inception! DeFi has particularly developed in Asia and South America, where the rate of banking access is relatively low.

THE ADVANTAGES...

DeFi offers several advantages:
- **Fund control**: You have real control over your money as it is stored on a decentralized network. No central authority can prevent you from accessing it (unlike centralized exchanges like Binance or the now-defunct FTX). This financial autonomy is one of the main advantages of DeFi, providing users with increased trust and independence compared to traditional financial systems.
- **Availability**: Through the use of blockchain and smart contracts, individuals can access financial services 24/7, 365 days a year. This constant availability allows users to manage their financial assets, conduct transactions, borrow or lend funds at any time.
- **Transparency**: Smart contracts enable direct interaction between buyers and sellers. Numerous on-chain analysis tools allow real-time tracking of where the money goes and how it is used, thanks to the transparency of the blockchain.
- **Reduced fees**: With DeFi, most intermediaries such as banks and brokers are eliminated, resulting in reduced fees.

...AND THE DRAWBACKS!

However, DeFi also comes with its share of issues.
- The first problem is **hacks**. The removal of intermediaries means that the only authority is the source code of the protocols. Therefore, like any application, these protocols can be targeted for major attacks or hacks. This phenomenon is amplified in DeFi due to the presence of significant amounts of money. As of December 2022, the cumulative losses in DeFi amounted to nearly $75 billion, with only $6 billion recovered[243].
- The second problem is "**rug pulls**." A DeFi rug pull is a crypto scam where the developers of a DeFi project create a new token and suddenly abandon the project after taking the funds of early investors. Unlike traditional lending platforms, DeFi still lacks regulations to protect its users from these scams.
- The third problem is "**impermanent losses**." An impermanent loss occurs when the price of the crypto locked in a liquidity pool changes. Typically, this happens when there is an unequal token ratio in the liquidity pool. However, impermanent loss cannot occur as long as the funds are not withdrawn from the liquidity pool.

DEFI ABSORBED BY CEX: THE CASE OF FTX CRASH

The FTX crash had a negative impact on the image of crypto. It all started with a tweet from Changpeng Zhao (CZ), the CEO of Binance. The Chinese billionaire made waves by announcing that Binance plans to sell all its FTT, the cryptocurrency of the FTX platform. Referring to a Coindesk report[244], CZ implied that FTX, the second-largest platform after Binance, could face a severe liquidity problem. The report pointed out questionable financial practices by FTX, with its sister company Alameda Research (also owned by FTX CEO Sam Bankman-Fried, aka SBF) holding 60% of all circulating FTT. This tweet caused panic, and many people began to withdraw their funds from the platform, starting a bank run. It's worth noting that the crash of UST in May 2022[245] and the specter of Celsius in June 2022[246] were still fresh in memory, prompting depositors to withdraw their funds as soon as possible. A few days later, no funds could be withdrawn. The crisis of confidence worsened, and the price of FTT plummeted, dragging the FTX platform down with it.

The key takeaway from the FTX crash is that: with centralized exchanges, you do not control your money. That's why some users couldn't withdraw their funds. These centralized exchanges replicate the traditional financial system identically, and the blockchain brings no benefits, quite the opposite. That's why DeFi is so important.

NFTFI: COMBINING DEFI AND NFTS

NFTFI: WHAT IS IT?

NFTFI is the combination of NFTs (Non-Fungible Tokens) and DeFi (Decentralized Finance). Instead of using decentralized protocols with fungible cryptocurrencies, NFTFI utilizes these decentralized protocols with NFTs. This emerging trend emerged in 2022 following the DeFi Summer and the NFT boom. The goal is to merge the best of both worlds by making it easier to invest in NFTs, almost as easily as investing in cryptocurrencies within DeFi. NFTFI facilitates the purchase of rare NFTs through fractionalized NFTs.

FRACTIONALIZED NFTs: PRINCIPLE AND FUNCTIONING

Note: We described the process of <u>collectivization</u> (1 NFT => 10,000 ERC20 tokens) here. The reverse process is also possible to regain access to the locked NFT: 10,000 PUNK tokens ⇒ CryptoPunk NFT, which is <u>privatization</u>.

BENEFITS OF FRACTIONALIZED NFTs FOR DEFI

Fractionalized NFTs allow investors with less capital to own a portion of the NFT. It makes the non-fungible fungible. Similar to how investment funds have allowed individuals to own a portion of real estate, fractionalized NFTs enable ownership of a fraction of a high-value NFT (although you might not be willing to trade your house for a Bored Ape Yacht Club NFT!). It also provides a new avenue for collectors to monetize their NFTs. They can now use them for lending, borrowing, and staking, instead of solely buying them for resale.

EXAMPLES

 AAVE Protocol was created in 2017 and derived its name from the Finnish word for "ghost." It is an open-source, decentralized lending and borrowing protocol. AAVE is one of the most widely used DeFi protocols today.

Curve Finance is a liquidity pool created in 2020 with the aim of facilitating decentralized trading of stablecoins (such as USDT, USDC, DAI, etc.) more easily, which was challenging at the time.

36. METAVERSE

THE METAVERSE: WHAT IS IT?

THE METAVERSE HAS BEEN AROUND FOR A WHILE

Despite the recent buzz around the metaverse (#Meta), the idea is not new. Two key milestones are worth mentioning here. In 1992, the term first appeared in Neal Stephenson's book _Snow Crash_. In this cyberpunk novel, the science fiction author describes the metaverse as follows: "_People are software called avatars. They are the audiovisual bodies that people use to communicate with each other in the Metaverse._" In 2003, the popular game "Second Life" was launched, which truly popularized the concept of the metaverse. At its peak, it had 11 million "residents" and 50,000 businesses.

THE METAVERSE: A BLEND OF AR AND VR

There are various definitions of the metaverse: a 3D virtual universe where users can interact with each other, explore environments, play games, and experience immersive activities; a digital space where users can have experiences similar to real life; a network of interconnected virtual worlds that offer social, commercial, cultural, and gaming experiences. However, the best definition is perhaps this: it is a digital world at the intersection of blockchain, social networks, augmented reality (AR), and virtual reality (VR).

AN INFINITE WORLD OF POSSIBILITIES

Imagine yourself in 1492. You are Christopher Columbus. You arrive in unexplored territories that were previously unknown to Europeans. In awe, you can only imagine the possibilities that lie ahead. Well, in 2023, we find ourselves in a similar situation with a vastly larger world, the metaverse. It is a world without borders, with space-time that can extend almost infinitely. Experts predict that the size of this market will reach $800 billion by 2024[247]. Startups building in this universe today may become the giants of tomorrow.

A MUCH MORE IMMERSIVE WORLD

The metaverse is a virtual universe where reality and fiction blend. To enter, you first need to connect to a dedicated platform that allows you to interact with other users and experience immersive 3D activities. Once connected, users can create their avatars to represent them in the virtual world and start exploring various environments. They can interact with other avatars, participate in recreational or educational activities, and even engage in commercial transactions using virtual currency. Entering the metaverse opens up new possibilities for socializing, entertainment, learning, and many other aspects of our lives.

NFTS: ESSENTIAL PILLARS OF THE METAVERSE

NO METAVERSE WITHOUT NFTS

It's hard to imagine a metaverse without NFTs because the metaverse relies heavily on the concept of digital ownership. Without digital ownership, the essence and depth of the metaverse would diminish. The immersive aspect would be less prominent. With NFTs, digital ownership is ensured, and it is arguably the most fundamental aspect. NFTs enable the creation of digital scarcity and a true digital identity. That's why industry players are investing heavily in NFTs to master the technology and protect their brands.

MANY INDUSTRIES IMPACTED

The metaverse offers numerous opportunities for various sectors such as entertainment, e-commerce, education, healthcare, and real estate. Companies can provide immersive and personalized experiences to their customers, such as live concerts, virtual stores, online courses, virtual property tours, and virtual healthcare services. Businesses that can establish themselves in the metaverse will have a significant competitive advantage and be at the forefront of innovation.

GOVERNANCE TOKENS THROUGH NFTS

Governance is a crucial aspect of metaverse development as it allows users to shape the future of the virtual world in a participatory and democratic manner. By using governance tokens, users can have direct control over network decisions and actions. Tokens can be used for voting on governance proposals, which can include decisions like adding new features, modifying protocol rules, or distributing rewards. Users can transfer their governance tokens to others, enabling them to participate in metaverse decisions. The most active users can accumulate more tokens, giving them greater weight in decision-making.

GAMIFICATION THROUGH NFTS

Platforms increasingly use gamification to make the user experience more immersive and engaging. NFTs will be the gateway to this gamification. Players can receive NFTs by completing specific tasks, such as playing games or finishing quests. Some players are willing to invest a lot of effort if they are assured that their rewards will be rare or even unique, creating a genuine economy of digital scarcity. NFTs are at the core of metaverse gamification by creating incentives for participation and enhancing user engagement.

THE IMPORTANCE OF COMMUNITIES IN THE METAVERSE

Communities play a crucial role in the success of businesses. They provide a way for companies to get closer to their customers and better understand their needs, preferences, and behaviors. Communities also help reinforce brand image by establishing trust and proximity with consumers. In the metaverse, communities are even more important as they can contribute to creating a more vibrant, dynamic, and collaborative virtual world. They can be highly involved in content and service creation by offering ideas, suggestions, and feedback to improve the experiences. Communities can also play a key role in promoting and sharing content with other users, commenting on it, and driving its dissemination.

A NEW SALES CHANNEL AND ADVERTISING TOOL

For some brands, particularly luxury brands, being present in the metaverse will become a necessity. The future of advertising and marketing will partly rely on the metaverse, presenting a massive market opportunity. Numerous advertising spots can be displayed in this world. More and more people will use the metaverse for their shopping. Landowners can rent out their advertising space to generate passive income.

VIRTUAL REAL ESTATE AND THE METAVERSE

The purchase of virtual land can be considered a long-term investment, as land value can increase with metaverse growth and rising demand. Some have not hesitated to spend large sums of money to acquire virtual land. A land of The Otherside metaverse was even sold for $1.6 million[248]! However, the virtual land market in the metaverse has been in freefall since November 2021. According to data collected by WeMeta and reported by The Information, virtual land sales on platforms like Decentraland and The Sandbox dropped by 97% between November 2021 and June 2022[249].

EXAMPLES

The Sandbox was co-founded by two French entrepreneurs, Arthur Madrid and Sébastien Borget. It is a community-based metaverse where players can design, share, and experience virtual worlds.

Decentraland is an open-source interactive platform where users can buy, use, and build on virtual lands.

37. COLLECTIBLE CARDS

COLLECTIBLE CARDS: FROM PANINI TO NFT CARDS

THE BEGINNING OF COLLECTIBLE CARDS FROM THE 1950s WITH PANINI

The history of collectible cards began in the 1950s in Modena. Two Italian brothers, Giovanni and Bénito Panini, both newspaper vendors, came up with the idea of inserting free images of football players in the newspaper pages to attract children and encourage parents to buy them. And Bingo! Success followed. They quickly stopped giving them away and started selling them. 3 million images were sold in just the first year. In 1961, the *Panini* company was established. Initially focused on Italy, it expanded internationally during the 1970 FIFA World Cup in Mexico with its first international album. This album truly marked the beginning of the *Panini* craze.

MAGIC AND THE RISE OF DECKBUILDING (1993)

August 5, 1993, marked a turning point in the history of collectible cards. Magic launched a collection of 300 unique cards that could be collected, traded, and used to play with friends. Each card had its own identity and characteristics. Magic introduced the concept of deckbuilding, allowing players to create their own deck with the cards they desired based on their strategy. And success followed suit: in 2020, there were over 20,000 unique Magic cards, including all expansions. This allowed for the creation of numerous decks! Today, there are more than 20 million players worldwide. Other competitors subsequently entered this market (Pokemon in 1996, Yu-Gi-Oh! in 1999).

THE RISE OF NFT CARDS: FROM RARE PEPE (2016) TO DONALD TRUMP (2023)

No, the first NFT cards did not appear with Sorare and were not minted on Ethereum either. They emerged with "Rare Pepe" cards. The first card was minted on Bitcoin (block 428,919, on September 9, 2016)[250]. It was a variation of the meme "Pepe The Frog" (originally created in 2005 by Matt Furie). Other collectible card trends emerged afterward, especially during the 2021 bull run. For example, NBA Top Shot gained popularity (including LeBron James' dunk card sold for over $380,000). In late 2022, Donald Trump also had NFT cards featuring his likeness.

PAUL LOGAN AND THE FAMOUS $5.3 MILLION PIKACHU ILLUSTRATOR CARD

The collectible card market is enormous and continues to grow each year. Just imagine that Paul Logan (a professional wrestler and YouTuber) spent a whopping $5.3 million to acquire the Pikachu Illustrator card. His video explaining his choice garnered 7 million views on YouTube[251]. Only 39 to 40 Pikachu Illustrator cards were produced, as they were rewards for winners of a contest in Japan, and there is only one card in the world with a "10/10" condition—Paul Logan's!

ADVANTAGES OF NFTS FOR COLLECTIBLE CARDS

CARD AUTHENTICATION

Previously, when you wanted to buy a rare collectible card, you had to have it authenticated by an expert to ensure you weren't being scammed. This process was slow and costly. However, with NFT cards, there's no need for that anymore. Since the blockchain is a public and transparent ledger, anyone can see who created the card, who owns it, and how many editions of the card exist. This eliminates the risk of counterfeiting and greatly improves the ease of purchasing collectible cards.

TRUE OWNERSHIP OF ONLINE CARDS

When you play online collectible card games (like Hearthstone, for example), the cards you purchase don't actually belong to you. You simply have access to the servers hosting your cards. If the servers no longer exist or if the game stops for any reason, you can say goodbye to your precious cards. By using NFTs, all the cards and rare items you acquire will be truly yours. You can do whatever you want with them, including selling them on marketplaces like OpenSea, which are not owned by the game's license.

EARNING MONEY WHILE HAVING FUN

What if all the hours you spend playing your favorite collectible card game could be monetized? This will soon be possible thanks to NFTs. For example, the winner of a tournament could receive a unique NFT card as a prize, which they can later sell at a higher price (or keep and use in other tournaments). This card will have a complete history showing its previous owners, which will increase its value if it passes into the hands of famous personalities. One can also imagine that this card provides access to exclusive benefits, such as participating in a special event or having one-year access to the game's full premium version, and more.

NO RISK OF DAMAGING PHYSICAL CARDS (-95% OTHERWISE)

Physical card collectors face a major problem: general wear and tear of the cards. They are susceptible to folds, tears, scratches, stains, and so on. Collectors must always take care of their cards, or else their investments of thousands of dollars can plummet to nearly zero. A damaged card can lose up to 95% of its value. NFT cards, on the other hand, are entirely digital, completely eliminating the risk of damage.

SHOULD PHYSICAL CARDS BE DISCARDED? NOT REALLY

NFT cards raise significant concerns among some collectors because they are not physical. You can't touch them, manipulate them, or use them in real-world physical tournaments. After all, collectible card games are also a means of creating real-life connections and not just staring at a screen, right? There are two objections to this. First, augmented reality will allow for maintaining social interactions in a physical setting while benefiting from NFT technology. All it will take is wearing augmented reality glasses (e-sports will likely benefit from this technology as tournament spectators can experience what professional players see in first-person). Second, for rare cards, it will be possible to incorporate an NFC chip inside them, enabling a physical card to be linked to its digital NFT counterpart.

EXAMPLES

Gods Unchained is like a Blockchain version of *Hearthstone*. The game was launched in 2018 by two brothers, James and Robbie Ferguson. Chris Clay, the former Game Director of Magic: The Gathering Arena, is behind the project.

Cross the Ages is a unique blend of NFTs, literature, and science fiction. Founded in 2019 by Sami Chlagou (head of PixelHeart studio, which has produced over 50 games), Cross the Ages is more than just a game—it's a complex universe that will span 7 volumes over 10 years of creation (releasing one chapter per week).

38. ECOLOGY

YES, YOU READ THAT RIGHT, ECOLOGY!

LET'S LOOK AT THINGS FROM A DIFFERENT PERSPECTIVE

Yes, you read the chapter title correctly. NFTs and... ecology. Of course, this chapter is not here to deceive you by saying that NFTs are all beautiful and eco-friendly. Just like watching cat videos on YouTube in 4K, playing Fortnite all night, or having a Zoom meeting with your colleagues, NFTs pose ecological problems. This chapter aims to provide a different perspective to nuance the usual clichés.

ENERGY CONSUMPTION: A DROP IN THE OCEAN

Let's start by recalling some figures. The global annual electricity consumption was 25,300 TWh in 2021[252]. For comparison, the annual consumption of Bitcoin (supposedly the most energy-consuming blockchain) was around 129 TWh per year in March 2023[253] (equivalent to 0.5% of the world's electricity consumption). The University of Cambridge regularly updates these figures, and they fluctuate between 125 and 150 TWh per year[254]. The Internet consumes 1500 TWh per year. As for the NFTs, most of them are based on the Ethereum blockchain. Since Ethereum transitioned to Proof of Stake* with The Merge*, its consumption has been reduced by 99.84%, reaching approximately 0.01 TWh per year only[255]. This represents a negligible fraction (0.00004%) of the world's electricity consumption. We are still far from an ecological catastrophe…

USING PROOF OF STAKE INSTEAD OF PROOF OF WORK

Every blockchain requires a consensus mechanism to function properly. There are primarily two types of consensus:
- **Proof of Work** (PoW*): This consensus involves solving complex mathematical problems that require a significant amount of computational power. The consumed computational power makes PoW secure because it is impossible to gather enough computational power to corrupt the network. The early blockchains operated on PoW (Bitcoin, Litecoin, Ethereum until 2022, etc.). Very few initially adopted PoS (Proof of Stake) as their consensus mechanism (Cosmos being one of the exceptions). However, at present, almost all blockchains operate on PoS.
- **Proof of Stake** (PoS*): This consensus does not require computational power to validate transactions. It only requires staking the native cryptocurrency of the blockchain (e.g., ETH for Ethereum). Validators are then responsible for verifying all transactions. If they attempt to corrupt the network, they risk being

"slashed," meaning they will lose a portion of the delegated cryptocurrency. Since everything on the blockchain is transparent and public, anyone attempting to corrupt the network would be immediately exposed. Therefore, seeking to corrupt the network would be futile. Given that no computational power is needed, PoS consumes significantly less energy than PoW.

EVEN IF IT WERE PROOF OF WORK...

Even if NFTs operated solely on Proof of Work, things would still need to be nuanced. Let's take the example of Bitcoin, which is perhaps the most illustrative. Did you know that Bitcoin primarily utilizes green energy? The reason is quite pragmatic: green energy is cheaper. Energy from sources like hydroelectric dams, for instance, cannot be stored, so some actors prefer to sell it at a lower price rather than wasting it. Bitcoin miners strategically position themselves in these areas to benefit from favorable prices. Therefore, regarding Bitcoin's 0.6% share of global electricity consumption, it is important to note that most of this consumption actually comes from green energy sources.

NFTS AND THE ENVIRONMENT: NOT CRAZY, AFTER ALL!

BETTER SUPPLY CHAIN MANAGEMENT

By assigning a unique NFT to each product, it becomes possible to track its lifecycle from production to end-of-life. This traceability enables a better understanding of the different stages of the supply chain, identifying inefficiencies, and taking measures to improve them. This traceability can be particularly useful, for example, in the case of defective cars, where it will be easier to target the specific vehicles to be recalled by tracing back to the source of the problem. Similarly, it will be easier to track the carbon footprint of a product, enabling companies to better understand the environmental impact of their production.

CERTIFIED ECO-LABELS ON THE BLOCKCHAIN

NFTs can be used to certify the environmental origin of products. By associating an NFT with an environmental certification, it becomes possible to track the product's journey from production to sale and ensure that environmentally friendly practices have been applied throughout the supply chain. NFTs could help prevent certain scams related to organic labels by guaranteeing that a particular product was indeed produced under environmentally friendly conditions. For example, forestry certifications could use NFTs to ensure that the wood used in their production comes from responsibly managed forests.

ADMINISTRATION: REDUCING UNNECESSARY TRAVEL AND PAPERWORK

NFTs could help eliminate unnecessary paperwork in administration. This advancement would be beneficial considering that, in addition to generating mental clutter (it's always difficult to organize papers), it also contributes to environmental pollution. Paper production requires large amounts of wood, water, and energy, contributing to deforestation. Most of the paper we print is used only once before being discarded. NFTs could also eliminate unnecessary travel for submitting official documents to the administration since the blockchain is sufficient to guarantee document authenticity.

FUNDING ECO-FRIENDLY PROJECTS

Tokenizing environmental projects offers investors the opportunity to invest in these initiatives while ensuring that the funds are used responsibly through blockchain transparency. For example, NFTs can be used to authenticate carbon credits, which can then be traded or used to finance CO_2 emissions reduction projects. The blockchain ensures the transparency and authenticity of these certificates, thus increasing investor confidence and encouraging their engagement in the fight against climate change. Investors could also benefit from a share of the profits generated by the project.

EXAMPLES

 Carbonable is a startup that allows people to invest in decarbonization projects through carbon credits. Previously, carbon credits were only accessible to major players like Total, but Carbonable makes them accessible to individuals through NFTs.

Tresorio is specializing in recovering thermal energy from digital sources. They have developed a water heater that can mine Bitcoin. Mining chips replace the electric resistance, utilizing the excess heat for cryptocurrency mining.

39. MEDIA

FROM MEDIA 1.0 TO MEDIA 3.0

MEDIA 1.0: READ CONTENT

At its beginning, the internet only allowed for content reading. The early websites were static spaces created by web professionals for individuals. The interaction between the two parties was limited, with users in a "read-only" mode. It was akin to reading a newspaper or a magazine, with a "one-to-many" approach that lacked interactivity.

MEDIA 2.0: CREATING CONTENT

The advent of Web 2.0 changed the landscape. Instead of distributing data from a static file, data was managed through dynamic HTML databases, allowing for more personalized content. Internet users could now write and publish their own content. This led to the rise of blogs and social media platforms such as Facebook, YouTube, and Instagram. The range of content expanded from text to various multimedia formats such as images, audio, and video. Websites like TripAdvisor and Amazon started incorporating user reviews and ratings. Online news outlets emerged, some managed not by traditional media but by individuals or independent organizations.

MEDIA 3.0: OWNING CONTENT

Web 3.0 takes another step forward: content ownership. It allows creators not only to produce content but also to have full ownership of it. In contrast to Web 2.0, where content creators often faced exploitation of their work without proper compensation, Web 3.0 introduces the concept of digital ownership through non-fungible tokens (NFTs). With NFTs, creators can irrefutably certify their authorship of a piece of content. In the realm of media, this opens up unexplored possibilities.

NFTS FOR MEDIA: WHAT USE CASES?

PARTICIPATING IN THE EDITORIAL BOARD

Ever dreamed of being part of a newspaper's editorial board? NFTs now make that possible. A newspaper can offer NFTs for sale, granting holders the opportunity to participate in the editorial decision-making process. This allows the newspaper to generate revenue while involving loyal readers in suggesting topics, providing opinions on ongoing articles, and even submitting their own articles. Coordination for these activities could be facilitated through platforms like Discord. Some newspapers have already initiated interesting projects in this regard. One such example is 20Mint, which sold 999 NFTs representing typewriters. The committee formed by the 999 buyers contributed to the release of 800,000 copies of the newspaper's first issue[256].

FUNDING INVESTIGATIVE JOURNALISM AND REAL-TIME ACCESS TO NEWS

NFTs can be leveraged to finance specific investigative journalism projects, such as an in-depth investigation into the situation in Iraq or Syria. Interested individuals can acquire the corresponding NFT, providing funding for the investigation. Once the funding goal is reached, journalists can dive into their investigation. NFT buyers would gain access to a dedicated Discord channel, receiving exclusive information and behind-the-scenes content. They can directly interact with the journalists leading the investigation, obtaining real-time updates and the opportunity to ask questions.

NFTs, MEDIA, AND CENSORSHIP

By utilizing NFTs, it becomes possible to ensure that content cannot be altered or removed without authorization. For example, if you are a journalist publishing an article on a sensitive topic on your website, you can use an NFT to protect it, guaranteeing its accessibility to the public even in the face of censorship for any reason. It would also be possible to restrict access to the article to specific users who possess the corresponding NFT, providing greater control over who can read it and how it is used.

THE IDEAL SOLUTION FOR A COLLABORATIVE MEDIA PLATFORM:

NFTs (Non-Fungible Tokens) allow content creators to work together more efficiently by providing a means to share copyright and associated remuneration in an automated and transparent manner. In the case of a news publication, for example, a team of journalists can use a smart contract associated with an NFT to manage the intellectual property of their articles and the distribution of advertising revenues. Each article would be represented by an NFT owned by the author, which would verify its authorship, ensure copyright protection, and allocate the advertising revenues generated by the article's publication.

MICRO-PAYMENTS FOR ACCESSING ARTICLES:

In the context of NFTs, it is conceivable that micro-payments could become more common for accessing exclusive articles. Instead of paying a monthly or yearly subscription, readers could purchase a specific NFT for each article they want to read. Micro-payments are advantageous in this case because they allow readers to pay only for the content they are genuinely interested in. The payment process would be simplified: for each article purchase, one would simply need to connect their digital wallet (which would likely have a small amount of money) and click "pay," without having to enter banking details.

ENSURING JOURNALISTS' COPYRIGHTS:

Copyright is a fundamental aspect of content creation for journalists. They need to be able to protect their work and prevent unauthorized reproduction and use. NFTs can help protect journalists' copyrights. By creating an NFT for an article, journalists can prove ownership and all reproduction and usage rights. This specific use of NFTs would make it easier for journalists to have legal evidence to exploit their work. According to Article L. 121-8 of the French Intellectual Property Code, authors have the exclusive right to collect their articles and speeches in a collection and publish or authorize their publication in that form. Therefore, works (texts, drawings, etc.) published in a newspaper can be exploited by their author. NFTs provide tangible and immutable proof of this exploitation.

AUTHENTICATING CONTENT ORIGIN TO COMBAT MISINFORMATION:

With the proliferation of fake news and misleading content, it is becoming increasingly important to be able to prove the authenticity and source of published online content. NFTs can be used for this purpose by creating proof of ownership and authenticity for informational content. For example, a media outlet could create an NFT for an exclusive photo or video to prove that it was created by their journalists. This proof of authenticity could then be used to verify the source of information or counter false information created to deceive gullible individuals.

EXAMPLES

20Mint is a media outlet launched by 20 Minutes, initiated by Laurent Bainier, its editor-in-chief. The media is co-piloted and financed through a collection of 999 NFT typewriters, which allowed them to release the first issue with over 800,000 copies.

Cryptoast is one of the leading crypto and NFT media outlets in France. Starting as a simple blog in September 2017, the media quickly expanded. Cryptoast launched an edition of its second print newspaper by associating it with a collection of 400 NFTs, with each NFT representing 1/400th of the cover.

TheBigWhale is a media co-founded by Grégory Raymond and Raphaël Bloch, both former journalists, and aims to dive into the web3. The media launched a collection of 2022 NFTs.

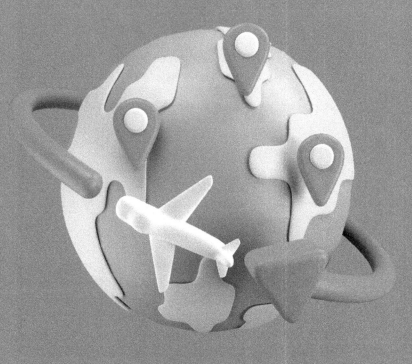

40. TOURISM

2040: MR. X PREPARING HIS TRIP... THANKS TO NFTS

LET'S PROJECT OURSELVES INTO THE FUTURE, SHALL WE?

To imagine how NFTs could be used in the world of tourism, how about we take a leap forward in time (2040) and accompany Mr. X on his trip to Mexico? In 2040, Blockchain technology is used almost everywhere, much like the Internet was in 2023. Everyone is using NFTs. People may not necessarily understand the underlying technology, but they find NFTs very convenient. That's what we'll discover as we travel with Mr. X.
Take your seats, fasten your seat belts, and let's go.

SMOOTH MANAGEMENT OF ADMINISTRATIVE IDENTITIES

To begin his trip to Mexico, Monsieur X heads to the airport. In the past, identity management at airports was a tedious process for both tourists and airport staff. However, with the use of blockchain technology, identity checks have become streamlined and automated. Each traveler now possesses an NFT that serves as proof of their identity and up-to-date passport. At the airport, Monsieur X simply scans his NFT at the checkpoint, and he's good to go. He receives a temporary NFT for the duration of his trip, which can be presented during other identity checks. With this thought in mind, Monsieur X feels reassured as he heads to the airport.

COLLECTIBLE AIRLINE TICKETS

As Monsieur X arrives in his taxi, he takes a look at his airline ticket in the form of an NFT on his smartphone. A smile appears on his face as he realizes he struck gold with his NFT ticket. He took the risky bet of purchasing it before the reveal and was pleasantly surprised to find a "Super Rare" NFT, granting him exclusive benefits. He admires the intricate 3D design of his ticket, created by a renowned artist (whose name he can't recall). Monsieur X is confident he can easily resell his airline ticket to collectors even after he has completed his journey.

AUTOMATED INSURANCE CLAIMS

Upon arrival at the airport, Monsieur X receives some bad news: his flight is delayed, and he will have to wait until the following day to depart. This situation troubles him because the last time he experienced a flight delay, 22 years ago, he had to go through a lengthy process of filling out forms, providing evidence, and waiting for days on end, only to ultimately abandon his claim. Fortunately, with blockchain technology, everything now operates seamlessly. Airport data is updated in real-time, and the smart contracts associated with the tickets ensure automatic compensation in the event of a flight delay. Within an hour, Monsieur X will receive his compensation in his wallet.

DURING THE JOURNEY: EXPLORING POSSIBILITIES

AUTOMATION OF PROCESSES IN HOTELS (IDENTITY VERIFICATION, PAYMENT METHODS, ETC.)

Monsieur X finally arrives at his hotel and proceeds with the well-known check-in process. Having worked in a hotel for two years, he is well aware of how time-consuming and tedious this step used to be. Verifying reservation information, checking identification documents, and ensuring accurate payment details for each guest was a cumbersome task. Additionally, making photocopies of all these documents only to discard them shortly after was wasteful. Fortunately, now there are NFTs. Monsieur X is confident that his reservation has been properly recorded, and he knows that the payment process is reliable and automated. He has locked the amount for his hotel stay in a smart contract, which will be debited only once he locks his room door using the NFT associated with his reservation. This arrangement provides security both for him and the hotel.

100% SECURE REVIEWS (E-REPUTATION)

As soon as Monsieur X enters his hotel room, he realizes that he made an excellent decision by choosing this establishment. Everything is impeccably as described in the listing, and the high rating given by previous tourists is well justified. In the past, Monsieur X had difficulty trusting hotel reviews, aware of the potential for manipulation. However, today he is convinced of the authenticity of the comments, which can only be written by people who have actually stayed at the hotel, thanks to the activation of an NFT by the hotel itself. The most appreciated reviews on the application, those that are the most detailed and realistic, receive token rewards, encouraging users to be maximally objective.

TRACEABILITY OF LOCAL PRODUCTS

Once settled in, Monsieur X decides to explore the city. After all, that's what he came for, right? Monsieur X strolls through the streets, seeking authenticity and a desire to buy local products. He passes by a souvenir shop that catches his attention. Curious, he decides to enter. He spots an object he likes. He then scans it using the available NFT and verifies for himself that the item was indeed produced locally. He has access to all the information (place of production, production date, etc.). He buys the item and continues to explore the city. He will give this souvenir to his daughter back home.

EXCLUSIVE RIGHTS THROUGH NFTs

Two days later, we find Monsieur X again. He visited his family, but today is his day to indulge in solo activities. His schedule is packed: his "Super Rare" NFT ticket grants him 24-hour access to all attractions and tourist sites on the island. It's 6:30 in the morning, and he decides to activate the NFT. All he has to do is scan his NFT (without waiting in line) to gain access to his desired activities.

MONSIEUR X'S DAILY ITINERARY:

06h30 : Activation du NFT « Super Rare »	**16h10** : Excursion en bateau vers une île voisine
08h00 : Découverte du parc zoologique	**19h40** : Spectacle de danse traditionnelle de l'île
09h45 : Randonnée guidée à travers les sentiers de l'île	**21h00** : Dîner dans un restaurant gastronomique spécialisé en fruits de mer
12h30 : Pause déjeuner dans un restaurant avec vue sur l'océan	**03h00** : Boîte de nuit VIP
14h00 : Visite du musée d'art contemporain	**15h10** : Fin du voyage pour Monsieur X. Retour au bercail !

END OF THE TRIP? NOT REALLY, ACTUALLY!

EXTENDING THE TOURISTS' EXPERIENCE

This short escapade with Monsieur X has demonstrated the potential of NFTs in travel, both during the trip and beyond. However, the use of NFTs doesn't stop there! They can be equally useful even after the journey. For travel agencies, NFTs represent an opportunity for innovation and differentiation in the market. They not only enhance the travel experience but also foster customer loyalty by extending the experience beyond the trip itself. By creating a lasting connection with travelers, agencies increase the chances of them returning for future trips and recommending their services to others. This adds value to their offerings, which go beyond simple travel bookings and encompass a broader and continuous experience.

MEMORIES OF THE TRIP THROUGH NFTs

This extended experience is reflected, for example, in the memories of the journey, engraved in both memory and the blockchain. This can help travel agencies foster customer loyalty and create a community around the proposed tourism experiences. They can allow tourists to obtain unique souvenirs, such as keeping the boarding pass in their wallet* or a 3D visualization of their villa hotel room in Bali. Every moment of the trip can be transformed into an NFT, creating a connection between the tourist, their experiences, and the digital world.

THE RISE OF VIRTUAL TOURS AND THE POTENTIAL OF THE METAVERSE

In a time where travel is limited and constraints of time and money increasingly influence travel decisions, virtual tours offer an affordable and convenient alternative to satisfy the new needs of customers. It is always cheaper and more practical to explore from the comfort of home without leaving the couch than to pay for a flight to the other side of the world! It is now possible to visit the Louvre[257], Lascaux Cave, Dubai[258], and many other places without leaving home. Some travel agencies even offer time travel experiences, such as visiting Notre-Dame de Paris or the Great Pyramid of Giza[259].

With the advent of the metaverse, the concept of tourism takes on a whole new dimension. In the metaverse, the full potential of NFTs can be realized. Travelers could acquire NFTs that allow them to interact uniquely with the metaverse environment, such as sitting in the front row of a virtual concert or participating in exclusive events. A special NFT could enable a tour with a historical figure rather than a regular assigned guide.

INCREASING COLLABORATIONS WITH ARTISTS

In the pursuit of differentiation, travel agencies will increasingly collaborate with artists to design their NFTs. These collaborations will create visually appealing and unique NFTs, as well as generate digital memories that reflect the artistic identity of their creators. For example, an NFT representing a historical monument could be used in an advertising campaign to attract visitors. This NFT could have increased value if specially created by a recognized artist in that field. Similarly, an artist could design an interactive art tour in the metaverse, accessible only through an NFT.

EXAMPLES

 Travala.com was co-founded in 2017 by Juan Otero and Steve Hipwell. The company is an alternative to Airbnb, which is currently marred by centralized control, high fees, limited payment options, and low levels of trust.

Travel Prime is a subscription-based travel service. With commission redistribution through the blockchain, it enables subscribers to save for their vacations and guarantee the lowest possible price.

41. PERSONAL DATA

BIG DATA IS WATCHING YOU

THE DATA IN THE AGE OF GAFAM

Today, everyone knows that the GAFAM (Google, Apple, Facebook, Amazon, Microsoft) have taken control of our personal data. This is largely due to them becoming the main providers of online services and information technologies. Many individuals and businesses use their products and services, which gives them access to a considerable amount of personal data.

THE CRUCIAL IMPORTANCE OF DATA

The GAFAM collect and use this data in various ways, including targeting advertising, improving their products and services, and developing new technologies. This data can be very valuable to the GAFAM as it allows them to understand consumer habits and preferences, which can give them a significant competitive advantage. They can display ads that are more likely to be of interest to individuals, resulting in higher click-through rates and better profitability for advertisers. To give you an idea, the data market is projected to exceed $100 billion worldwide by 2027[260].

GIVING AWAY DATA? NO, MONETIZING IT WITH NFTS!

THE FUNDAMENTAL PARADOX OF DATA TODAY

We are facing a paradox today: we have accepted the notion of ownership in the physical world for thousands of years, but since the advent of the digital age, we have accepted the fact that we do not own anything, especially our data. This paradox is even more evident in the case of data storage in the cloud. By carefully reading the terms of use, we not only realize that we do not own our data, but also that the cloud provider reserves the right to access all the information contained in the stored files! Similarly, we all know that our COVID vaccine-related health data was stored on Amazon servers, meaning sensitive French data was accessible by Amazon. This raises obvious sovereignty issues.

LIBERTY, EQUALITY... PROPRIETY ?

In the face of this problem, NFTs can bring about a revolution. They will allow for the preservation of data privacy and ownership. The idea itself is revolutionary, in the true sense of the word. By the way, in France, one of the founding principles of the French Revolution of 1789 is the notion of property.

Art. 2 : « The aim of every political association is the preservation of the natural and imprescriptible rights of Man. These **rights** are Liberty, **Property**, Safety and Resistance to Oppression. »

Art. 17 : « Since the **right to Property** is inviolable and sacred, no one may be deprived thereof, unless public necessity, legally ascertained, obviously requires it, and just and prior indemnity has been paid. »

The rule of law has a duty to guarantee citizens the means to secure their private property. But why shouldn't private property also extend to the digital world?

HOW WOULD A DECENTRALIZED CLOUD WORK?

Blockchain and NFTs offer the possibility of creating a decentralized cloud, with thousands of participants offering their hard drives to backup files that are fragmented and encrypted. Essentially, data is divided into several pieces (e.g., 10), and each piece is stored on different servers. Each server only has a fraction of the data. The NFT becomes the encryption/decryption key, allowing for the separation and reconstruction of all the data pieces. You alone have control over this NFT, which you can potentially transfer. With this model, data is no longer managed by a single central entity but by a multitude of independent nodes.

DATAS, AI, BLOCKCHAIN, AND DATA ANONYMITY

Major companies are currently developing AIs that will allow them to optimize targeted advertising, as mentioned earlier. To be precise, these AIs require a vast amount of data. However, the data market is currently very opaque, as companies have no incentive to share their data. As a result, only 1% of the data in the world is being utilized by AIs. Yet, it would be possible to monetize this data to make it profitable enough to use. The question then arises: How can we monetize our data while retaining ownership and preserving anonymity? To solve this problem, projects like Ocean Protocol propose creating a data exchange marketplace and connecting entities that want to monetize their data with those who need it. Through the blockchain, this connection is made automatically while preserving anonymity.

Of course, this project is extremely complex to implement and is still in its early stages, but the idea is there.

CURRENT OBSTACLES

MANAGING A HUGE AMOUNT OF DATA IS IMPOSSIBLE

There is currently such a massive amount of data that it will be absolutely impossible to put everything on the blockchain. To give you an idea of the exponential growth of data, here are some figures for the data generated every minute in 2021[261]: 400,000 hours of video streamed on Netflix, 41 million messages sent on WhatsApp, 147,000 photos shared on Facebook. And we are talking about just one minute. Faced with such a deluge of data, we will have to choose what we decide to store on the blockchain or not. For example, in a company, will all documents deserve to be put on the blockchain? Probably not. The question will be more about identifying the truly important and confidential documents. For these documents, using a blockchain infrastructure will be relevant for encrypted, secure, and decentralized storage.

NOT EVERYONE IS READY TO TAKE RESPONSIBILITY FOR THEIR DATA

Not everyone is inclined to take responsibility for their personal data. Some are willing to accept the collection of their personal data in exchange for services or products they find useful or interesting. Others may lack the knowledge or skills to understand how to protect their privacy online and control their personal data. Still, others are inclined to trust the companies and organizations that collect and use their data, believing that they have adequate privacy and data protection policies in place.

EXAMPLES

 Ocean Protocol allows organizations from all sectors to share their data while retaining ownership of that data through the use of Blockchain and artificial intelligence.

Filecoin is a decentralized data storage network. It operates on a peer-to-peer basis and connects people who want to sell unused storage capacity with those who want to rent it.

 The Graph enables data indexing through the Blockchain. Anyone can create and publish open APIs called "Subgraphs," making the data easily accessible.

42. INTELLECTUAL PROPERTY

INTELLECTUAL PROPERTY IN FRANCE AND WORLDWIDE

INPI IN FRANCE AND WIPO WORLDWIDE

INPI (National Institute of Industrial Property), founded in 1951, is the French organization responsible for the protection of industrial property. It is responsible for issuing and managing patents, trademarks, designs, and protected geographical indications. According to INPI's figures[262], in 2021, the platform processed 14,758 patent applications and 113,070 trademark applications. On a global scale, the World Intellectual Property Organization (WIPO), established in 1967 in Switzerland, manages the protection of industrial property. It is a United Nations institution and currently has 193 member states. Around 250 non-governmental organizations (NGOs) and intergovernmental international organizations have official observer status for WIPO meetings.

TRADEMARK APPLICATION IN FRANCE... (IT'S LOOOONG)

When you want to file a trademark in France, you have to go through INPI, and the process can take time... a lot of time. After checking the availability of the brand name you want to register, you can file your trademark. INPI then sends you an acknowledgment of receipt with the date and national number of your application. You have to wait for 6 weeks for your application to be published in the Official Bulletin of Industrial Property (BOPI) published by INPI. INPI sends you the notice of publication in BOPI, which lists the information you provided during the filing. You review it and send it back, ensuring there are no errors. INPI then examines your application and raises any objections if necessary. They may also transmit any observations or oppositions received. You may need to respond to these objections. Finally, after a minimum period of five months, once the examination process is complete, INPI publishes the registration of your trademark in BOPI. Following this publication, INPI sends you a certificate confirming the registration of your trademark. If you've followed along, this process takes a minimum of 6 months, which is quite lengthy. With blockchain, this process would be much faster due to process automation.

INTELLECTUAL PROPERTY AND NFTS: CHALLENGES AND DEBATES

MAJOR BRANDS EMBRACE THEM...

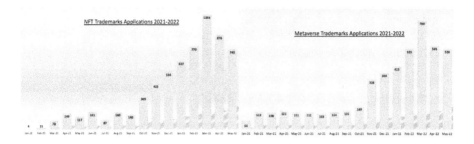

Since Mark Zuckerberg announced on October 28, 2021, the transformation of Facebook into Meta[263], more and more major brands have started taking the metaverse and NFTs seriously. Trademark filings related to NFTs significantly increased from November 2021, reaching over 1000 filings in March 2022. At that time, the NFT market was at its peak. Since then, the hype has slightly diminished (as shown in the graph below shared by Mike Kondoudis)[264], but it hasn't discouraged companies from filing their trademarks. In total, 7746 NFT-related trademark applications were filed in 2022, compared to 2154 in 2021 and only 27 in 2020.

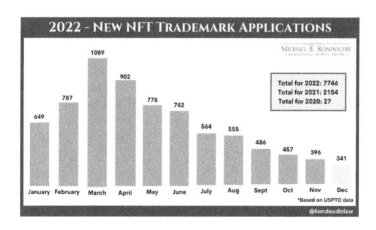

...TO PROTECT THEMSELVES (E.G., THE HERMÈS CASE)

Major brands have already registered their trademarks with WIPO, including names such as LVMH, Ralph Lauren, Playboy, Levi's, Vans, Dolce & Gabbana, Louis Vuitton, Mastercard, and more. And they are right to do so: some brands have had to take legal action against NFT creators who were using their brands inappropriately. For example, there was the case of Hermès versus Mason Rotherschild, the creator of Metabirkin (see the chapter on justice for more details). As the proverb goes, "prevention is better than cure." Hence, other brands have taken preemptive measures, like Nike, which obtained a patent for "CryptoKicks"[265], giving rise to a whole new type of shoe: "phygital" shoes.

FOR INDIVIDUALS: ANTICIPATING NEW TRENDS

NFTs and the metaverse being very recent topics, it's not just major brands seeking to protect their ideas. All it takes is a good idea and protecting that idea by filing a trademark... and anyone can file a trademark, both large companies and individuals. However, the process may differ in countries within the European Union. In the United States, the trademark filing system is based on usage. This means that the first person to use a trademark in a commercial context holds the intellectual property rights to that trademark, even if it hasn't been filed with the *United States Patent and Trademark Office* (USPTO).

CC0 LICENSE: WHY DID THE MOONBIRD COLLECTION CAUSE CONTROVERSY?

A tweet from August 4, 2022[266], sparked discord. Kevin Rose (the collection's creator) announced that Moonbird would enter the public domain by becoming a CC0 public license. Essentially, this meant that people who had purchased Moonbirds (some selling for over 1 million dollars, like Moonbird #2642 sold for 350 ETH[267]) and expected to use them commercially found themselves with JPEG images that could be used and commercialized by anyone without the owner's permission. According to Kevin Rose, this decision aimed to align with a free and shared vision of Web 3.0. However, the community did not necessarily agree, as the collection's floor price dropped from 16 ETH at the time of the announcement to less than 7 ETH at the time of writing[268].

THE MONKEY MAKES A GRIMACE: YUGA LABS AND INTELLECTUAL PROPERTY

JUNE 2022: LAWSUIT AGAINST RYDER RIPPS REGARDING RR/BAYC

Although Yuga Labs' Bored Ape Yacht Club (BAYC) collection is its most iconic, the company has had some troubles regarding the ownership of its images, as indicated by the lawsuit filed in June 2022 against Ryder Ripps. Ripps had launched the NFT collection RR/BAYC (very similar to the original)[269] in which he displayed alleged connections between BAYC and neo-Nazi symbols. Yuga Labs immediately accused him of plagiarism and attempting to profit from the collection's reputation, which Ripps vehemently denied. This case put Yuga Labs in an embarrassing situation since the company claimed that NFT owners would be the only ones with ownership rights over their apes (allowing them, for example, to create a collection of T-shirts, a restaurant chain, or other ventures). Ultimately, Yuga Labs obtained a summary judgment in their favor, resulting in the condemnation of Ryder Ripps[270].

FEBRUARY 2023: YUGA LABS FORCED TO REMOVE THEIR BAKC LOGO

A few months later, Yuga Labs faced new legal problems. The company was compelled to change the logo of their Bored Ape Kennel Club (BAKC) collection because they did not have the rights to the image. The image was taken from a drawing application (Easy Drawing), which was protected by copyright. The drawing had been published in May 2021 and used for BAKC in June 2021, a month later. The case came to light on February 17, 2023, through a tweet by @Jdotcolombo[271]. Confronted with the situation, Yuga Labs had no choice but to abandon the logo. These two cases once again reignite the debate on the intellectual property of NFTs.

WHAT DO WE ACTUALLY OWN WITH NFTs? THE CASE OF RICH BULLS

When considering the question of copyright and ownership, the example of Moonbird and Yuga Labs raises a question about what we truly own when we own an NFT. Remember that an NFT is nothing more than a piece of code stored on a blockchain through a smart contract*. What you truly own is the piece of code, not the image itself. Some collections have even reserved the right to modify the image of the NFT without the owner's consent. After all, everything is specified in the smart contract (which is immutable), so it was a matter of reading it carefully. This is the case with the infamous Rich Bull Clubs NFTs: if you sold your NFT below the floor price*, your image would be directly transformed into a bull with excrement on its head and marked as "Banned"[272].

43. NOTARIES

NFTS, THE GRAND NOTARY OF THE WORLD

THE MODERNIZATION OF NOTARY WITH MICEN IN FRANCE (2008)

In 2008, the French Notarial Profession adopted digital technology to enable the signing of the first authentic electronic deed. The MICEN (Central Electronic Register of Notarial Deeds in France) was created to secure all Electronic Authentic Deeds (EADs) recorded by notaries. Since its launch, EADs have become widespread, with over 90% of authentic deeds being signed electronically, resulting in the deposition of more than 20 million EADs since 2008[273].

Note: In law, "minute" refers to the original version of a written decision or notarial deed. This is why the term "Minutier" is used for the MICEN (Central Electronic Register of Notarial Deeds in France).

ADVANTAGES OF A DECENTRALIZED NETWORK

Although notarial services have embraced digital advancements like MICEN, there are occasional issues of slowness and system failures, which can be inconvenient. For example, some notaries have found themselves stuck with their clients for 30 minutes in front of a frozen screen due to network issues. While such situations are rare, it remains problematic when signed deeds cannot be deposited due to a centralized server receiving excessive demands. By using NFTs as Electronic Authentic Deeds, this issue would be eliminated as blockchain networks are decentralized enough to avoid such *Single Points of Failure**.

IMPOSSIBLE TO FALSIFY THE CONTRACT RETROACTIVELY

Notarized contracts are legal agreements signed in the presence of a notary. However, even with a notary present, it is still possible for malicious parties to falsify a contract afterward. This can be done by modifying the terms of the contract, signatures, or other essential elements of the document. By utilizing NFTs, each notarized contract can be recorded on the blockchain, creating an irrefutable proof that the document was indeed signed by both parties. The document itself cannot be modified once the NFT is created. Such NFT-based contracts could be used for lease agreements to ensure that neither the landlord nor the tenant can falsify the contract retroactively.

REDUCING PAPERWORK FOR NOTARIZED DEEDS

Despite the digitization efforts in the notarial field, a significant portion of deed copies still exist in paper format. Unfortunately, these paper copies can easily get lost, destroyed (accidentally or intentionally), or even forged. Moreover, locating paper copies takes significantly more time compared to retrieving digital copies through a well-organized archival system. While current digital means can be utilized to store these copies in a digital format, human errors can still occur. To avoid these problems, the use of NFTs is essential to ensure the integrity and availability of deed copies while generating less unnecessary paperwork for administrative purposes. The integrity of deed copies can be automatically verified without the need for human intervention.

THE CASE OF DYNAMIC NFTs

Dynamic NFTs (dNFTs*) have gained popularity since 2023 as they solve a problem associated with current NFTs: their immutability*. This use of dynamic NFTs could be particularly useful for notarized deeds. Let's consider a scenario where someone wants to purchase a house and verify information about it through the blockchain. If you are the owner and have made renovations to the house, you would have an interest in disclosing that information. With dNFTs, you can do just that. For example, if a garage has been added to your house, you could directly include it in the characteristics of your dNFT, along with proof of the renovations. It would work as follows[274]:

2022	2037
House dNFT Metadata	**House dNFT Metadata**
ADDRESS	ADDRESS
1001 Blockchain Rd.	1001 Blockchain Rd.
MAINTENANCE HISTORY	MAINTENANCE HISTORY
None	2027 / New Door
	2029 / New Roof
AGE	AGE
1 Year	16 Years
PAST SALES	PAST SALES
2021 / $400,000	2021 / $400,000
	2025 / $450,000
	2027 / $500,000

ACCESSING CONFIDENTIAL DATA WITHOUT A NOTARY

By utilizing blockchain technology, we could potentially eliminate the need for physical presence of a notary to authenticate real estate transactions. Verifications would be automated and reliable, thanks to the use of proven mathematical protocols (unlike notaries who, being human, can be subjected to pressures or corruption). The transparency of the blockchain would allow anyone to access the sales history of a property and its successive owners, offering complete traceability of transactions and mitigating disputes and fraud. The transfer of property ownership from one person to another would be immediate and irreversible, simply by linking the contract to the individual's wallet address.

NFT TRANSFER IN THE CONTEXT OF A WILL

How can the transfer of NFT ownership to heirs be managed in the event of the owner's death? The difficulty lies in the fact that only the person in possession of the private key can access their NFTs. If this key is lost upon the owner's death, the transfer may become impossible, resulting in the loss of the inheritance. To avoid this, the solution would be to store the codes related to the private key in a highly secure location. Once the person has passed away, the notary could transfer the safe, containing all the NFTs, using the private key. Of course, the notary would not know what is inside the safe; they would only know that there is a safe. Other solutions could also be considered, such as posthumous mandates, involving multiple notaries, code fragmentation, engaging an authorized service provider, or even a dedicated notarial blockchain.

WILL NOTARIES DISAPPEAR ALTOGETHER?

SPOILER ALERT: THE ANSWER IS NO

Those familiar with Betteridge's Law[275] already know the answer: no. No, blockchain technology will not render notaries obsolete or send them back to university. It will not make them disappear, just as Artificial Intelligence will not eliminate web designers or blockchain developers. We will always need specialists to ensure that notarized deeds are properly drafted. However, the use of blockchain will bring about an evolution in their profession. Notaries will become more efficient and cost-effective, leading to higher expectations from clients.

IT IS IMPOSSIBLE FOR AN INDIVIDUAL TO DRAFT THEIR OWN NOTARIZED DEEDS

Individuals will not be able to draft their own notarized deeds. If that were the case, lawsuits would multiply exponentially, and everyone would lose out except for the few lawyers who are not already overwhelmed with work. Many cases would pose problems: What would happen if one of the property owners (e.g., a donor still holding a usufruct) was forgotten in the sale? The forgotten owner could force the parties to go to court. What would happen if the parties did not use valid diagnostics? The sale could be canceled, the price reduced, or damages awarded. Lastly, what would happen if the parties failed to inform the holder of a pre-emptive right? The sale could be annulled, and the parties would eventually end up in court. The list goes on...

A NOTARY IS NOT JUST A DOCUMENT-RECORDING MACHINE

The role of a notary is not merely to authenticate the signing of a deed but also to exercise judgment on the signatory's capacity and verify the legality of the transaction. They must ensure that the parties fully understand the implications of the contract. Notaries primarily have an advisory role, leveraging their legal knowledge to have a broad overview and anticipate potential issues—an aspect that blockchain can never replace. However, gradually, their advice will focus on mastering these new tools available in the blockchain ecosystem.

EXAMPLE

Ternoa enables the creation of time capsules in the form of NFTs. The company recently introduced *Time Guardian*, an application that will allow managing digital assets with NFTs.

44. ONLINE REVIEWS

THE ONLINE REVIEWS MARKET

TRIPADVISOR: NO LESS THAN 270 REVIEWS PER MINUTE..!

We all use them without really paying attention: online reviews. Whether it's buying a new laptop, going to an unfamiliar restaurant, or booking a hotel, we rely on reviews to guide our choices. Big players like Google, Amazon, and Facebook have long understood this, as well as smaller players like TripAdvisor. This website was one of the first to focus on customer comments and reviews. However, it started as a simple search engine (which actually disregarded customer reviews), and today, the site has over 200 million users, references 890,000 hotels, and receives 270 reviews per minute![276]

ONLINE REVIEWS SHOULD NOT BE TAKEN LIGHTLY...

When a company ignores its online reviews, it makes one of the worst mistakes possible. Managing online reputation is a delicate task that can easily go sour if not handled correctly. However, it is possible to recover from a problematic situation by taking appropriate measures and acting proactively. Reviews are valuable tools for assessing a company's performance, identifying areas for improvement, and understanding customer expectations. This helps maintain a positive image while strengthening customer trust.

95% OF CUSTOMERS READ ONLINE REVIEWS BEFORE MAKING A PURCHASE

It's understandable why these players have entered this market, considering that the majority of (potential) customers read reviews before buying or visiting a place. According to a 2017 study by the Spiegel Research Centre, this applies to 95% of consumers![277] Hence, it is crucial for businesses to receive positive ratings and respond to customer comments. Positive reviews can boost sales and a company's reputation, while negative reviews can have the opposite effect.

SOMETIMES, A SINGLE NEGATIVE REVIEW IS ENOUGH...

It is common for us to pay more attention to negative reviews than positive ones. Even if a company has twenty positive reviews, sometimes a single negative review, particularly one that is long and well-argued, can harm its image. According to a study conducted by *Harvard Business Review*[278], a negative review, on average, decreases the likelihood of a purchase by 51% and increases the chances of seeking an alternative product elsewhere by 11%. Just consider the importance we place on Google reviews when choosing a good restaurant, for example: if we see a single long and well-argued negative comment, we tend to not choose that restaurant, even if there are many other positive reviews.

USING NFTS FOR CUSTOMER REVIEWS: 5/5

1. AUTHENTICITY

Problem: Some reviews can be deceptive or fake because they are written by people who haven't actually used the product or service in question. Dishonest competitors can also write fake negative reviews to harm the targeted company. This situation can confuse consumers who rely on reviews to make purchasing decisions.

Solution: NFTs can certify that a review has been written by someone who has purchased the product or used the service. It is possible to verify the person's identity and ensure it is not a fake profile.

2. PROMOTING CONSTRUCTIVE COMMENTS

Problem: Online reviews can be of poor quality, written inadequately or incoherently. The context may be poorly explained, leading to confusion among potential customers, which also harms the selling company.

Solution: Implement a system where consumers are rewarded for providing precise and objective reviews. The more likes a comment receives from other users, the more the author will be rewarded with tokens. These tokens can then be exchanged for dollars or used for vouchers.

3. COMPANY CREDIBILITY

Problem: Companies can be accused of manipulating reviews or being non-transparent about their product or service, which can harm their credibility. If consumers perceive that reviews are biased or that the company does not provide complete information about its products or services, they may lose trust and turn to more reliable companies.

Solution: Using NFTs could bring more transparency and legitimacy to a company. Since everything is transparent on the blockchain, there can be more certainty about the absence of review manipulation (particularly by the company itself), thus reinforcing trust in product or service reviews.

4. DECENTRALIZATION OF COMMENTS

Problem: A centralized system for online reviews has advantages, including ease of management and organization. However, it also presents a risk of a single point of failure, meaning that if the system crashes, all the information will be lost or inaccessible. This can be detrimental to both the platform, businesses, and customers.

Solution: Decentralizing online reviews through the blockchain helps avoid this problem as data is not stored on a single centralized server but rather distributed across an interconnected network of nodes. This distributed architecture ensures greater security and resistance to malicious attacks.

5. EXCLUSIVE RIGHTS FOR TOP REVIEWERS

Problem: The top contributors on online review sites are not always recognized for their engagement, which is problematic since their contribution is often very valuable to other users. These highly active commenters are often experts in their field and can provide detailed and accurate information.

Solution: To incentivize others to become top contributors on the platform, a form of gamification could be implemented with a leaderboard. The most active contributors (provided their comments receive a minimum number of likes from certified accounts) could compete to receive special NFTs.

EXAMPLE

 Lum Network was founded by Sarah-Diane Eck in 2017. It is a decentralized protocol in the Cosmos ecosystem that establishes an authentic trust relationship with their clients.

45. EDUCATION

« I GUESS YOU GUYS ARE NOT READY FOR THAT YET. BUT YOUR KIDS GONNA LOVE IT! »

YOUR CHILDREN PROBABLY ALREADY KNOW MORE ABOUT NFTS THAN YOU

Blockchain, NFT, Bitcoin, metaverse... Most young people under the age of 20 are already familiar with these terms. Many of them spend time on Twitter accounts or Discord servers. They subscribe to YouTube channels like Hasheur, Hardisk, or Micode. They have all heard influencers talk about crypto or NFTs at some point. They are immersed in this culture and will be even more so in the years to come. An increasing number of young people are investing time (and sometimes money) in this field. And this interest in NFTs could be put to good use in schools.

MORE GAMIFICATION IN THE LEARNING PROCESS

We know how much children love games. So why not use this inclination for gaming to encourage students to learn? Innovative teaching methods like the Montessori method[279] have already emerged, but NFTs could add another dimension to the gamification of learning. For example, it is possible to imagine a level-up system for the most active students in their classes. After reaching a certain level, they could be awarded skill acquisition badges certified by the blockchain. They could then showcase their acquired skills to the educational institutions they aim to attend in the future.

GIVING STUDENTS MORE SAY IN SCHOOL OPERATIONS

There is no better way to engage students than involving them in the decision-making process, especially when their involvement is permanent. Students who actively participate in school life could be rewarded with NFTs created specifically for them. For example, class representatives and mediators could receive an NFT symbolizing their important roles in the school community. Similarly, students who excel in their achievements could receive an NFT of appreciation, acknowledging their hard work and success. These NFTs could serve as inspiration for other students aspiring to push their limits and become more engaged in their education.

METAVERSE: RELIVING THE BEST MOMENTS IN HISTORY OR EXPLORING THE WORLD

Imagine being able to relive the storming of the Bastille as if you were there, thanks to the metaverse. You could explore the cobblestone streets of Paris, hear the cries of the crowd, smell the gunpowder, and see the barricades against the royal troops. You could even actively participate in the event, joining the crowd to storm the fortress or hiding in the alleys to evade gunfire. The experiences could be incredible. For example, imagine being able to immerse yourself in the Battle of Waterloo in 1815, alongside Napoleon... Or sailing with Magellan and his crew during their voyage from 1519 to 1522. To relive these historical moments, a platform could be created that is accessible only through a special NFT (known as "token-gating access").

ENSURING THE AUTHENTICITY OF MICRO CERTIFICATIONS

Micro-certifications have become a popular way to validate specific skills acquired in various fields. To ensure their authenticity, integrity, and portability, NFTs appear to be a promising solution. Each micro-certification could be represented by a unique NFT that details the acquired skills. This NFT would be immutably recorded on the blockchain, making falsification impossible. Employers and institutions could then quickly and confidently verify candidates' micro-certifications, strengthening trust and the value of these certifications.

NOT JUST FOR CHILDREN!

SUBMITTING HOMEWORK ON THE BLOCKCHAIN = NO MORE CHEATING!

"My dog ate it last night... But I swear I did it!" Or "It wasn't me who cheated, it was him!" We've all heard these excuses, more or less justifiable. In a school that utilizes blockchain technology, teachers could ask students to submit their assignments as NFTs, minted on the blockchain. This would provide an infallible timestamp (confirming that the assignment was created on a specific day and time, as confirmed by the blockchain). By using dynamic NFTs, teachers could add their corrections directly to students' assignments. This would be a good way to address the issue, although students could still claim internet outages!

SCHOLARSHIPS

NFTs could play a vital role in scholarships, offering benefits for both administrations and students. Administrations could be confident that the documents sent by students are authentic. They could also require students to prove their attendance at each class by scanning a QR code (or NFC chip) presented by the teacher. The student would validate their attendance using the wallet containing their private key and the NFT that certifies their eligibility for the scholarship. For students, they could have formal proof that the administration has granted them the scholarship. Some scholarships could even be accessible only through special NFTs that can be earned through competitions or other means.

ENSURING EXCLUSIVE ACCESS TO ONLINE COURSE PLATFORMS

Online course platforms have multiplied in recent years. Sites like Udemy, Coursera, Udacity, and Skillshare have emerged as interesting alternatives for developing new skills. They offer significant advantages: flexibility (courses are often pre-recorded and can be accessed at any time), convenience (no need to travel, saving time and money), variety (a wide range of courses), and cost-effectiveness (often cheaper due to no tuition fees, travel, accommodation, or dining expenses). In this new education landscape, NFTs could be used to create exclusive content on these platforms (known as "token-gating access").

BENEFITS OF HAVING DIPLOMAS ON THE BLOCKCHAIN

Using NFTs for diplomas could revolutionize how they are issued, stored, and verified. Traditionally, diplomas are issued as paper or electronic documents that can be easily falsified or lost. Utilizing NFTs would create unique and tamper-proof digital certificates stored on the blockchain. Graduates could easily prove their possession and authenticity of these certificates to prospective employers. This would reduce the costs and delays associated with diploma verification, as everything would be automated, transparent, and secure through the blockchain.

EXAMPLE

Token for Good is a mentoring platform dedicated to prestigious schools. Alumni offer mentoring sessions to students and are rewarded with tokens. They can then use these tokens to access various services

46. POLLS AND PETITIONS

NFTS: A TRUSTED SOLUTION FOR POLLS?

RELIABLE AND VERIFIED SOURCES FOR STATISTICS

NFTs offer the undeniable advantage of being transparent and fully traceable, which opens up interesting opportunities for polling institutions. These features can enhance trust and transparency in their surveys. With NFTs, participants will have the ability to verify the correct recording of their response on the blockchain. They can be certain that they are participating in a public, transparent, and traceable poll. They only need to have the contract address on which the vote was cast and verify with their wallet address if their vote has been properly recorded. They can also see in real-time how many people have voted.

THE PROBLEM OF PARTICIPATION INCENTIVES

It is possible for some polling institutions to incentivize respondents to participate by offering token rewards in exchange for their participation. For example, a company could use NFTs to offer rewards to individuals who participate in a survey about their products. These rewards could include discounts on future purchases, free products, or reward tokens that can be exchanged for goods or services. However, this use of NFTs could introduce cognitive biases among participants, as they might be motivated to respond in a biased manner or provide false answers simply to obtain the reward.

SURVEYS ENGRAVED IN DIGITAL MARBLE

DECENTRALIZATION AND STORAGE OF RESPONSES

When it comes to storing survey responses, decentralization is a major asset as it helps avoid issues of data reliability and accuracy. When data is stored in a centralized manner, it becomes vulnerable to human errors, manipulation, and malicious attacks. On the other hand, when data is stored in a decentralized manner across multiple network nodes, each node needs to validate the data to ensure its accuracy. The decentralization of the blockchain also ensures transparency and security of the collected data. Each network node has a copy of all the stored data, making the survey data more reliable.

MAKING SURVEYS UNCENSORABLE

Surveys can be censored for various reasons, including political, social, or economic motivations. Individuals or organizations that control the media or dissemination channels can delete or manipulate survey results to serve their interests or influence public opinion. Since voting results are typically managed on a single database, it can be easier for a lobbying group to pressure for survey censorship. However, since the blockchain is decentralized, it becomes much more difficult to censor or exert pressure on the content of a survey.

ANONYMOUS PARTICIPATION THROUGH ZERO KNOWLEDGE PROOF

Anonymity is crucial for credible surveys as it allows respondents to provide their honest opinions without fear of retaliation or judgment. If responses are associated with respondents' names or personal information, they may fear that their opinions could be used against them or that they might face criticism for their views. The blockchain helps preserve this anonymity while maintaining voting transparency. This is made possible, in part, through Zero Knowledge Proof (ZKP). By using NFTs to store each response, it would be possible to separate responses from respondents' personal information.

THE USE OF NFTS FOR ONLINE PETITIONS

USING NFTS FOR ONLINE PETITIONS

Who hasn't signed an online petition against an injustice or in support of a citizen initiative? In 2020, 47% of individuals aged 18-30 signed a petition or advocated for a cause on the internet or social media[280]. Online petitions have become a fast and effective way to mobilize citizens around a cause, gather support, and make their voices heard by decision-makers. Several dedicated websites for online petitions have emerged in recent years, such as change.org and avaaz.org, and have gathered millions of signatures for various causes ranging from environmental protection to the defense of human rights and social justice.

CLEARLY IDENTIFYING THE PETITION AUTHOR AND SOURCES

Online petitions are a simple and free service, but exercising critical thinking, especially regarding authenticity, is important. To assess the authenticity of a petition, the first step is to identify its author, which can sometimes be challenging given the widespread use of pseudonyms on the internet. With NFTs, the petition author could provide assurance, through the transparency of the blockchain, that they are indeed the author. The same applies to the sources used in the petition content: NFTs would enable verification of their origin and ensure they come from reliable and verified sources.

ARTIFICIALLY INFLATING THE NUMBER OF SIGNATORIES

It is not uncommon for a petition to quickly gather thousands of signatures, sometimes even upon launch. This mass of petitioners can give the appearance of legitimacy, but caution is advised. It is easy to artificially increase the number of signatories. In France, a test conducted in March 2016 on the petition demanding the withdrawal of the El Khomri law on change.org clearly demonstrated this. Journalists had used fake email addresses and borrowed names (Léon Blum, Jean Jaurès, etc.) to sign the petition. After revealing the subterfuge to the platform, the fake signatories were removed, but the proof had already been provided. The use of NFTs could partially solve this problem by verifying the identity of each signatory and authenticating each signature.

IT'S FREE? THEN, YOU ARE THE PRODUCT!

As you may know, signing an online petition is free... well, not really. As the famous saying goes, "When something is free, you are the product." When you sign an online petition, you automatically accept their terms of use, in accordance with the General Data Protection Regulation (GDPR), which requires consent for commercial use of data. However, we often tend to accept these terms without much thought. Platforms usually have no trouble obtaining our consent, whether or not it is fully informed.

ONLINE PETITIONS: DATA COLLECTION AND MONEY

When you wish to participate in a petition, you have to agree to share your data. The platforms collecting this data are private companies, with Change.org being the most prominent. These platforms face a dilemma: either they strictly adhere to their civic mission, even if it means being unprofitable and forgoing growth, or they turn it into a business by monetizing their services and the collected data. The use of blockchain technology could offer a third path for these platforms, a hybrid approach that reconciles civic mission and economic development.

47. GAMBLING

THE ONLINE GAMBLING MARKET

THE ONLINE GAMBLING MARKET: A LOOK BACK

The history of online gambling began in 1994 with the development of downloadable gambling software by Microgaming, which could be accessed via a CD-ROM. Then, in 1996, the introduction of JavaScript revolutionized virtual gaming by allowing instant online play without the need to download any software. This advancement enabled Microgaming to launch the first virtual slot machine jackpot in 1998. The introduction of JavaScript also facilitated the development of mobile applications, allowing players to directly play on their smartphones. This advancement contributed to the growth of online casinos in many countries.

A MARKET PROJECTED TO BE WORTH $150 BILLION BY 2030

The online gambling market was valued at approximately $61 billion in 2021[281]. According to estimates, this figure could reach over $110 billion by 2028[282], representing a multiple of at least 2.5 in 7 years and an annual growth rate of 12%. Easy access to the internet and smartphones has contributed to this growth. The COVID-19 pandemic may have also played a role in the expansion of this market. With physical casinos closed, the only option for gambling was to do it online, which led to the digitalization of the gambling industry.

ONLINE GAMBLING AND SCAMS: A BRIEF OVERVIEW

In the world of online casinos, there are three common types of scams:
- **Rigged games**: These games are designed to give the illusion of easy and quick wins, but they end up draining players of their money. They leave players with no chance of recovering their initial bets.
- **Deposit theft**: This scam involves enticing players to deposit money into their online casino accounts and then denying them the withdrawal of their winnings. This method is often associated with casinos that have not obtained the necessary licenses to operate legally.
- **Identity theft**: Scammers using this method attempt to impersonate others or sell personal information to malicious third parties.

GAMBLING GAMES AND NFTs: NOT A RANDOM CONNECTION

The line between the blockchain world and gambling games is sometimes blurred. It is not surprising to find many players showing a keen interest in blockchain technology and cryptocurrencies in general. Some early adopters of Bitcoin were avid casino and gambling players. This can be explained by the fact that certain gambling platforms accepted cryptocurrencies early on. The next step will be the adoption of NFTs. Some casinos have already started launching their own collections, such as the Partouche Group with their Joker collection[283].

THE POTENTIAL OF NFTS: PLACE YOUR BETS!

AUTHENTICATING UNDERAGE INDIVIDUALS

In many countries, it is illegal for minors to participate in online gambling. Websites offering gambling services must ensure compliance by verifying the age of players. As gambling can be addictive and cause financial problems, non-compliant sites face legal action, which can result in financial penalties and loss of credibility. Platforms implement age verification measures, but they are often insufficient, leading to criticism regarding player protection. This is where the use of NFTs could represent a significant advancement, as they offer a more secure (and anonymous) means of verifying a player's age.

100% PUBLIC AND TRANSPARENT RULES OF THE GAME

One of the biggest concerns for those engaging in online gambling is whether they can trust the platforms. Do they offer players a fair chance to win? Are the rules of the game followed 100%? It would be easy for these platforms to cheat since they have control over the results and mechanisms. However, with blockchain technology, everything is transparent and immutable. Once the rules of the game are written on a smart contract, they cannot be changed, and everyone can see these rules. This brings more transparency to an.

EXCLUSIVE RIGHTS FOR NFT HOLDERS

In the context of casinos, NFTs can be used to offer exclusive rights to privileged players. For example, an online casino can use NFTs to represent VIP seats or exclusive gaming experiences that players can purchase with real money or cryptocurrency. Players who own these NFTs then have the right to participate in these exclusive gaming experiences or receive special treatment in the casino. NFTs could also grant the right to participate in competitions reserved for owners of the same type of NFT or receive discounts on drinks sold by the casino, hotel rooms, and more.

CASINOS IN THE METAVERSE

The metaverse represents a revolution in the casino world in many ways. Firstly, the metaverse offers an immersive and interactive gaming experience, pushing the boundaries of physical environments. Players can explore detailed virtual worlds and interact with other players in real-time, as if they were there. Secondly, NFTs allow players to own unique and authentic virtual assets. This gives real value and rarity to these digital assets, allowing players to collect, trade, and sell them directly in the casino metaverse.

CUSTOMER RETENTION THROUGH NFT STAKING AND LOOTBOXES

It is always more beneficial for a business to retain existing customers than to acquire new ones. In this case, casinos could implement an NFT staking service to attract and, more importantly, retain customers. Staking involves putting cryptocurrency or NFTs at stake, which are locked for a certain period in exchange for rewards. This method helps secure the network and maintain a stronger treasury. These rewards could be issued in the form of lootboxes, which may hide a big prize! Casino customers would have the choice to open them directly or sell them on the secondary market.

WHAT BET ON THE FUTURE?

A GAME OF DECEPTION WITH MANY SCAMS

Like any new technology, NFTs are unfortunately subject to numerous scams, including in the online casino world. On October 20, 2022, a press release from Texan authorities condemned the Slotie project for fraud[284]. The project aimed to "fund" a casino in the metaverse with a collection of 10,000 NFTs, which would have provided passive returns on the casino's profits. Although the collection design was well-crafted, it turned out to be a scam, and there were numerous red flags: no way to verify who was really behind the project, many fake followers, no partners despite an existing tab, and more. The list goes on. Their Twitter account had been inactive since October 31, 2022[285], 10 days after the accusation. This game of deception did not escape US regulators, who also condemned other casinos for attempted fraud with NFTs, such as *Flamingo Casino Club*[286] and *Sand Vegas Casino Club*[287].

LEGAL DEFINITION OF GAMBLING (IN A FRENCH PERSPECTIVE)

Games of chance and gambling are defined in Article L. 320-1 of the French Internal Security Code as "*any operation offered to the public, under any name whatsoever, to create an expectation of a gain that would be due, even partially, to chance and for which a financial sacrifice is required from the participants.*" Thus, a game is classified as gambling as soon as it imposes a financial sacrifice on participants that creates an expectation of gain. The question is whether NFTs fall into this category. This question recently arose for Sorare, which was accused of offering disguised sports betting[288]. This question has not yet been publicly settled by French courts and the French National Gaming Authority (ANJ), which is why the principle of prohibition applies[289].

EXAMPLES

 Lucky Block is an application based on the BSC (Binance Smart Chain). It offers games, slot machines, and a live casino.

Yes or No (YoN) stands out for its extremely simplified interface (only two possible responses: YES or NO). All possible and imaginable subjects can be the subject of a bet.

48. SOULBOUND TOKENS

WHAT ARE SOULBOUND TOKENS (SBT)?

A VERY RECENT CONCEPT BY VITALIK BUTERIN (2022)

Vitalik Buterin, the founder of Ethereum, mentioned a mysterious project called Soulbound on his blog in January 2022[290]. He explained that the term "Soulbound" originated from the game World of Warcraft, where Soulbound items are the most powerful in the game. Vitalik pondered the idea of making NFTs non-transferable. Four months later, on May 11, 2022, he published a 37-page document[291] in collaboration with E. Glen Weyl and Puja Ohlhaver to explain what SBTs are.

SOULBOUND TOKENS: DEFINITION AND EXAMPLES

Unlike transferable NFTs, Soulbound Tokens (SBT) are non-transferable. They can be considered as non-transferable NFTs. SBTs are linked to the "soul" of a person or entity and represent their characteristics or achievements. This can include medical records, official documents (passports, driver's licenses, etc.), and any type of information about a person or entity. SBTs are issued by a competent authority, but they can also be revoked at any time (for example, if you lose all the points on your driver's license). They essentially represent your "digital reputation."

NON-SPECULATIVE FORMS OF NFTS

SBTs aim to transform the concept of NFTs into something beyond money. Since SBTs are tied to a person's characteristics and cannot be traded, it is impossible to speculate on them. They are simply designed to serve as a measure of trust and social value, reflecting a person's reputation and contributions in a particular domain.

POSSIBLE USE CASES OF SBTS

FOR DIPLOMAS

Unlike NFTs, SBTs are designed to be "soulbound" to their owner. This characteristic can be useful in the case of diplomas. Imagine that when a student obtains a diploma, they also receive an SBT that is stored on the blockchain and accessible from their wallet. This means that each SBT is unique and associated with a specific individual, making it an ideal way to represent ownership and validity of diplomas. This innovation in diploma management offers numerous advantages, including reducing fraud and forgery, facilitating qualification verification, and enhancing portability.

FOR HEALTH RECORDS

Health records in the form of SBTs could greatly simplify the lives of doctors and patients. When a patient changes doctors or healthcare providers, an SBT containing their complete medical records could significantly streamline the process. Instead of manually filling out customary forms and contacting different medical institutions to transfer medical records, the patient could simply share their SBT with the new healthcare provider. Through this SBT, the doctor would have instant access to the patient's entire medical history, including diagnoses, test results, past treatments, and allergies. This facilitated access to patient information could be invaluable in emergency situations and could save lives each year.

GAMIFICATION

Gamification has become a proven method to encourage engagement and participation among users. By incorporating game elements such as rewards, challenges, levels, and goals to achieve, gamification can motivate users to actively involve themselves in a task. The rewards offered to users could be provided in the form of SBTs. For example, imagine SBT badges on *Call of Duty* that certify your position as one of the top 50 players in the world or being recognized as the best player of the year 2023 based on a community vote. In the future, a professional esports player could have their entire career documented in their wallet in SBT format, including victories and championships they participated in.

ELECTORAL CARDS

In the near future, it is possible that, like in Estonia, a digital card may allow online voting. Instead of storing the data in centralized systems, this digitization of voting could leverage SBTs to provide a complete and indisputable proof of each individual's participation. Election results could be recorded in a more secure and efficient manner through the use of SBTs, reducing the risks of electoral fraud and ensuring transparency and integrity in the electoral process. This would reassure voters about the possibility of voting from home without having to go to a polling station.

FOR ARTISTS

SBTs also offer interesting advantages for artists. They can provide a new way to protect and value their work. Identity theft is a major concern for artists today. With the proliferation of online platforms, it becomes easier for malicious individuals to impersonate an artist and distribute their work without permission. By using SBTs, artists could protect their digital identity, and by extension, their digital artworks.

FOCUS ON SPECIFIC SOULBOUND TOKENS: POAP

POAP* (Proof of Attendance Protocol) is one of the most widely used variants of SBTs currently. POAPs function by assigning a unique token to each person attending an event, providing tangible and verifiable proof of their presence at a specific event, whether it's a conference, concert, festival, or any other gathering. They can be used as mementos, allowing participants to keep a tangible record of the event. POAPs offer sentimental and symbolic value to participants, enabling them to relive their memories by referring to their POAPs. Organizers can also leverage POAPs to track and analyze event attendance, helping them improve future events.

SOME ASPECTS REQUIRING PARTICULAR ATTENTION

THE COMMUNITY RECOVERY SYSTEM SOLUTION (ERC-4337)

After explaining what SBTs are and how they can be used, you may have wondered: what happens if someone loses the wallet where all their SBTs are stored? Is it impossible to recover them? This concern is legitimate, and you're right to ask that question. That's why ERC-4337[292] was created in March 2023. It will enable a community recovery system. In practical terms, this means that a 12 or 24-word speed phrase will no longer be necessarily required to regain access to one's private key.

CONFIDENTIALITY OF SBTs

Data confidentiality is a central concern regarding SBTs. As everything is public on the blockchain, how can the confidentiality of data stored in SBTs be preserved? Finding a solution to program access to SBTs is one of the current challenges. For instance, regarding passports or medical records, individuals holding SBTs should be able to choose which information to show to relevant authorities. Techniques such as Zero-Knowledge Proofs (ZKPs) are being explored to prove information without revealing it. For example, it would be possible to prove possession of a specific SBT among a group of other SBT holders without disclosing the associated wallet.

AN EPISODE STRAIGHT OUT OF BLACK MIRROR?

You may have already watched the episode "Nosedive" from the TV series _Black Mirror_ (Season 3, Episode 1). In that episode, the story follows characters living in a society based on a rating system. Each individual is assigned a rating from 0 to 5, evaluated by other members of society based on their daily interactions. This rating system creates a social pressure where individuals are constantly judged and ranked based on their behavior and relationships. Similar systems are already in place (such as the social credit system in China), and SBTs could potentially be used in such a context. It's still challenging to envision living in such a society.

IMAGINING SBTs IN AN AUTHORITARIAN GOVERNMENT

Vitalik envisions a "Decentralized Society," but it's not without its problems. As the famous saying goes, _"With great power comes great responsibility."_ Therefore, potential abuses must be considered, especially in cases where an authoritarian government has control over the issuance of these SBTs. Excessive centralization of power in SBT issuance could lead to manipulation, abuse, and increased surveillance of the population. This would compromise the principles of freedom and autonomy at the core of Vitalik Buterin's "Decentralized Society" and potentially steer us toward a dystopian society reminiscent of George Orwell's _1984_.

49. AI AND DEEP FAKE

THE IMPACT OF AI ON THE NFT ECOSYSTEM

AI, MACHINE LEARNING, DEEP LEARNING: DEFINITIONS

Artificial Intelligence (AI) is a broad term that refers to any technology that enables machines to simulate human intelligence. It includes two subcategories:

- **Machine Learning**: It is a form of AI that allows machines to adapt and improve by learning from data without being explicitly programmed for a specific task. Machine learning is often used to analyze and predict trends from data, such as product recommendations on e-commerce websites.
- **Deep Learning**: It is a form of machine learning that uses deep neural networks to learn from data. Deep learning is often used to analyze and process complex data, such as images or voice recordings, and is commonly applied in speech recognition, image recognition, and text generation tasks.

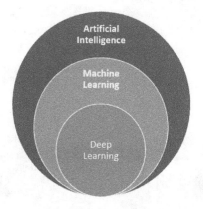

CHATGPT: THE TEXTUAL REVOLUTION

Among various AI tools, ChatGPT is undoubtedly one of the most well-known. Released by OpenAI in November 2022, it gained one million users within just five days[293]. This rapid adoption demonstrates its massive popularity. ChatGPT has paved the way for an unprecedented revolution that both fascinates and raises concerns. It has been prohibited, for example, by institutions or even entire countries like Italy (over privacy concerns)[294].

MIDJOURNEY: THE VISUAL REVOLUTION

Midjourney is the visual counterpart of ChatGPT, providing image-related capabilities. It was developed by David Holz, co-founder of Leap Motion, and its beta version was launched on Discord in July 2022. Midjourney has been trained on billions of images, and its numerous parameters contribute to its advanced functionality. Due to its high usage, the CEO was compelled to end the free trials in March 2023. Midjourney's Discord community now boasts nearly 14 million users[295].

HOW AI COULD BE USED TO CREATE NFTs?

With the growing popularity of NFTs, artists and creators are exploring new ways to generate unique digital assets. AI offers an innovative solution by enabling creators to automate the generation of images, videos, music, and other digital content. For example, developers can leverage ChatGPT to code smart contracts more efficiently, detect errors, or convert code into different programming languages like Python or Rust.

INCORPORATING AI INTO NFTs: A 2022 TREND

Since 2022, a new trend has emerged: incorporating AI directly into NFTs. These NFTs, known as "dynamic" NFTs, evolve based on various parameters and data. One example is Alice, an "iNFT" (intelligent NFT) created by Alethea AI. Alice combines blockchain technology with AI, making the NFT dynamic. It utilizes ChatGPT's technology to produce realistic human-like interactions.

AI AND DEEPFAKES: WHY NFTS WILL BE NECESSARY?

AI AND THE EMERGENCE OF DEEPFAKES: DEFINITION AND HISTORY

In 2014, Ian Goodfellow and his team of researchers introduced the concept of deepfakes with the publication of a paper[296] on Generative Adversarial Networks (GANs). GANs consist of two algorithms that train each other: one tries to generate as realistic counterfeits as possible, while the other tries to detect the fakes. Through this process, both algorithms improve over time through their respective training. As the number of available samples increases, the quality of the generated counterfeits improves.

However, the term "deepfake" first appeared on the internet in the fall of 2017 on Reddit when an anonymous user under the pseudonym "Deepfakes" uploaded adult videos featuring celebrities. These videos quickly spread like wildfire.

THE CHALLENGES OF DEEPFAKES: THE EXAMPLE OF OBAMA

« *President Trump is a total and complete deep shit* » - **Obama, avril 2018.**

Consider what former U.S. President Barack Obama said about Donald Trump in 2018 in a video[297] where he appears calm and composed. Did he really say that? Of course not! It was all fake, as explicitly shown in the video that uses deepfake technology. In the video, the impersonator, after demonstrating the power of deepfakes, emphasizes the following point: "It's time when we need to rely on trusted news sources." These trusted sources will be NFTs, the only means to prove the authenticity of multimedia files such as photos and videos. This video alone highlights the challenges posed by AI and deepfakes: disinformation, defamation, mass manipulation, and more. While deepfakes can be used for legitimate purposes (such as in the film industry[298]), they also raise serious ethical and societal concerns. In the coming years, deepfakes in the form of videos won't even require source videos anymore; they can be created from scratch, making it necessary for us to be even more vigilant...

So, as Obama says, "Stay woke, bitches"!

AUTOMATED SCAMS: THE GATEWAY

AI has opened Pandora's box, for better or worse. Just imagine how devastating a scam could be if someone used ChatGPT to send an automated email associated with a deepfake video during a crypto fundraising event or the release of a long-awaited token. This combination of AI and deepfakes could create a highly convincing illusion, perfectly mimicking the official communication of a company or influential figure. It could mislead potential investors into investing in a scam. The consequences could be catastrophic, not only financially but also for trust in the cryptocurrency and investment domains in general. Malicious individuals are already exploiting AI to carry out scams, such as impersonating loved ones in distress to extort money[299].

CONTENT WILL LOSE VALUE, SO VALUE MUST BE SOUGHT ELSEWHERE

In addition to verifying the authenticity of content, NFTs will be used to attribute value to that content. As the creation of high-quality images and text becomes easier, the intrinsic value of content will inevitably decrease. Therefore, we need to find value elsewhere: in digital scarcity. And what better way to attribute digital scarcity to content than through the use of blockchain and NFTs?

THE ISSUE OF CENTRALIZATION OF AI PROVIDERS

The use of AI raises another problem: data centralization. The past two decades have clearly demonstrated that when we entrust our personal data to a few private entities, we grant them unprecedented power. And we're talking about platforms that were initially just social networks or marketplaces. Now, imagine if an oligopoly of a few companies were to control the provision of AI-related services. They could have access to all the data we give them. The power conferred by AI is too great to be centralized, and some are already realizing this (for example, banning the use of ChatGPT in companies where certain data may be sensitive). To counter this problem, the best solution is to turn to decentralization and data encryption through the blockchain.

NFTs WILL ENABLE SELF-VERIFICATION OF INFORMATION

AI and deepfakes are indeed a real problem, and it's not just Donald Trump who would agree (#fakenews). The only true solution that can be provided is NFTs because they will transparently and securely guarantee the origin of information. In case of doubt, it will be possible to verify the origin of the information on the blockchain. If it cannot be verified, it is most likely a fake. Of course, NFTs will not be the ultimate solution to combat deepfakes. There will always be a human element involved. However, NFTs can add an additional layer of trust and transparency in the verification of information.

IS BLOCKCHAIN REALLY THE SOLUTION? THE WORRISOME WORLD COIN PROJECT BY SAM ALTMAN

Sam Altman, the co-founder of ChatGPT, recently raised $200 million for his project Worldcoin, aimed at solving AI-related problems. According to Altman, given the speed at which AI is progressing, it will soon be impossible to know if you are talking to a real human or not. It will feel like you are having a conversation with someone, but in reality, it will be an AI. Altman wants to use the blockchain to identify "real" humans, utilizing eye retina data stored on the blockchain. Altman's second hypothesis is that in a few decades, AI will have destroyed so many jobs that governments will be forced to implement a universal basic income. The only way to do this would be by using Altman's proposed trio: "World ID," "Worldcoin," and the "World App." Something like WeChat on steroids with Blockchain integration...

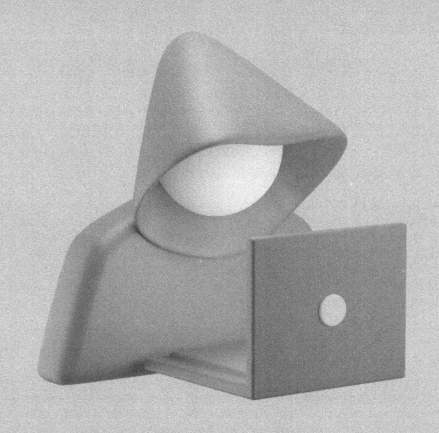

50. SCAMS AND FRAUDS

YES, NFTS CAN ALSO BE USED FOR SCAMS

WHAT IS A SCAM?

The purpose of this chapter is to warn you. Besides the fact that NFTs can be amazing, they can also be subject to numerous scams... But let's start from the beginning. What is a scam? A scam is a fraud, a deception, a swindle, a trickery, a hoax... Call it what you want, you get the idea. Scammers seek to gain your trust in order to extort your hard-earned NFTs from you by any means necessary.

$100 MILLION STOLEN IN NFTs IN 2021-2022

As you know, the NFT market is still very new. This market is not yet fully regulated, and in some aspects, it's still the Wild West. Considering that some NFTs can be worth hundreds of thousands of dollars, it's not surprising to see an increase in scams. According to a report[300] published by *Elliptic* in August 2022, over $100 million in NFTs were stolen between July 2021 and July 2022, earning scammers an average of $300,000 per scam. In July 2022, over 4,600 high-value NFTs were stolen. Tornado Cash was reportedly the preferred "money laundering" tool for 52% of NFTs before being sanctioned by OFAC on August 8, 2022[301].

IN 2021/2022, MANY NFT PROJECTS WERE SCAMS

There have been countless scams that emerged during the 2021/2022 bull run. Just one example among many others: Bored Bunny (a copycat of the Bored Ape Yacht Club). The marketing campaign was well-executed, featuring celebrities like Jake Paul, DJ Khaled, David Dorbik, and Floyd Mayweather. The collection was announced in December 2021 and released in January 2022. With a mint price of 0.4 ETH each, the creators raised 2,000 ETH in a matter of hours (equivalent to $20 million at that time). They took all the funds and disappeared, leaving investors in complete dismay. This example clearly shows that you need to remain extremely vigilant. You can lose everything in just a couple of clicks. Remember: if you're not 100% sure about what you're doing, simply don't do it. One can never be too cautious in this world. Scammers will try every means to deceive you, so don't fall for their tricks. And I know what I'm talking about—I've lost a few feathers myself...

SCAMS: A SAMPLING IN 7 POINTS

1. PUMP AND DUMP

If you're not familiar with English, "Pump" means a sudden rise, and "Dump" means a sudden fall. No, we're not talking about roller coasters... But the excitement is somewhat similar. As you can guess, it involves artificially pumping and dumping the price of an NFT. Usually, it's the whales (large holders) who engage in this kind of fraud. They artificially inflate the price of an asset by injecting a massive amount of liquidity and then suddenly sell off their holdings, causing the market price to plummet. It's common for multiple whales to coordinate their actions.

2. PHISHING

The operation of phishing is quite simple: scammers impersonate an organization or website you're familiar with (such as Ledger) by sending you a message, often via email. Everything is designed to make you believe that it's a legitimate sender (logo, signature, similar email address, etc.). They inform you that there is some issue with your account. Of course, in their great mercy, they are ready to help you. But for that, you need to click on a link or download a file. If you do what they ask, it is possible that you may never recover your funds. And due to the immutability principle* of the Blockchain, it is impossible to reverse transactions, unlike with a bank. Once the funds are sent, they cannot be retrieved.

3. RUG PULL

The objective of a rug pull is to create a project that initially appears credible (even if there is nothing behind it) to attract gullible investors who put money into it. To gain visibility and attract attention, scammers are often willing to spend a lot of money on marketing. Once the project is well underway and enough funds have been invested, the scammers disappear with the money, leaving nothing behind. A well-known example is the case of Evolved Apes (also referencing Bored Ape Yacht Club). This collection of 10,000 NFTs was launched in October 2021. The project promised investors the creation of a blockchain game in which monkeys would battle each other (ah... the games of our time). The NFTs were supposed to finance the game, which was claimed to be in the development phase. However, all of this was false. The developer, known as "Evil Ape," had amassed a whopping 798 ETH (approximately $2.7 million at the time) before disappearing, leaving only a simple JPEG file for those who believed in the project.

4. IDENTITY OR WEBSITE IMPERSONATION

If you're on Twitter or Discord (and I'm sure you are!), you've probably come across dozens of fake profiles that closely resemble influencers you already know. Strangely, they may even contact you themselves (as influencers have nothing else to do, it's well known) and offer to give you NFTs or provide access to airdrops for free. Like magic. And then you realize there's something fishy going on. Upon investigation, you discover that it's obviously a fake profile that promises you wonders in order to pick your pockets. More elaborate techniques include copying websites down to the smallest details.

5. FAKE TECHNICAL SUPPORT

The technique is quite simple: impersonate a member of the NFT project team. Again, the idea is to establish trust between you and the scammer, making you believe that they are indeed a team member. It is legitimate to be in contact with a team member if you have a question about the project. And it's normal for someone to respond, right? Except that it could very well be a malicious person trying to direct you to a third-party website that requests access to your Metamask*. These scams typically take place on Telegram or Discord.

6. COUNTERFEIT NFTs

This involves creating an exact replica of a well-known and highly valued collection, considered a blue chip* (such as Bored Ape, CryptoPunks, etc.), and selling it on an NFT marketplace. The aim of this type of scam is to deceive investors by leading them to believe that they are purchasing the official collection when, in fact, they are buying a worthless copy. It can also involve a scammer claiming that a famous personality has created an NFT collection and selling it without the consent of that person. Some buyers have spent large sums of money only to end up with a simple JPEG image without value.

7. FAKE AIRDROPS

As you probably already know, an airdrop involves distributing an NFT (or crypto) for free to a third party, provided that the recipient meets certain eligibility criteria. Airdrop dates are always announced in advance to create buzz and FOMO*. During these periods of excitement, you need to be particularly vigilant as many fake accounts send you private messages claiming that the airdrop is happening earlier and all you have to do is follow the link they provide. They emphasize that only the first XX individuals will be able to benefit from the airdrop. In the rush, you may inadvertently click on a fraudulent link.

HOW TO PROTECT YOURSELF FROM SCAMS IN THESE CASES?

DYOR (DO YOUR OWN RESEARCH)

DYOR is a term you'll often come across in the world of NFTs. It essentially means that you should do your own research before investing in anything. Remember: never invest in something you don't understand. Investing solely to make money is the best way to lose it. Before investing, check the following points:
- Social media: How many followers on social media (Twitter, Discord, Telegram)? Is the community active? Are there many fake profiles?
- Team: Are the founders doxxed*? What have they done before? Have they successfully completed similar projects?
- Project: Is there a well-defined roadmap? If yes, has it been followed so far? Is there documentation available? What is the relevance and value of the project? Does the project offer something new?

BASIC SECURITY RULES

In addition to DYOR, there is another basic security measure specific to the world of NFTs and blockchain. You should never, under any circumstances, share your seed phrase*. Do not share it with your family, spouse, or even your cat (well, yes, you can share it with your cat!). You must keep your seed phrase in a safe place, disconnected from the internet, where no one else has access except for you. It's also best to divide your seed phrase into 3 parts and alternately distribute the 2/3 parts in at least 3 different locations. This method allows you to reassemble your seed phrase even if you lose the paper hidden in one of your locations.

AVOID FOMO, STAY LEVEL-HEADED

FOMO (Fear Of Missing Out) refers to the fear of missing out on an opportunity, which leads you to enter a market even if it's already in full swing, risking significant losses. These are periods when the price of NFTs keeps rising, and you think it can go even higher... Emotions run high, speculations abound, and the fear of missing out on the continuous price increase becomes almost unbearable. However, it is crucial to exercise caution and assess the situation rationally. Jumping into impulsive investments without evaluating the risks can lead to regrettable consequences.

Remember: Never try to catch a falling knife... You could get hurt, even if it worked once.

EXAMPLES

 Ledger is the undisputed leader in securing digital assets (crypto and NFTs) in France and worldwide. The company was founded in 2014 by several experts in the cryptocurrency and security fields, including the co-founders of La Maison du Bitcoin (2013), Éric Larchevêque and Thomas France.

Bubblemaps is a tool for visualizing the distribution of a cryptocurrency or NFT collection. Each wallet is represented by a bubble, with the size proportional to the wallet's holdings. This tool also allows for visualizing relationships between wallets: if the bubbles are linked, it indicates that there has been a transfer between the wallets.

CLOSING WORDS

Thank you so much for reading this book until the end. You hold in your hands the result of over 8 months of research, writing, and rewriting. I hope it has been useful to you, and that you enjoyed reading it as much as I enjoyed writing it.

Throughout the pages, we have explored 50 use cases of NFTs, whether in ticketing, music, books or tourism.

I firmly believe that this new technology is a true revolution that will profoundly change our relationship with digital ownership.

And as a reader of this book, you are an integral part of this revolution. Your curiosity and open-mindedness have led you to discover NFTs. I encourage you to continue your journey in the world of NFTs.

Take part in this revolution, create, collect, support the artists and creators who embrace this new era.

As for me, I don't plan on stopping here.

This book was only the first step. It's just the beginning of the journey.

I have a much more ambitious project in mind for the future...

And I intend to lead the revolution in the publishing industry myself.

See you soon.

GLOSSARY

BAYC (Bored Ape Yacht Club): It is a collection of 10,000 NFTs, with each NFT representing a different ape with varying degrees of rarity. The collection was created by Yuga Labs in April 2021 and is considered a Blue chip*.

Bear market: This term refers to a "downward market" and is the opposite of the term "Bull run". It is used when the market enters a prolonged period of decline (several months or even years).

Bitcoin: A blockchain created in 2009 by Satoshi Nakamoto (pseudonym). It should not be confused with bitcoin, which refers to the currency.

BIP (Bitcoin Improvement Proposal): Bitcoin allows the community to propose improvements to the protocol (including consensus rules). This system was formalized by Amir Taaki on August 19, 2011, shortly after Satoshi Nakamoto's permanent departure.

Blue chip: Blue chip NFTs have demonstrated price stability over time and are often considered safe investments.

Bull market: This term refers to an "upward market" and is the opposite of the term "Bear market". It is used when the market enters a prolonged period of growth.

CBDC (Central Bank Digital Currency): A **CBDC** is a digital currency issued by a central bank. Unlike cryptocurrencies, CBDCs have legal tender status and must be accepted by merchants.

CEX (Centralized Exchange): These are platforms for buying, selling, and trading digital assets through an intermediary, the exchange website.

Copycat: A person or company that copies the ideas or products of others.

CryptoPunks: CryptoPunks are a collection of 10,000 NFTs representing pixelated punks. The collection was created in 2017 and is now considered a Blue chip*.

Cypherpunk: A portmanteau of the English words "cipher" (encryption) and "punk." The term was coined by Jude Milhon and is a play on words to describe cyberpunks who used cryptography.

DAO (Decentralized Autonomous Organization): A DAO is a decentralized autonomous organization. In a DAO, governance rules are automated and immutably and transparently recorded on a blockchain. The DAO is collectively managed by its members.

DDoS (Distributed Denial of Service): This type of attack involves sending a large number of requests to a computer system in order to overload it and cause it to crash.

DEX (Decentralized Exchange): A DEX refers to a decentralized exchange platform. Created to address the centralization issue of CEX*, a DEX stands out by being fully developed on the blockchain using smart contracts.

DID: An acronym for Decentralized Identifier, referring to a decentralized identity.

Discord: The primary instant messaging software used by NFT projects to communicate with their community.

Doxxed: The term "doxxed" refers to the intentional or accidental revelation of a person's real identity on the Internet.

ERC (Ethereum Request for Comments): ERC is a technical standard used on the Ethereum blockchain to propose new standards, protocols, and improvements.

Ethereum: A blockchain created by Vitalik Buterin in 2014 to address the lack of programmability in Bitcoin. It enables the execution of smart contracts* and the deployment of decentralized applications (dApps).

FOMO (Fear Of Missing Out): Refers to the fear of missing out on something, specifically putting money into an NFT when the price is already high, in the hope of selling it for an even higher price.

Gas fees: Payments that users of a Blockchain network have to make to perform a transaction. The functioning is similar to toll fees on a highway.

Immutability: A characteristic of a computer system that ensures that data cannot be modified once it is recorded.

IPFS (InterPlanetary File System): A distributed file storage system that allows files to be stored and distributed across multiple computers. IPFS is widely used for storing NFT collection metadata.

Lootbox: A box that contains random items, often used in video games to encourage players to pay money to unlock new items.

Meme: An image or video that has become popular on the internet and is often used to express an idea or emotion.

Metamask: Metamask is a browser extension that allows users to easily interact with decentralized applications.

The Merge: Refers to Ethereum's transition from Proof of Work to Proof of Stake.

Metaverse: A digital world at the intersection of Blockchain, social networks, augmented reality (AR), and virtual reality (VR).

Miner: A person who engages in mining to validate transactions on a Proof of Work blockchain through mathematical calculations. Miners secure the blockchain through this process.

Mint: The term "Mint" means to create a new NFT for the first time.

NFT (Non-Fungible Token): An NFT is a digital token that uses the Blockchain to certify the authenticity, ownership, and traceability of a digital asset.

Node: A node in a blockchain is a computer or device that participates in the network by maintaining a complete and verifiable copy of the blockchain. Nodes are responsible for validating transactions, verifying block compliance, and disseminating this information to other nodes in the network.

Oracle: An oracle is a device that provides external data to a smart contract. Oracles are used to connect smart contracts to real-world data sources, such as financial prices, weather data, or sports results.

Liquidity pool: A liquidity pool is a collection of funds deposited by users in a decentralized finance (DeFi) protocol to facilitate the exchange of different digital assets.

POAP (Proof of Attendance Protocol): A protocol used to certify participation or attendance at physical or online events.

Private Blockchain: A ledger that enables the storage and transmission of information securely and in a decentralized manner, but with stricter reading and verification systems than a public blockchain.

Proof of Authority (PoA): This is a consensus mechanism that gives a limited and designated number of actors in a blockchain the power to validate transactions and update its distributed ledger.

Proof of Stake (PoS): A consensus mechanism used in blockchain protocols where block validation is based on the ownership and staking of a certain amount of cryptocurrency.

Proof of Work (PoW): Proof of Work is a consensus algorithm used in blockchain protocols where miners must solve complex mathematical problems to validate transactions and create new blocks.

Reveal: The reveal phase is when the NFTs in a collection take form and differentiate from each other. This is when each unique characteristic of the NFT becomes visible to its holder.

Roadmap: The roadmap is intended for users and investors of a specific project. It lists all the different milestones that the project aims to achieve and the associated dates.

Rug pull: A rug pull refers to a type of scam. It occurs when the creators of a project abruptly sell off their tokens, causing a drastic drop in value and leaving investors with no opportunity to recover their money.

Royalties: In the context of NFTs, royalties are percentages of subsequent sales of an NFT that are paid to the original creator of the digital artwork.

Scalability: Scalability refers to the capacity of a blockchain to adapt to fluctuations in the number of transactions and users using the network at the same time.

Seed phrase: A seed phrase is a series of randomly generated words or phrases created when setting up a wallet. This phrase is used as a means of backup and recovery for the wallet. It typically consists of 12 or 24 words that should be securely stored.

Shitcoin: The term "shitcoin" is often used derogatorily to describe a cryptocurrency considered to be unreliable or lacking technical, economic, or conceptual solidity.

Smart contract: A smart contract is a computer protocol that automatically defines and executes specific conditions of a "contract." It is based on the blockchain, which ensures its transparency, security, and immutability.

Solidity: Solidity is a high-level programming language specifically designed for developing smart contracts on the Ethereum blockchain. This language was created by Vitalik Buterin.

Staking: Staking involves locking or holding a certain amount of cryptocurrency on a platform in order to receive rewards in return.

Tokenomics: Tokenomics refers to the economic and financial principles underlying a particular crypto or token ecosystem. It encompasses the design and implementation of tokens, their distribution, supply, and utility within a blockchain network.

Trilemma of Blockchains: This concept highlights the difficulty of simultaneously achieving three essential characteristics of a blockchain: scalability, security, and decentralization. It is challenging to maximize all three aspects at the same time as they often conflict with each other.

TVL (Total Value Locked): TVL refers to the total value of financial assets (cryptocurrencies, tokens, etc.) locked in a decentralized finance (DeFi) protocol or platform.

Web3: Web3 refers to the next evolution of the Internet that focuses on decentralization, security, privacy, and user autonomy.

Wallet: A wallet is a digital wallet used to store, manage, and secure cryptocurrencies and NFTs.
Whale: A "whale" is a term used to describe an individual or entity that holds a large amount of cryptocurrencies or NFTs.

Whitepaper: A whitepaper is a detailed technical document that presents a project, technology, or proposal in the blockchain domain. It provides in-depth information about the objectives, principles, technical features, architecture, and use cases of a specific project.

ZKP (Zero Knowledge Proof): ZKP is a cryptographic method that allows proving the truth of a statement without revealing the underlying information.

ESSENTIAL TOOLS

Website	Description
Bubblemaps	Visual Explorer of Crypto/NFT Holders: Allows visual exploration of the structure of cryptocurrency or NFT holders.
CoinMarketCap	Reference website to check cryptocurrency prices. Nearly 25,000 cryptocurrencies referenced.
CoinGecko	Alternative to CoinMarketCap.
Defi llama	The ideal tool for *on-chain* analysis.
DEXTools	Numerous interesting tools for advanced users.
Etherscan	The go-to tool for on-chain analysis on Ethereum.
Follower Audit	Allows you to verify fake followers of a Twitter account.
Nansen	One of the references in terms of Blockchain data.
NFT GO	Excellent tool for tracking NFT *whale* movements.
Revoke.cash	Allows you to view and revoke permissions you have granted to smart contracts you have interacted with.
Rarity Tools	Allows you to check the rarity traits of a collection's NFTs.
Remix	Facilitates coding and easy deployment of your first smart contracts.
Token Terminal	Offers a very useful dashboard.
Tx Street	Allows real-time visualization of block fillings on Bitcoin and Ethereum.
Ultrasound Money	Allows you to check the supply of ETH in relation to its burn.

FOOTNOTES

[1] https://www.whatisemerging.com/videos/gavin-wood-on-web3

[2] more details here: https://www.forbes.com/advisor/ca/investing/cryptocurrency/proof-of-work/

[3] https://twitter.com/zemnmez/status/1443821271045845005

[4] https://www.statista.com/statistics/1202503/global-cryptocurrency-user-base/

[5] https://propy.com/browse/propy-nft/

[6] https://coinmarketcap.com/currencies/the-sandbox/

[7] https://www.visualcapitalist.com/cp/visualized-the-rise-and-fall-of-music-sales-by-format/

[8] https://nft.olympiahall.com/

[9] https://dittomusic.com/en/blog/how-much-does-spotify-pay-per-stream/

[10] https://twitter.com/theweeknd/status/1565778353465933824

[11] https://www.jeanmicheljarre.com/live/oxygen-in-moscow

[12] https://www.npr.org/sections/coronavirus-live-updates/2020/04/24/843631981/travis-scotts-fortnite-event-draws-record-audience

[13] https://www.youtube.com/watch?v=wYeFAIVC8qU

[14] https://decentraland.org/blog/announcements/looking-back-at-decentraland-metaverse-music-festival-2022/

[15] https://cryptoast.fr/comment-nfts-web3-stimulent-creativite-industrie-musicale/ (translation)

[16] https://www.youtube.com/watch?v=RjrA-slMoZ4

[17] https://www.nme.com/news/music/muses-will-of-the-people-on-track-to-bag-first-uk-number-one-album-with-nft-technology-3301707

[18] https://www.fortunebusinessinsights.com/supply-chain-management-market-102977

[19] PwC study, 2016

[20] https://en.wikipedia.org/wiki/2013_horse_meat_scandal

[21] https://techland.time.com/2012/03/06/youd-need-76-work-days-to-read-all-your-privacy-policies-each-year/

[22] https://socialimpact.facebook.com/news-and-more/news/the-facebook-company-is-now-meta

[23] https://about.fb.com/news/2022/05/introducing-digital-collectibles-to-showcase-nfts-instagram/

[24] https://nftnow.com/news/breaking-instagram-is-sunsetting-digital-collectibles-nfts/

[25] https://www.coindesk.com/business/2022/04/13/jack-dorseys-first-tweet-nft-went-on-sale-for-48m-it-ended-with-a-top-bid-of-just-280/

[26] https://twitter.com/TwitterBlue/status/1484226494708662273

[27] https://techcrunch.com/2022/10/18/redditors-have-created-millions-of-crypto-wallets-to-buy-nft-avatars/

[28] https://dune.com/dunetester/reddit-avatar-nft-holder-stats

[29] https://capitalcounselor.com/how-much-tiktok-pays-for-1-million-views/

[30] https://www.godaddy.com/

[31] https://domainnamewire.com/2021/12/21/nfts-trip-up-uniregistrys-top-level-domain-auctions/

[32] You can refer to the website almonit.eth, which indexes decentralized websites, for more information on this topic.

[33] https://brave.com/transparency/

[34] https://dune.com/hildobby/ENS-Airdrop

[35] https://opensea.io/collection/ens/activity

[36] on Ulule, for example, publishing is at the top of the rankings: https://fr.ulule.com/stats/

[37] https://goodereader.com/blog/electronic-readers/amazon-has-sold-between-20-million-and-90-million-kindles

[38] https://newsroom.spotify.com/2021-11-11/spotify-to-acquire-leading-audiobook-platform-findaway/

[39] more details about ZKP: https://www.leewayhertz.com/zero-knowledge-proof-and-blockchain/

[40] https://www.entrepreneur.com/growing-a-business/how-gary-vaynerchuk-sold-1-million-books-in-24-hours-and/412931

[41] https://nftevening.com/veefriends-how-gary-vee-made-utility-the-new-thing-with-his-top-nft-collection/

[42] https://www.hachette.fr/actualites/ego-de-maxime-girardeau-des-nft-collectors-offerts-aux-50-premiers-lecteurs

[43] https://www.statista.com/statistics/456500/daily-number-of-e-mails-worldwide/

[44] https://postmarkapp.com/blog/transactional-vs-marketing-email

[45] https://www.radicati.com/?p=16892

[46] https://ividence.com/infographie-2020-les-chiffres-cles-de-lemail/ (french article)

[47] https://www.sciencedirect.com/science/article/abs/pii/S1389128622004418

48 https://www.sciencedirect.com/science/article/abs/pii/S1389128622004418

49 https://www.worldgovernmentsummit.org/press/releases/adopting-digital-health-to-unlock

50 https://www.blockchainpartner.fr/wp-content/uploads/2017/06/Sante-Industrie-Pharmaceutique-Blockchain.pdf

51 https://www.who.int/news/item/28-11-2017-1-in-10-medical-products-in-developing-countries-is-substandard-or-falsified

52 https://www.forbes.com/sites/sap/2019/10/03/counterfeit-drugs-a-bitter-pill-to-swallow/

53 https://www.lequotidiendumedecin.fr/actus-medicales/politique-de-sante/fraude-sociale-lassurance-maladie-flouee-de-200-millions-deuros-en-2014

54 https://journals.plos.org/plosmedicine/article?id=10.1371/journal.pmed.0020124

55 https://www.blockchainpartner.fr/wp-content/uploads/2017/06/Sante-Industrie-Pharmaceutique-Blockchain.pdf

56 https://www.leewayhertz.com/zero-knowledge-proof-and-blockchain/

57 https://digiexpo.e-estonia.com/healthcare/national-electronic-health-record/

58 https://www.persuadersrh.com/blog/considerations-sur-le-big-data-en-sante/ (french article)

59 https://www.cnbc.com/2020/02/19/how-many-job-seekers-lie-on-their-job-application.html

60 https://www.cnbc.com/2020/02/19/how-many-job-seekers-lie-on-their-job-application.html

61 https://thefootballlovers.com/football-questions/what-is-the-stade-de-france-scandal

62 https://cryptopotato.com/france-could-deploy-blockchain-ticketing-for-paris-2024-olympic-games-report/

63 https://www.bbc.com/news/technology-28055678

64 https://www.lefigaro.fr/presidentielle-2012/2012/04/04/01039-20120404ARTFIG00826-organiser-des-elections-coute-1-euro-par-electeur.php (french article)

65 https://harris-interactive.fr/opinion_polls/les-francais-l-abstention-et-le-vote-par-internet/

66 https://www.nasdaq.com/articles/russias-supreme-court-makes-landmark-vote-with-blockchain-system-from-kaspersky-lab-2020

67 https://www.swissinfo.ch/eng/business/crypto-valley-_-switzerland-s-first-municipal-blockchain-vote-hailed-a-success/44230928

68 https://www.ledgerinsights.com/blockchain-voting-voatz-app-us-postal-service-patent/

69 https://coinnounce.com/french-researcher-cracks-moscow-blockchain-voting-system-month-before-elections/

70 more details here: https://medium.com/vechain-foundation/what-does-scalability-really-mean-in-blockchain-b8b13b3181c6

71 https://cryptonews.com/news/the-mysterious-sale-of-cryptokitty-for-eth-600-2568.htm

72 https://www.europeanbusinessreview.com/the-most-expensive-axie-to-be-sold-a-rundown-of-the-highest-selling-crypto-collectibles/

73https://www.outsourceaccelerator.com/articles/how-a-usd-300-monthly-salary-supports-decent-living-standards-in-the-philippines/

74 https://restofworld.org/2021/axie-players-are-facing-taxes/

75 https://nftnow.com/guides/a-guide-to-stepn-the-app-that-lets-you-earn-crypto-while-you-exercise/

76 https://ancient8.gg/research/en/articles/erc-4907-making-web3-nft-marketplace-more-efficient

77 https://www.crosstheages.com/

78 https://www.beyondgames.biz/22051/louis-vuittons-nft-game-amasses-more-than-2-million-downloads/

79 https://www.eurogamer.net/gabe-newell-explains-why-steam-banned-nfts

80 https://www.dexerto.com/gaming/ubisoft-giving-nfts-to-employees-despite-quartz-backlash-1756988/

81 https://www.nintendolife.com/news/2022/02/team17-confirms-an-end-to-its-metaworms-nft-project

82 https://venturebeat.com/games/forte-raises-725m-for-compliant-blockchain-gaming-platform/

83 https://quartz.ubisoft.com/

84 https://legal.ubi.com/ubisoftquartzterms/fr-FR

85 https://www.theverge.com/2021/3/11/22325054/beeple-christies-nft-sale-cost-everydays-69-million

86 https://bigthink.com/high-culture/salvator-mundi-leonardo-da-vinci/

87 https://nonfungible.com/news/analysis/yearly-nft-market-report-2021

88 https://nonfungible.com/news/analysis/yearly-nft-market-report-2021

89 https://iq.wiki/wiki/fewocious

90 https://nftevening.com/eminem-is-confirmed-as-a-new-member-of-the-bored-ape-yacht-club

91 Hash of the transaction: https://etherscan.io/tx/0x0f5e735a0791ef6fd88dc2263904ea941957b400a522cfbf859279710de54b46

92 https://news.bitcoin.com/bored-ape-yacht-clubs-apecoin-dao-airdrops-millions-of-apecoins-to-nft-owners/

93 https://opensea.io/collection/richbullsclub

94 https://mpost.io/a-bored-ape-yacht-club-nft-holder-opens-a-bayc-themed-cafe-in-switzerland/

95 https://www.fauveparis.com/le-marche-de-lart-francais-va-t-il-manquer-la-revolution-nft/

96 https://www.statista.com/statistics/1192960/forecast-global-insurance-market/

97 https://www.coindesk.com/markets/2017/09/13/axa-is-using-ethereums-blockchain-for-a-new-flight-insurance-product/

98 https://reassurez-moi.fr/guide/assurance-auto/fraude (french article)

99 https://thegivingblock.com/annual-report/ (figures may have changed)

100 https://www.indiatoday.in/technology/news/story/vitalik-donates-1-billion-worth-shiba-inu-and-ethereum-to-india-covid-19-relief-fund-1802009-2021-05-13

101 https://blockworks.co/news/assangedao-raises-55m-in-six-days-to-help-liberate-wikileaks-founder

102 wallet address: https://etherscan.io/address/0x165cd37b4c644c2921454429e7f9358d18a45e14

103 https://www.elliptic.co/blog/live-updates-millions-in-crypto-crowdfunded-for-the-ukrainian-military

104 https://coins.fr/ukraine-cede-nft-soutenir-effort-guerre/ (french article)

105 https://variety.com/2021/digital/news/ellen-degeneres-nft-sale-prices-1234961319/

106 https://twitter.com/jack/status/1374071729467707394

107 https://ec.europa.eu/health/ph_threats/human_substance/documents/ebs272d_en.pdf

108 https://www.thebigwhale.io/article/macron-linnovation-et-la-prise-de-risque-font-echo-a-lhistoire-profonde-de-notre-pays

109 https://www.numerama.com/politique/857771-quelles-sont-les-propositions-sur-la-tech-et-le-numerique-danne-hidalgo.html

110 https://twitter.com/zemmoureric/status/1493340013031047169

111 https://coins.fr/jean-noel-barrot-nft-crypto-pas-faire-revolution-technologique-decret/

112 https://www.youtube.com/watch?v=XlnQ801wWf4

113 https://www.artnews.com/art-news/news/beeple-nft-artwork-nifty-gateway-sale-1234584701/

114 https://www.huffpost.com/entry/donald-trump-nft-sold-out_n_639d75c9e4b0a13a9506dd6f

115 https://www.cryptoslam.io/trumpdigitaltradingcards?tab=historical_sales_volume

116 https://www.dailymail.co.uk/news/article-10317173/Melania-puts-NFT-sale-bitcoin-auction-painting-eyes-audio-message.html

117 https://en.bitcoin.it/wiki/BitDNS

118 "Cypherpunks write code," as explicitly stated by Eric Hughes in the *Cypherpunk Manifesto* (https://www.activism.net/cypherpunk/manifesto.html)

119 https://twitter.com/danheld/status/1405243560039956481

120 Asymmetric cryptography is based on mathematics, unlike symmetric cryptography which has existed for much longer, like Enigma during World War II.

121 https://groups.csail.mit.edu/mac/classes/6.805/articles/crypto/cypherpunks/may-crypto-manifesto.html

122 https://www.ladn.eu/blockchain-en/cypherpunks-parrains-bitcoin/

123 https://www.wired.com/insights/2014/04/bitcoin-ultimate-democratic-tool/

124 https://www.coindaily.co/tomorrow-it-will-be-10-years-since-satoshi-created-the-genesis-block/

125 https://bitcoin.org/bitcoin.pdf

126 https://www.wired.com/insights/2014/04/bitcoin-ultimate-democratic-tool/

127 downloadable here: https://thenetworkstate.com/

128 https://www.monde-diplomatique.fr/cartes/PPA

129 https://twitter.com/OliynykovaUA/status/1370777064559771651

130 https://www.highsnobiety.com/p/rtfkt-cryptokicks-irl/

131 https://about.nike.com/en/newsroom/releases/nike-acquires-rtfkt

132 https://www.wsj.com/articles/nfts-and-fashion-collectors-pay-big-money-for-virtual-sneakers-11615829266

133 https://twitter.com/socios/status/1508776236193140738

134 https://twitter.com/binance/status/1539969367726620674

135 https://sports.yahoo.com/nba-top-shot-wild-1-095529854.html

136 https://www.si.com/nba/pacers/news/lebron-james-nba-top-shot-sells-for-over-387000

137 https://nft.ballondor.com/

138 https://coinmarketcap.com/currencies/paris-saint-germain-fan-token/

139 https://finance.yahoo.com/news/fc-barcelona-cancels-marketing-agreement-025100607.html

140 https://www.coinalist.io/manchester-city-suspend-accord-3key-technologies/

141 https://sorareintelligence.substack.com/p/distribution-of-wealth-in-sorare?

142 https://www.researchandmarkets.com/reports/5742936/precious-metals-market-gl

[143] https://or.fr/cours/or#historical-chart

[144] See on this subject the excellent animated graphic created by James Eagle: https://www.youtube.com/watch?v=-lrprsWauPk

[145] https://www.insee.fr/fr/statistiques/5354766?sommaire=5354786

[146] https://www.euronews.com/next/2022/12/02/the-eu-threw-a-gala-launch-party-for-its-387000-metaverse-and-just-6-people-showed-up

[147] https://www.lemonde.fr/police-justice/article/2017/04/19/affaire-thevenoud-la-phobie-administrative-de-l-ex-secretaire-d-etat-devant-la-justice_5113291_1653578.html

[148] https://petapixel.com/2022/03/03/this-is-the-most-expensive-photography-nft-ever-sold/

[149] https://www.republicworld.com/technology-news/social-media-news/disaster-girl-cashes-in-on-nft-of-her-meme-for-whopping-rs-3-dot-20-crore.html

[150] https://en.wikipedia.org/wiki/2022%E2%80%932023_Pentagon_document_leaks

[151] See the chapter on justice.

[152] https://www.wordstream.com/blog/ws/2017/04/20/instagram-statistics

[153] https://www.youtube.com/watch?v=RjrA-slMoZ4

[154] https://www.cnet.com/personal-finance/bored-ape-yacht-club-is-getting-its-own-film-trilogy/

[155] https://coinmarketcap.com/nft/collections/

[156] https://www.storiesout.com/porntech-chapitre-1-chiffres-cles-et-premieres-innovations-technologiques-a-servir-lindustrie-du-x/

[157] https://www.webroot.com/us/en/resources/tips-articles/internet-pornography-by-the-numbers

[158] https://fr.beincrypto.com/marches/28742/lancement-rareporn-pkn-marketplace-nft/ (french article)

[159] https://www.ladn.eu/nouveaux-usages/nft-industrie-porno/

[160] https://www.instagram.com/cryptosisnft/

[161] https://www.youtube.com/watch?v=ljtPe1h4Ca0

[162] https://www.leoo.fr/fr/actualites/de-la-fidelisation-transactionnelle-la-fidelisation-experientielle (french article)

[163] https://olympus-assets.com/coca-cola-nft-collection-celebrates-friendship-day/

[164] https://www.republicworld.com/technology-news/other-tech-news/spider-man-no-way-home-amc-theatres-sony-to-offer-86000-nfts-to-early-ticket-buyers.html

[165] https://www.cnet.com/personal-finance/bored-ape-yacht-club-is-getting-its-own-film-trilogy/

[166] https://www.kinodao.com/Whitepaper.html

[167] https://nftevening.com/stoner-cats-nft-raises-8-million-in-35-minutes-sending-gas-fees-to-600-gwei/

[168] https://www.youtube.com/watch?v=v-a7d2xqF3s

[169] https://deadline.com/2022/10/warner-bros-discovery-the-lord-of-the-rings-the-fellowship-of-the-ring-nfts-1235150456/

[170] https://hypebeast.com/2022/7/netflix-stranger-things-nft-candy-digital

[171] https://www.mediaplaynews.com/new-nfts-of-anthony-hopkins-feature-zero-contact-available/

[172] https://hypebeast.com/2022/1/quentin-tarantino-pulp-fiction-nft-sold-1-1-million-usd-miramax-lawsuit-scrt-labs

[173] https://variety.com/2022/film/news/quentin-tarantino-miramax-pulp-fiction-nft-settlement-1235365550/

[174] https://www.mediapart.fr/journal/france/230423/nounours-et-cryptomonnaies-dubai-le-mauvais-film-de-kev-adams

[175] https://www.youtube.com/watch?v=HPP4r72JLQs&t=451s (french video)

[176] https://www.legifrance.gouv.fr/codes/article_lc/LEGIARTI000006278911

[177] https://twitter.com/Giambroneintern/status/1546878457136783366

[178] https://www.lemonde.fr/m-le-mag/article/2022/01/04/la-crypto-contrefacon-crispe-le-monde-de-l-art_6108105_4500055.html

[179] https://fashionunited.fr/actualite/business/metabirkins-l-artiste-rothschild-demande-le-reexamen-de-l-affaire-qui-l-oppose-a-hermes/2023032031673 (french article)

[180] https://www.europarl.europa.eu/news/en/headlines/society/20190313STO31218/co2-emissions-from-cars-facts-and-figures-infographics

[181] https://www.consilium.europa.eu/fr/policies/green-deal/

[182] https://en.wikipedia.org/wiki/Volkswagen_emissions_scandal

[183] https://www.bbc.com/news/technology-33650491

[184] https://twitter.com/eth_porsche/status/1617942323563991040

[185] https://www.redpoints.com/blog/fashion-counterfeit-impact/

[186] https://dune.com/kingjames23/nft-project-possible-data-to-use

[187] https://about.nike.com/en/newsroom/releases/nike-acquires-rtfkt

[188] https://www.designboom.com/design/nike-rtfkt-sneaker-nft-real-life-cryptokicks-irl-12-06-2022/

293

189 https://www.millenium.org/news/382365.html

190 https://www.blogdumoderateur.com/chiffres-cles-gaming-france-monde-2022/

191 https://www.ledgerinsights.com/gartners-hype-cycle-metaverse-10-year/

192 https://www.montres-de-luxe.com/attachment/2369586

193 https://www.fhs.swiss/fre/stopthefakes.html

194 https://corsearch.com/content-library/blog/counterfeiting-in-the-watch-industry-the-rise-of-the-superfakes-luxury-daily/

195 https://www.hublot.com/fr-fr/news/hublot-launches-two-nfts-takashi-murakami

196 https://hypebeast.com/2021/4/jacob-co-nft-sf24-tourbillon-watch-release

197 https://gothammag.com/jacob-and-co-sells-nft-watch

198 https://www.cointribune.com/jacob-and-co-montre-astronomia-solar-bitcoin/

199 https://jacobandco.com/nft

200 https://www.retaildive.com/news/tag-heuer-accepts-crypto-payment/624211/

201 https://retailinasia.com/in-sectors/tag-heuer-calibre-e4-smartwatch-nft-display/

202 https://opensea.io/collection/genwatch

203 https://opensea.io/assets/ethereum/0xc323f3b39ab0779fc6300cad7d7e3f47c1b86c27/148

204 https://opensea.io/assets/ethereum/0xc323f3b39ab0779fc6300cad7d7e3f47c1b86c27/58

205 https://www.lvmh.com/news-documents/news/bulgari-unveils-octo-finissimo-ultra-the-worlds-thinnest-watch-celebrating-the-10th-anniversary-of-the-octo-collection/

206 https://tsdr.uspto.gov/#caseNumber=97655284&caseType=SERIAL_NO&searchType=statusSearch

207 https://twitter.com/KondoudisLaw/status/1589591456251273217

208 https://www.worldbank.org/en/news/press-release/2017/10/12/11-billion-invisible-people-without-id-are-priority-for-new-high-level-advisory-council-on-identification-for-development

209 https://cryptoast.fr/zero-knowledge-proofs-zkp-principe-applications/ (french article)

210 https://www.wired.co.uk/article/digital-estonia

211 https://cointelegraph.com/news/estonian-e-residency-and-bitnation-launch-new-public-notary-in-blockchain-jurisdiction

212 https://www.silicon.fr/faille-e-carte-identite-moitie-estoniens-prives-services-numeriques-189365.html

213 https://twitter.com/koeppelmann/status/1570436882483523585. For updated figures, see: https://defillama.com/chain/Ethereum?tvl=true

214 https://www.terredevins.com/actualites/les-cotes-de-provence-se-protegent-en-chine (french article)

215 Examples here: https://opensea.io/collection/winebottleclub

216 https://bitcoinmagazine.com/technical/bootstrapping-a-decentralized-autonomous-corporation-part-i-1379644274

217 https://journalducoin.com/defi/gouvernance-blockchains-vitalik-buterin-dan-larimer/

218 https://www.youtube.com/watch?v=E91l7qsg614 (french video)

219 Downloadable here: https://thenetworkstate.com/

220 https://cryptoast.fr/salvador-adopte-officiellement-bitcoin-btc-monnaie-legale/

221 https://ipfs.io/ipfs/QmRanZDLabLRvzrFZgNuS4noRekLKt1V2FWLhkaKJauysx

222 https://desci.world/

223 https://www.desci.berlin/

224 https://www.youtube.com/playlist?list=PLYCWARA8YNdpVj31TutmnxptIK8Wy7O6D

225 https://www.vox.com/2016/7/14/12016710/science-challeges-research-funding-peer-review-process#1

226 https://www.molecule.to/blog/we-have-raised-12-7-million-in-seed-funding-to-build-the-future-of-decentralized-science-and-biotech

227 https://discover.molecule.to/projects/cl4o3qj2u023009joilcqgf85

228 https://www.youtube.com/watch?v=QstuPwCPE_s&t=17s

229 https://www.shopify.com/enterprise/global-ecommerce-statistics

230 https://fr.statista.com/infographie/17432/industries-les-plus-touchees-par-les-contrefacons/

231 https://www.marketplacepulse.com/articles/one-year-after-nike-stopped-selling-on-amazon

232 https://france.securitas.fr/newsroom/demarque-inconnue-definition (french article)

233 https://www.shopify.com/retail/token-gating

234 https://www.spatial.io/

235 https://en.wikipedia.org/wiki/Louvre

236 https://metahistory.gallery/

[237] Timeline: https://metahistory.gallery/collection/warline

[238] https://www.euronews.com/2022/02/13/nfts-representing-thousands-of-sections-of-klimt-s-the-kiss-sold-for-valentine-s-day

[239] https://jingculturecrypto.com/british-museum-lacollection-jmw-turner-nfts/

[240] https://news.artnet.com/art-world/uffizi-gallery-michelangelo-botticelli-nfts-1969045

[241] https://en.thevalue.com/articles/russia-state-hermitage-museum-nft-art-da-vinci-van-gogh-monet

[242] https://defillama.com/

[243] https://defiyield.app/rekt-database

[244] https://www.coindesk.com/business/2022/11/02/divisions-in-sam-bankman-frieds-crypto-empire-blur-on-his-trading-titan-alamedas-balance-sheet/

[245] https://www.coindesk.com/learn/the-fall-of-terra-a-timeline-of-the-meteoric-rise-and-crash-of-ust-and-luna/

[246] https://www.bqprime.com/crypto/why-did-celcius-crypto-crash-the-fall-of-celcius-network-explained

[247] https://www.bloomberg.com/professional/blog/metaverse-may-be-800-billion-market-next-tech-platform/

[248] https://www.todayscrypto.news/otherside-metaverse-land-sold-for-1-6-million/

[249] https://newsinfrance.com/the-real-estate-bubble-has-burst-in-the-metaverse/

[250] https://en.wikipedia.org/wiki/Rare_Pepe

[251] https://www.youtube.com/watch?v=N4PPGuW7czQ&ab_channel=LoganPaul

[252] https://www.statista.com/statistics/280704/world-power-consumption/

[253] https://bitcoin.fr/quelle-est-la-consommation-electrique-du-reseau-bitcoin/ (french article)

[254] https://ccaf.io/cbnsi/cbeci

[255] https://digiconomist.net/ethereum-energy-consumption

[256] More details: https://20mint.xyz/

[257] https://www.louvre.fr/en/online-tours

[258] https://dubai360.com/scene/375-above-atlantis-the-palm-hotel-palm-jumeirah/en

[259] https://immersive-expeditions.io/en/

[260] https://www.statista.com/statistics/254266/global-big-data-market-forecast/

[261] https://financesonline.com/how-much-data-is-created-every-day/

[262] https://www.inpi.fr/chiffres-cles-inpi-2021-record-de-depots-de-marques-pour-la-4e-annee-consecutive

[263] https://about.fb.com/news/2021/10/facebook-company-is-now-meta/

[264] More details: https://blog.cryptoflies.com/do-metaverse-and-nfts-have-a-future-these-statistics-on-trademark-fillings-will-convince-you

[265] https://www.modeintextile.fr/nike-obtient-le-brevet-pour-sa-technologie-cryptokicks/

[266] https://twitter.com/kevinrose/status/1555262099093200896

[267] https://www.nonfungible.com/market-tracker/moonbirds/MOONBIRD/2642

[268] updated price: https://nftpricefloor.com/proof-moonbirds

[269] https://rrbayc.com/

[270] https://edition.cnn.com/2023/04/25/business/yuga-ripps-bored-ape-lawsuit/index.html

[271] https://twitter.com/Jdotcolombo/status/1626538005581406208

[272] Official collection: https://opensea.io/collection/richbullsclub

[273] https://extranet-adsn.notaires.fr/front/actualite/28

[274] https://medium.com/geekculture/storage-of-dynamic-nft-metadata-based-on-db3-network-f39bd1fe2a77

[275] https://en.wikipedia.org/wiki/Betteridge%27s_law_of_headlines

[276] https://expandedramblings.com/index.php/tripadvisor-statistics/

[277] https://www.statheap.app/reports/spiegel-research-center-how-online-reviews-influence-sales

[278] https://blog.reputationx.com/check-reviews

[279] https://montessori-nw.org/about-montessori-education

[280] https://start.lesechos.fr/societe/engagement-societal/faut-il-se-mefier-des-petitions-en-ligne-1404492

[281] https://www.statista.com/statistics/270728/market-volume-of-online-gaming-worldwide/

[282] https://www.statista.com/statistics/270728/market-volume-of-online-gaming-worldwide/

[283] https://www.jokerclub.io/

[284] https://www.ssb.texas.gov/news-publications/three-state-securities-regulators-file-enforcement-actions-stop-sales-fra

[285] https://twitter.com/SlotieNft

[286] https://ssb.texas.gov/sites/default/files/2022-05/flamingocasinoclub_order_entered05102022.pdf

[287] https://www.ssb.texas.gov/sites/default/files/2022-04/Order_ENF_22_CDO_1860_.pdf

[288] https://en.thebigwhale.io/article/sorare-anj-regulation-jeux

[289] https://www.legifrance.gouv.fr/codes/article_lc/LEGIARTI000039169738/

[290] https://vitalik.ca/general/2022/01/26/soulbound.html

[291] Downloadable here: https://papers.ssrn.com/sol3/papers.cfm?abstract_id=4105763

[292] More details: https://hacken.io/discover/erc-4337-account-abstraction/

[293] https://www.statista.com/chart/29174/time-to-one-million-users/

[294] https://www.bbc.com/news/technology-65139406

[295] This figure may have changed since: https://discord.com/invite/midjourney

[296] https://arxiv.org/abs/1406.2661

[297] https://www.youtube.com/watch?v=cQ54GDm1eL0&t=6s&ab_channel=BuzzFeedVideo

[298] https://www.youtube.com/watch?v=wc1L_nzycus

[299] https://arstechnica.com/tech-policy/2023/03/rising-scams-use-ai-to-mimic-voices-of-loved-ones-in-financial-distress/

[300] https://www.elliptic.co/resources/nfts-financial-crime

[301] https://cryptoast.fr/sanctions-ofac-tornado-cash-retour-consequences-affaire-controversee/

www.ingramcontent.com/pod-product-compliance
Lightning Source LLC
Chambersburg PA
CBHW071924080326
R17960400001B/R179604PG40689CBX00011B/1